RSPCA

COMPLETE DOG CARE MANUAL

COMPLETE DOG CARE MANUAL

DR. BRUCE FOGLE

DORLING KINDERSLEY
LONDON • NEW YORK • STUTTGART

The RSPCA and Dog Care

The RSPCA – the Royal Society for the Prevention of Cruelty to Animals – is a charity that was founded in 1824 to promote kindness and prevent cruelty to animals. The Society's work with pet animals is often what comes first to mind. But it is just as concerned about helping wildlife, farm animals, and those used for research purposes. In short, the RSPCA cares about all animals. The Society carries out its law enforcement work with a force of 300 uniformed inspectors stationed throughout England and Wales. It also maintains a nationwide network of animal homes, hospitals, welfare centres, and clinics. Many of these are run by voluntary workers belonging to the 207 branches that are the backbone of the Society. Education has always been an important part of the RSPCA's work, and a major focus is teaching people about the responsibilities involved in keeping an animal. Many of the problems with which it deals are caused by thoughtless or irresponsible pet owners.

Dogs are the most popular pets, but sadly they are also the most frequent victims of mistreatment by irresponsible owners. A badly kept, untrained dog can also be a menace to society. Ignorance is the cause of many problems.

This book is essential reading for any existing or would-be dog owner. It tells you what makes your pet tick, so that you can create the best environment for a fit and happy dog. Only by understanding your dog's behaviour and needs can you be sure of looking after it properly and giving it the kind of life it deserves.

Terence Bate
Chief Veterinary Officer

A DORLING KINDERSLEY BOOK

Project Editors Alison Melvin, Lynn Parr
Art Editors Hazel Taylor, Nigel Hazle
Managing Editor Krystyna Mayer
Managing Art Editor Derek Coombes
Computer page make-up Patrizio Semproni
Production Controller Antony Heller

First published in Great Britain in 1993
by Dorling Kindersley Limited,
9 Henrietta Street, London WC2E 8PS
Reprinted 1994, 1995

A CIP catalogue record for this book is available from the British Library

ISBN 07513-0019-5

Colour reproduced by Colourscan, Singapore
Printed and bound by Mondadori, Italy

CONTENTS

INTRODUCTION

DOGS ARE AN INTEGRAL part of human society on every inhabited continent on Earth. They drive livestock and protect it; police property; scent and detect illicit substances; haul sleds; scavenge refuse; retrieve game; guide the blind; search for and rescue the lost and injured; comfort the lonely; hear for the deaf; or simply add a sparkling natural reality to the lives of hundreds of millions of people throughout the world.

The Origins of the Domestic Pet

In the course of history, through domestication and controlled, selective breeding, we have taken the genetic putty provided by the wolf and transformed it into breeds of dog as varied as the palm-sized miniature Yorkshire Terrier and the massive Great Dane. Just as we have altered the size and shape of dogs, we have altered their behaviour, too, emphasizing certain wolf characteristics, such as respect for the leader, while diminishing others, such as fearful shyness and scent marking. By doing so, however, we have created a species of animal almost wholly dependent upon humans for complete care.

Selective Breeding of Pedigree Dogs

Many breeds of dog exist today not because of survival of the fittest, but because of human whim. Canine coat lengths and densities can vary tremendously and need careful human management. Body size varies over one hundred-fold, far more than in any other living mammal species. Unfortunately, in the course of creating such a wide range of different breeds, we have also created structural and health problems. Dogs have more known inherited physical and medical disorders than any other domesticated species of animal in the world.

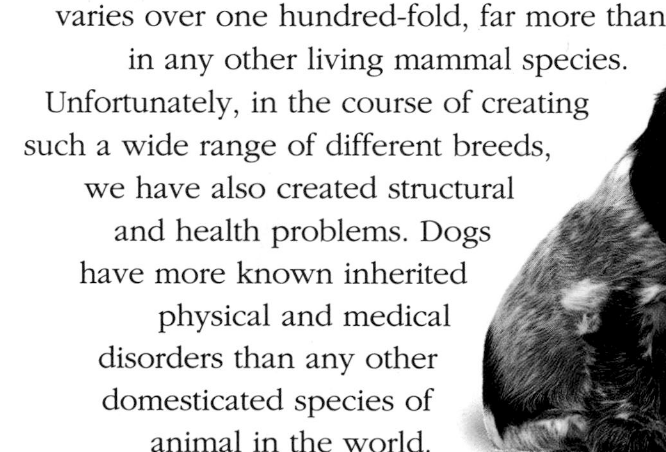

Caring for a Canine Companion

Every vet wishes he had enough time to sit down and talk with each dog owner, so that he could explain that dogs are not simply people in furry disguises, but are uniquely designed individuals with eating, grooming, training, and health needs that are different to our own and specific to their species. Practising good veterinary medicine does not mean treating problems when they occur. Prevention is invariably gentler, easier, and cheaper than cure. Using colour photographs and illustrations, this book shows and explains how best to care for your canine companion.

Bringing a Dog into Your Home

Although physically most dogs may look unlike their wolf relatives, they still retain the anatomical and behavioural foundations they inherited from their wild ancestors. Chapter One contains information on the canine senses and explains how different breeds evolved from the wolf and spread to all parts of the world. Because your dog will share your home for about 14 years or more, it is important that you select your canine companion carefully, handle and train it during its first, formative months, play with it, and plan ahead when you go on holidays. Basic dog care is discussed in Chapter Two.

Maintaining a Healthy Diet

Dogs are dependent on us to provide them with healthy food. Maintaining a nutritious and balanced diet is vital, although feeding requirements vary according to the age, size, state of health, and activity of the individual. Information on feeding your dog a well-balanced diet is contained in Chapter Three.

Pampering Your Pet

A dog's coat varies, too, from the velvety texture of the Dobermann's, to the deep luxuriousness of the Rough Collie's, and grooming requirements differ accordingly. The grooming of all coat types is described and illustrated with step-by-step photographs in Chapter Four.

The Dog Owner's Responsibilities

Keeping a dog as a pet is a joy and a privilege, but it is also a responsibility. Regardless of how attractive and well fed your dog is, if it is not properly trained, it is like a loose cannon, liable to misfire at any moment. Fortunately, training a dog to be a well-behaved pet is not difficult. Once more, prevention is easier than cure. If you teach your canine family member while it is still a puppy simply to sit and stay on command, you should be able to control it under almost any circumstance. Even when unwanted behaviour develops, if your dog understands and responds to the basic commands, you are more than halfway to correcting the problem. Dog training is discussed in Chapter Five.

Keeping Your Dog Healthy

Maintaining your pet's good health is, of course, central to complete dog care, which is why the health care chapter is the largest in the book. Disorders are described according to body system, and there is information on recognizing the symptoms of your pet's illness so that you can provide a vet with accurate information, enabling him to prescribe an appropriate course of treatment. Inherited disorders and dangers to humans from dogs are also discussed in Chapter Six. Dogs seem to get better faster when they are cared for in their own homes, and Chapter Seven concentrates on home nursing and looking after an elderly dog.

A Child in Canine Clothing

Succeeding chapters describe and illustrate dog breeding, dog shows and, perhaps most important of all, first aid for your pet. You should watch over your dog in the same way that you watch over young children. Both are inquisitive – if they find something interesting, they want to taste it. If something exciting catches their eye, they want to run over and examine it. Accidents do happen, but by understanding elementary first aid, you can provide vital, immediate care. You should know how to give cardiac massage and mouth-to-nose resuscitation, or how to stop bleeding and bandage minor wounds. In case of a road accident, you should be familiar with the principles of how to move an injured dog away from danger and to the nearest emergency facility.

The Last Link with the Natural World

It is a curious fact that almost every culture in the world keeps pets, and that the dog is the world's favourite. Looked at dispassionately, this is a totally illogical phenomenon. After all, why share our food and our homes with a species that, today, offers most of us no practical or utilitarian function in return? As we evolve from an agrarian to an urban culture, dogs are in many ways one of our last and most important links with the natural world. We get pleasure from caring for our gardens and for our pets. This is a primitive satisfaction, but the fact that it is vital is a good omen for the future of the natural world around us.

Chapter 1

INTRODUCING THE DOG

OUR RELATIONSHIP with the dog is much more varied, intense, and interdependent than with any other living species. The pact works because we understand each other so well. Both of us are naturally playful, gregariously sociable animals that instinctively defend our territories and hunt for our food. The dog's superior physical design and senses were obvious to our ancestors, and by harnessing these attributes, the dog became – and still remains throughout the world – our best animal friend. That relationship continues to evolve and develop, with dogs more popular now than they have ever been.

EARLY DOMESTICATION

Dogs were probably first domesticated from wolves throughout the northern hemisphere, and then in this altered form accompanied people, or were taken by them, to all other parts of the world. Wolves may originally have been simply camp followers, willing consumers of ancient refuse. It is equally likely that young wolves were raised in human settlements and treated as pets. Because of the wolf's adaptable nature, taming soon led to controlled breeding, or domestication. The first known domestic dogs date from around 12,000 years ago.

ORIGINS OF THE DOMESTIC DOG

Guardian *(right)*
According to ancient Chinese mythology, the "guardian" Foo Dog was a loyal protector of people and their property, and drove away evil spirits. As well as producing guard and protector dogs, the Chinese also bred the first small lap dogs, such as the Pekingese.

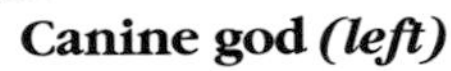

Canine god *(left)*
The dog was worshipped in Ancient Egypt as a messenger of the dead. It was represented by the jackal-headed god Anubis.

Ancient hunting dogs *(below)*
Mastiff-type hunting dogs appear in this frieze from Ashurbanipal's Palace at Nineveh in Assyria, carved over 2,600 years ago.

Beware of the dog *(above)*
By Roman times, a vast variety of breeds had evolved. To guard and protect remained a primary role, as shown in this Roman mosaic of a guard dog.

Aristocratic hounds *(right)*
In Renaissance Europe, dogs were specially bred to hunt with the aristocracy, as seen here in Andrea Mantegna's 15th-century portrait of the Duke of Mantua's grooms with their hounds.

Fashionable lap dogs *(left)*
Although lap dogs like the Pekingese had existed in China for thousands of years, and small breeds like the King Charles Spaniel had been kept by the European nobility for centuries, it was not until the 18th century that pet dogs became common. This painting by Richard Collins shows a pet spaniel enjoying tea with the family. Pedigree breeds were initially the companions of wealthy, aristocratic families, but gradually became widespread among the lower classes.

THE FIRST DOG BREEDS

Distinct dog breeds have been in existence for thousands of years. In Israel, archaeologists have found a grave over 10,000 years old, containing a human skeleton with its arm around a puppy. The puppy's skeleton was similar to that of the Canaan Dog, an indigenous species of that region today.

Dingoes arrived in Australia with settlers more than 3,000 years ago. Salukis have been bred in the Middle East for several thousand years, while the Pekingese in China has not changed in 2,000 years. In the New World, native people kept dogs, varying from the Alaskan Malamute to the Chihuahua in Mexico. Similar developments occurred in Europe, producing guarding and herding dogs from the indigenous wolf, while the smaller Asiatic wolf was the progenitor of breeds that spread through the Middle East into the heart of Africa.

Alaskan Malamute
This powerful, wolf-like dog was bred by the Malamute tribe of Alaska.

Newfoundland
The Newfoundland was the result of breeding European dogs with native island dogs.

Boston Terrier
One of the few wholly American breeds, the Boston Terrier was developed as a lap dog in New England.

Chihuahua
This tiny dog is the oldest breed on the American continent. It may have been introduced to Mexico by traders from China.

Wolf-free South America
Northern wolves migrated south as far as Central America but no further. By the time the Spanish Conquistadores came, however, dogs were found throughout the continent, probably having migrated with human traders.

WILD AND FERAL DOGS

Closely related to the Papua New Guinea Singing Dog, the Dingo first arrived in Australia with the Aborigines. Feral dogs, often called pariah dogs, still exist in many parts of the world. They usually form packs and breed successfully, unlike abandoned domestic dogs, which rarely do either.

Dingo

AMERICAN WOLF

The large variety of sizes and colours of the North American wolf provided ample genetic material for different dog breeds to develop.

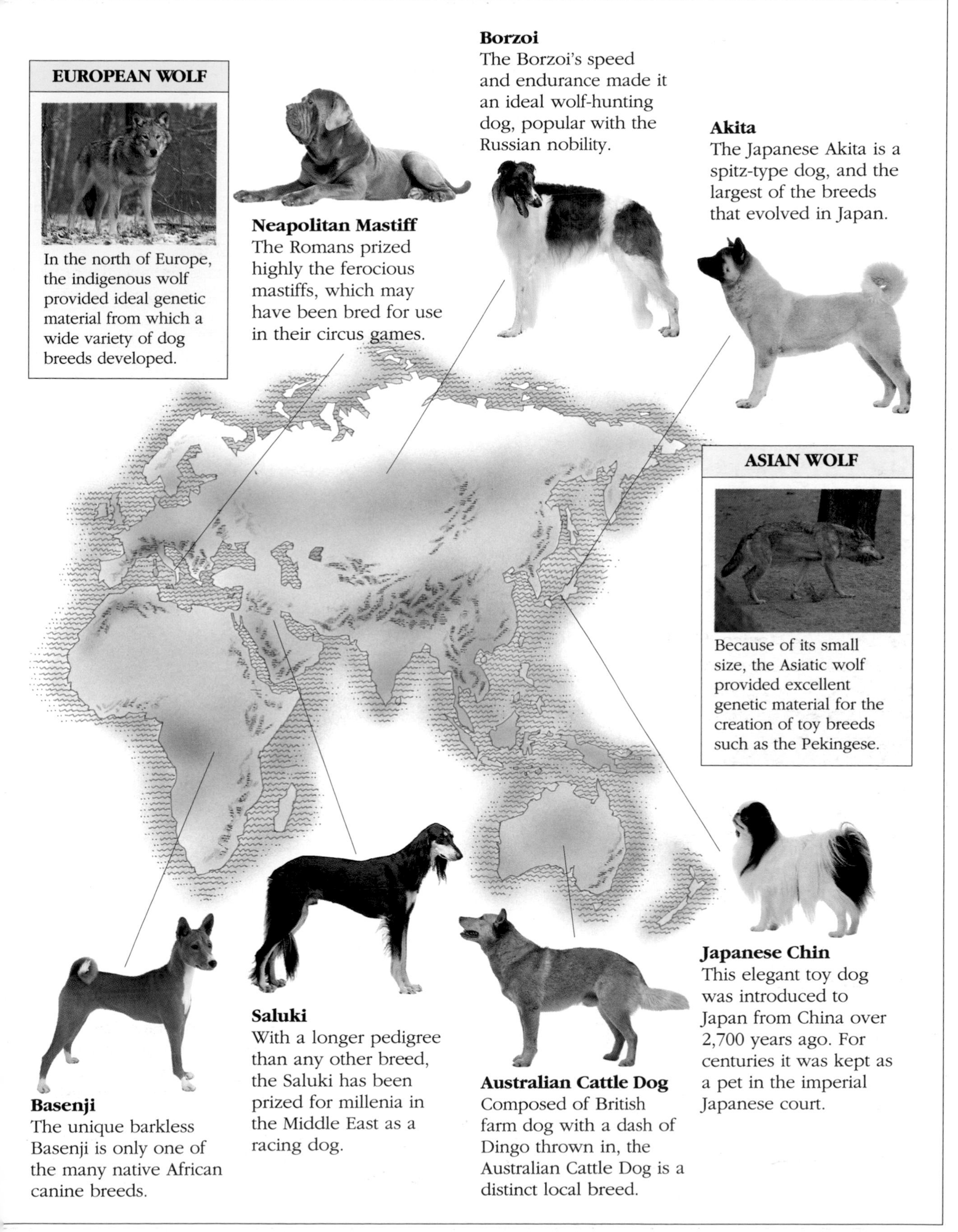

EUROPEAN WOLF

In the north of Europe, the indigenous wolf provided ideal genetic material from which a wide variety of dog breeds developed.

Neapolitan Mastiff
The Romans prized highly the ferocious mastiffs, which may have been bred for use in their circus games.

Borzoi
The Borzoi's speed and endurance made it an ideal wolf-hunting dog, popular with the Russian nobility.

Akita
The Japanese Akita is a spitz-type dog, and the largest of the breeds that evolved in Japan.

ASIAN WOLF

Because of its small size, the Asiatic wolf provided excellent genetic material for the creation of toy breeds such as the Pekingese.

Basenji
The unique barkless Basenji is only one of the many native African canine breeds.

Saluki
With a longer pedigree than any other breed, the Saluki has been prized for millenia in the Middle East as a racing dog.

Australian Cattle Dog
Composed of British farm dog with a dash of Dingo thrown in, the Australian Cattle Dog is a distinct local breed.

Japanese Chin
This elegant toy dog was introduced to Japan from China over 2,700 years ago. For centuries it was kept as a pet in the imperial Japanese court.

THE DESIGN OF THE DOG

The classic design of the dog is exemplified by the world's most popular breed, the German Shepherd Dog. This dog has a heavy coat for good insulation against the cold, no bony attachment between the front legs and shoulders, which allows for prolonged running on "shock absorbers", a long muzzle with specialized teeth to grip and crush, and powerful muscles that do not tire easily. This is the basic design of the wolf, and also of its relatives, the husky breeds of dog.

Through selective breeding, humans have improved certain aspects of this model but have also produced breeds with shortened life expectancies and many medical problems.

WHAT IS A DOG?

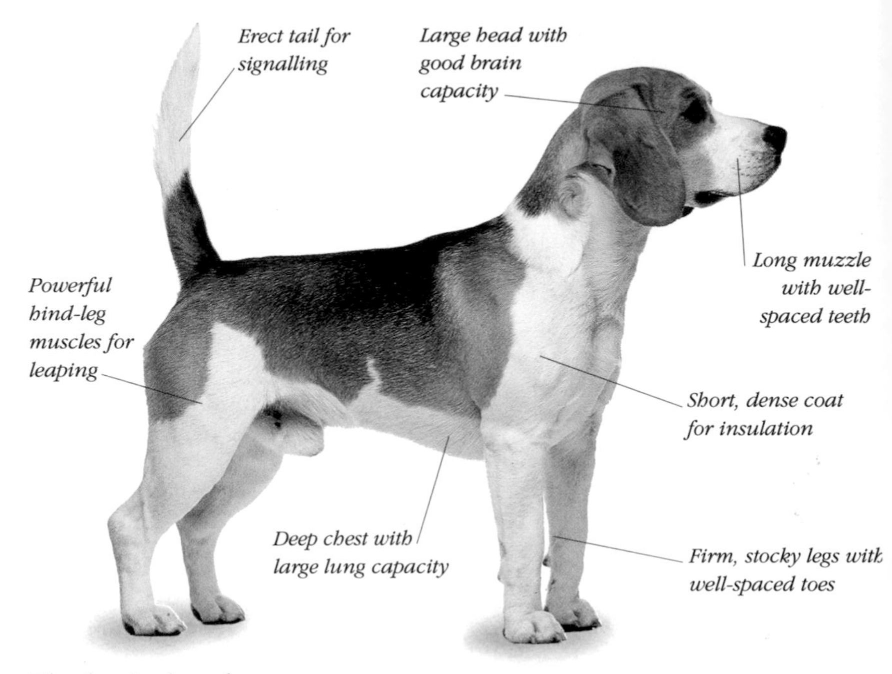

The basic dog shape
The typical dog is an all-rounder – well muscled, built for endurance, with balanced proportions of height to length, and with the ability to use all its senses to their maximum capacity.

SELECTIVE BREEDING

Giant breeds *(left)*
The St. Bernard has been selectively bred for size and thickness of coat. The result is a dog with great physical strength, able to work in freezing temperatures.

Miniature breeds
Because it once served as a mobile hot-water bottle, the Pekingese was designed to be compact, furry, and affectionate.

Agile strength
Powerful hind-leg muscles allow this German Shepherd Dog to jump effortlessly, an ability we utilize when we train dogs for specific tasks, such as police work.

Speed and endurance
This Lurcher can run much faster than the wolf from which it is descended. This breed is a classic example of how, through selective breeding, humans have redesigned the original model to emphasize one particular characteristic.

Playful temperament *(below)*
Redesign involves temperamental as well as physical changes. This Bichon Frise is typical of the breeds of dog in which humans have perpetuated life-long active, playful, puppy-like behaviour.

Faulty craftsmanship *(left)*
Lovable it may be, but with its bandy legs, squashed face, breathing problems, and skin disorders, the Bulldog shows how we have abused our control over dog design.

THE CANINE SENSES

The dog is a hunter and scavenger that lives within a pack structure in which it must recognize friend and foe. Its senses have therefore developed for these purposes – excellent sight to enable it to see the slightest movement of potential prey; a sense of smell far beyond human comprehension with which it scents game, territory odours, and even emotional states in other animals; acute hearing to distinguish sounds over great distances; but poorly defined taste, allowing it to eat things that other animals consider offensive. It also has a refined sense of touch, which is why the dog makes such a good companion to humans.

THE FIVE SENSES

Sight
Laterally placed eyes, as on this Whippet, provide good peripheral vision, which is important for dogs used for hunting and chasing. The more frontally placed eyes of the Pug offer better binocular vision, but are not very good at seeing things close up.

Pug

Whippet

Smell
Smell is the dog's most important sense. Inside its nose is a surface area as great as the area of its entire body. A moist nose can capture more molecules of scent than can a dry one.

Touch *(left)*
The contact comfort of infancy that most mammals enjoy is a life-long pleasure in dogs. Pleasure of touch is important in any animals that play together, huddle together for warmth, and use touch in the form of licking or pawing as a means of signalling rank within the pack.

Taste *(right)*
The sensation of taste is closely linked with that of smell. For example, this Boxer is dribbling saliva because it can see and smell something appetizing to eat. Dogs have far fewer taste buds than do humans, and can only register tastes as pleasant, indifferent, or unpleasant.

Hearing *(below)*
Erect ears, like on this Basenji, are more likely to take in sound than the exaggerated lop ears of the Bloodhound. Hearing is almost pitch perfect, for example allowing dogs to tell the difference in car engine sounds produced even by similar models.

Basenji

Bloodhound

CANINE SIXTH SENSE

Do dogs have extrasensory perception? Many owners believe that their dogs have a sixth sense. This enables them to know, for example, when the family's children are approaching the house on their way home from school, or to tell when it is time to go for a walk. Dogs are also credited with telepathic abilities that enable them to pick up their owners' feelings.

Scientific evidence suggests that dogs have an electromagnetic sense that makes them sensitive to earth tremors and vibrations. This may help them to predict earthquakes and find their way home across hundreds of miles.

UNDERSTANDING A DOG

Because they are pack animals, dogs, like their wolf relatives, have developed a subtle and sophisticated range of communication methods based upon body language and odours. Many of these actions are easily understood by humans, but some, such as urine marking, are open to misinterpretation.

Understanding canine communication is the best way to provide effective care and companionship for your dog.

PACK BEHAVIOUR

Pack members
These Siberian Huskies are able to work together as a true pack with a human leader. In the absence of fellow canines, dogs look upon humans as other members of the pack.

Separation anxiety
Howling, barking, pacing, and destroying objects are all signs of stress caused by being left alone *(see page 87)*.

Dominant dog
Some dogs, like this cross-bred terrier, are naturally more dominant than others. This behaviour is more common in males and requires firm control by human handlers.

Submissive dog
To avoid aggressive confrontations, dogs have a system of ritual submissive behaviour. By lying down and lifting a leg, this Lurcher signals to more dominant dogs, and to humans, that it is not a threat.

Ears are flattened
Leg is raised
Belly is exposed
Tail is tucked between legs

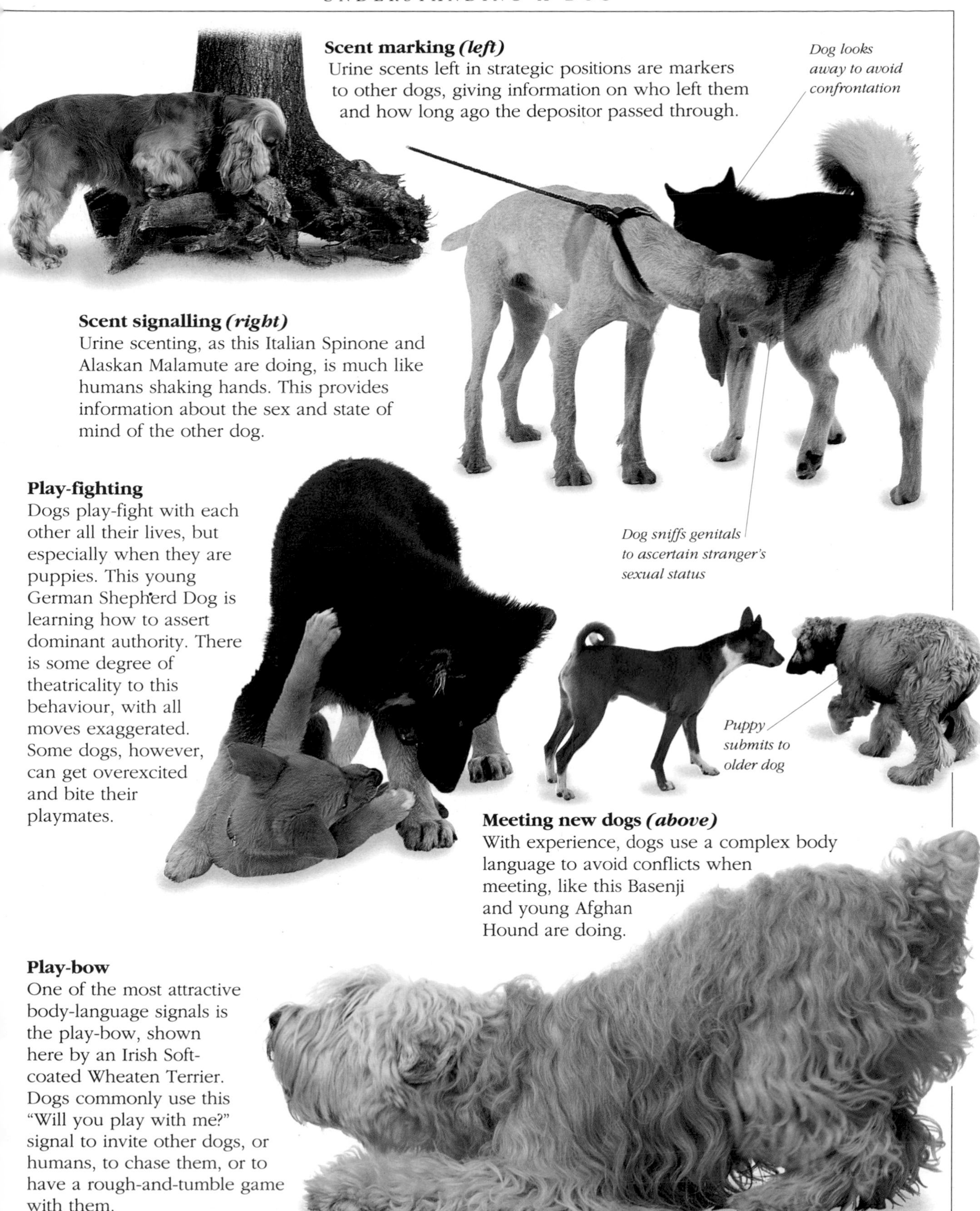

Scent marking *(left)*
Urine scents left in strategic positions are markers to other dogs, giving information on who left them and how long ago the depositor passed through.

Scent signalling *(right)*
Urine scenting, as this Italian Spinone and Alaskan Malamute are doing, is much like humans shaking hands. This provides information about the sex and state of mind of the other dog.

Play-fighting
Dogs play-fight with each other all their lives, but especially when they are puppies. This young German Shepherd Dog is learning how to assert dominant authority. There is some degree of theatricality to this behaviour, with all moves exaggerated. Some dogs, however, can get overexcited and bite their playmates.

Meeting new dogs *(above)*
With experience, dogs use a complex body language to avoid conflicts when meeting, like this Basenji and young Afghan Hound are doing.

Play-bow
One of the most attractive body-language signals is the play-bow, shown here by an Irish Soft-coated Wheaten Terrier. Dogs commonly use this "Will you play with me?" signal to invite other dogs, or humans, to chase them, or to have a rough-and-tumble game with them.

THE DOG AS A PET

When introduced into a home as young puppies, dogs readily adopt humans as members of their pack. Dogs do not think they are humans; they think we are very strange and powerful dogs. However human it may seem, your dog always thinks like a dog and acts like a dog.

A programme of breeding has enhanced the canine qualities that humans find desirable, such as affection and loyalty. At the same time, it has diminished other normal, but undesirable, characteristics such as constant territory marking, to make the dog the world's most popular pet.

BUILDING A GOOD RELATIONSHIP

The dog looks for attention from its owner

Physical contact is reassuring to the dog

The human pack
Dogs are social animals that thrive in a group where there is a well-established hierarchy. Your dog should become part of the family, a member of the human pack but always the lowest-ranking member. All dogs seek attention and physical contact from their owners.

DOG OWNERSHIP WORLDWIDE

Over 200 million dogs are kept as pets worldwide. Australia, North America, and France have the highest dog populations on a household basis, while Japan has the fastest increasing number of dogs. Germany has a relatively small dog population, while in China and Iceland, the number of dogs kept as pets is low because of strict controls.

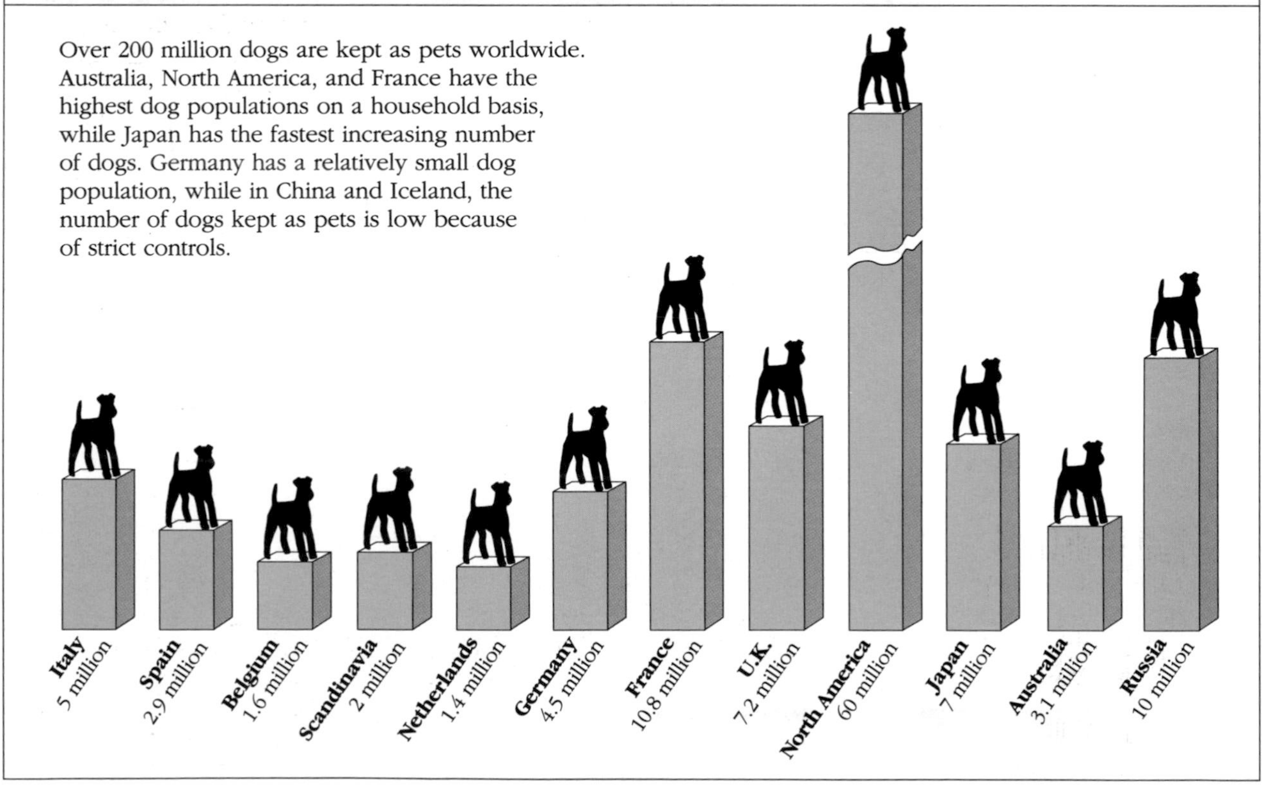

WHY DO YOU WANT A DOG?

Show dog
Showing dogs is a hobby for some and a passion for others. In order to win a show, the dog must be presented at the top of its form, fit, and well groomed *(see pages 182–183).*

WORKING DOGS

With their supple intelligence and desire to serve, dogs are trained to assist humans in different ways. A guide dog for the blind, such as this one, a hearing dog for the deaf, or a service dog for a physically disabled person, willingly fills the void created when an individual loses an important ability. Some dogs are trained to use their refined sense of smell to detect illicit drugs. Other dogs can follow ground or air scents to aid in avalanche and earthquake rescues.

Lap dog *(left)*
Small lap dogs can provide humans with an opportunity to satisfy their life-long enjoyment of caring for living things.

House dog *(left)*
A family pet gives you an enormous amount of companionship and affection. Dog owners take regular outdoor exercise more than non-owners and report fewer minor health problems. They might even be less at risk from heart disease.

Guard dog
Because of their natural desire to protect their pack and their territory, all canines, but especially the larger breeds, offer us security and protection.

Basic Dog Types

Dogs inherited a range of behaviour from wolves. But by accentuating or diminishing specific traits or characteristics, humans have created dog breeds with different personalities. They have also created a range of shapes and sizes. Some of these present-day breeds are less fearful than their ancestral relatives, while others are more aggressive. By Roman times there were shepherd dogs, warrior dogs, sight and scent hunters, terriers, and companions. Kennel clubs still emphasize such divisions in their classifications.

BREEDING FOR DIFFERENT TASKS

Herder
These collies are typical of herding breeds with an enhanced desire and ability to herd and control flocks of domestic animals.

Sight hound *(right)*
This Borzoi is typical of breeds already highly developed thousands of years ago to help in hunting by using their superior vision to sight game and their immense speed to chase it.

Companion *(above)*
Maltese Terriers like these two were first bred thousands of years ago. The breed is thought to have been named for the island of Malta. Today, companionship is the dog's most important role.

BREED CATEGORIES

Breeds are categorized by each country's national kennel club. The Kennel Club of Great Britain was the forerunner of all other organizations. It divides recognized breeds into six groups: Hounds, Utility, Gundogs, Terriers, Working, and Toy dogs.

Scent hound
These Bloodhounds have an infinitely superior ability to follow both air and ground scent. Scenting breeds invariably have long noses to house their larger-than-average smelling faculties.

Warrior
Historically, guard and attack dogs were massive in size, like this Neapolitan Mastiff. Today, however, guard dogs are bred more for physical dexterity than size.

Gundog *(below)*
In the 19th century, breeds like this Irish Setter, together with pointers and retrievers, were developed for use in recreational hunting. Today, setters are primarily companion dogs.

Terrier *(left)*
Although terriers have existed at least since Roman times, Britain has produced more breeds of terrier than any other country. This Border Terrier originated in the Scottish Border region.

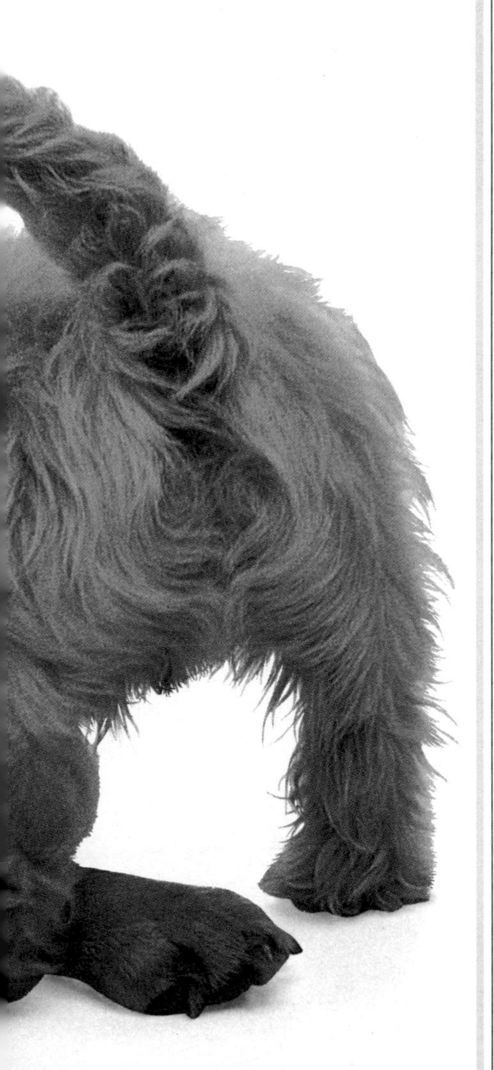

Chapter 2

BASIC CARE

OWNING A dog can enrich your life. By living with a canine companion we are reminded that we are not unique and separate from the rest of nature but have an interdependent relationship with it from which we both benefit. As the dominant member of the partnership with our dogs, we have an obligation to care for them as best we can. We are responsible for their proper training, feeding, handling, breeding, and housing, as well as acting as a leader of the family "pack", and providing them with companionship and security. Combined with grooming and health management, this care ensures a happy and secure future for our dogs.

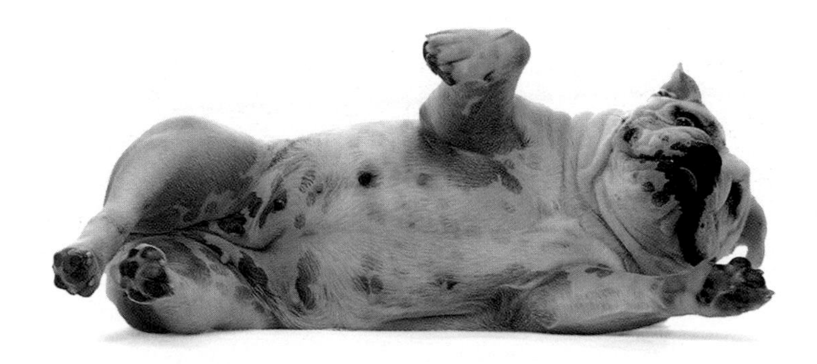

BECOMING A DOG OWNER

Make sure you select a dog that fits into your lifestyle both now and as you expect it to be in years to come. The amount of exercise, food, grooming, and general attention a dog needs varies with its shape and temperament. Size is not everything. Some small dogs can actually need more exercise than their much larger relatives.

DECIDING ON A DOG TYPE

Pedigree
By choosing a pedigree dog such as this Basenji you know in advance not only its potential size and energy requirements, but also a good deal about its temperament. Choose a temperament compatible with your own.

Facial expression is endearing and unique

Mongrel *(left)*
Mongrels are often endearing and in need of homes. Because of the randomness of their breeding they are less likely to suffer from inherited diseases and disabilities than are purebred dogs.

Cross breed *(right)*
A cross-bred dog like this Jack Russell and Border Terrier cross often combines beneficial attributes of both parents. The converse rarely occurs.

THE DOG FOR YOUR LIFESTYLE

Family pet *(right)*
This Large Munsterlander revels in human and canine companionship, and delights in vigorous exercise.

Large, active dog
This Rottweiler needs plenty of space for its daily exercise, but is wary of unfamiliar people and dogs. You should only acquire a breed like this if you have ample experience of dog handling, since a large dog can be hard to control without proper training.

Small companion
Compact but robust, this Chihuahua offers companionship like most toy breeds. Yet it is also a surprisingly effective little guard dog.

WHERE TO OBTAIN A DOG

Animal shelter *(left)*
Animal shelters always have surplus dogs requiring good homes. The best shelters interview you before letting you take home one of their charges. Because these dogs have had previous homes, be prepared for unexpected behavioural problems. Such dogs may take a while to settle down.

Purebred puppies
Recognized breeders or friends and neighbours are good sources for purebred puppies. You should not buy puppies from pet shops.

Essential Equipment

It is important to invest in proper equipment before bringing a dog into your home. You should provide it with a bed and a variety of toys. Feeding bowls should be slide-proof, and grooming utensils appropriate for the dog's coat. You should also have ready a collar, lead, identity tag, and, if necessary, a muzzle.

Bean bag bed
Form-fitting bean bags make ideal beds. They are soft, light, retain body heat, and are easy to wash. Most dogs enjoy the security they feel when nestled down on one.

Brass tag

Steel tag

Identity tags
Provide an identity tag on which you can have your dog's name, your telephone number, and that of your vet engraved.

Basket
Chew-proof plastic baskets are easier to clean and harder for a dog to damage than wicker models. Line the basket with a well-fitting, washable mattress.

Dog pull
Only use a tug-of-war toy like this with a dog that willingly gives it up when you command it to do so *(see page 43)*.

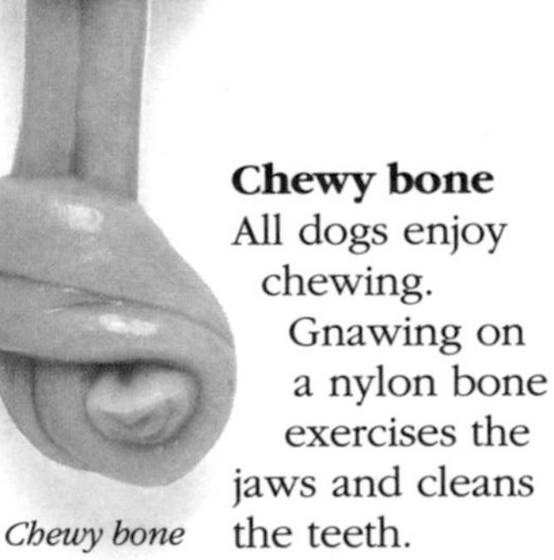

Chewy bone

Chewy bone
All dogs enjoy chewing. Gnawing on a nylon bone exercises the jaws and cleans the teeth.

Chewy toy

Chewy toy
This rubber toy is chewable and also bounces erratically when it is thrown, stimulating a dog to give chase.

Squeaky toy

Squeaky toy
This toy squeaks when chewed, appealing to a dog's hunting instincts. Beware of toys that can be swallowed.

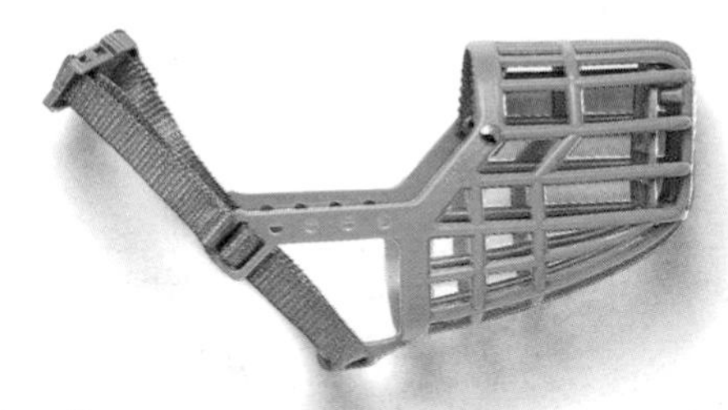

Muzzle
A dog should wear a muzzle to prevent it from scavenging, or if you do not know its personality and think there is even a remote possibility of it biting, especially children.

Basic grooming kit *(right)*
A good-quality bristle brush grooms the fine, downy coat close to the skin, while metal brushes and combs remove tangles, matts, and debris from the thicker, longer hair. Be sure to use brushes that are correct for your dog's breed *(see pages 66–69).*

Bristle brush *Wide-toothed comb* *Fine-toothed comb*

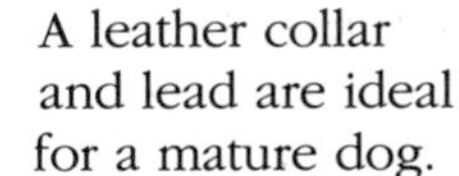

Leather lead

Leather collar

Collar and lead
A leather collar and lead are ideal for a mature dog. You might prefer using cheaper meshed nylon, especially given the variety of collars needed for a puppy that will grow to a large size. A dog should always wear a collar and identity tag *(see page 49).*

Bowls
Each dog should have its own food bowl, which should always be kept clean. Use either a heavy ceramic bowl or a stainless steel one rimmed with rubber so that it does not slide. Fresh water should always be available and replenished daily.

Stainless steel bowl

Ceramic bowl

Puppy bowl

CHOOSING A PUPPY

Owing to advances in preventative medicine, nutrition, and treatment of diseases such as cancer, it is likely you will share the next 14 years or so with your dog.

Choose one that is not only right for your lifestyle today, but also one that you think will still fit into your daily routine in ten years' time. Only choose a puppy that appears bright, alert, and healthy. Whenever possible, arrange to see the puppy with its mother, since this will tell you something about its temperament. A reputable breeder will let you have a puppy conditional upon a vet examining it and certifying that it is healthy. Puppies should stay with their mothers until they are eight weeks old.

WHAT TO LOOK FOR IN A PUPPY

Eleven-week-old puppy
This Boxer puppy is active, inquisitive, and alert. When it first meets new people it does not cower, but comes forward to investigate, which is a good sign of confidence. Puppies that are overconfident, however, can sometimes develop into dominant adults.

Facial expression is quizzical but relaxed, with no sign of fear

Fur is shiny and soft, and feels clean and smooth

Legs are straight, and there is no splaying to suggest poor growth

Muscles are well developed and symmetrical

Relatively hairless skin on the belly is pink and unstained

Feet should show no signs of deformity that could lead to lameness

EXAMINING A PUPPY

1 The eyes should be clear and bright, and free from any discharge. There should be good pigmentation, and no sign of inflammation or irritation.

2 The ears should be pink inside with neither an unpleasant odour nor any sign of crusty or waxy discharge, which may indicate ear mites.

3 The skin should not be oily or flaky, and it should not have any sores or lumps. The hair should be firm and not come out when it is stroked.

4 The gums should be pink and odour-free. Except in certain breeds, such as this Boxer, the teeth should meet perfectly in a scissor bite.

5 The anal region should be clean and dry. There should be no sign of either diarrhoea or other discharge from the genitals.

6 When it is picked up, the puppy should feel firm and heavier than you expect. If the puppy is relaxed while being lifted, this is an indication that it might be easygoing as an adult.

ASSESSING TEMPERAMENT

Observing the litter
Seeing the mother will give you an idea of the puppy's potential temperament. Watch how the puppy behaves with the rest of the litter. Bossy puppies often become dominant adults, while submissive puppies often develop into insecure adults. The best pets are usually those with temperaments between these extremes.

FIRST INTRODUCTIONS

When it is first brought into your home a new puppy might be disoriented. You should restrict it to one room and let it investigate its new environment, but keep it company so that it does not become afraid. You should provide water, food, a chewy toy, and a comfortable bed, preferably in an enclosed pen, which will soon become the puppy's personal "den". Newspaper on the floor will soak up accidents.

For the first few days you should give it the same food that it has previously been fed, and only change to a new diet once the puppy is over the initial excitement of coming into your home.

A secure den
A puppy pen offers security, and means that even when you are out of the room the puppy is being trained to relieve itself on newspaper *(see page 36).*

THE PUPPY PEN

Puppy can watch all activity of household

Newspaper will soak up accidents

Fresh water should always be available

MEETING OTHER PETS

Introducing a dog to a puppy
An older dog may resent the arrival of a puppy so it is important to supervise their first few meetings. Allow the dog to investigate the puppy when it is asleep.

Puppy demands attention from older dog

SAFETY IN THE HOME

Making your home safe
A puppy is naturally inquisitive and will want to investigate any new object by smelling and chewing it. Simple precautions, similar to those you would take to ensure that your home is safe for toddlers, should be taken to prevent damage or injuries to your dog. Remove all breakable items and ensure that the puppy does not chew dangerous objects such as electric flex.

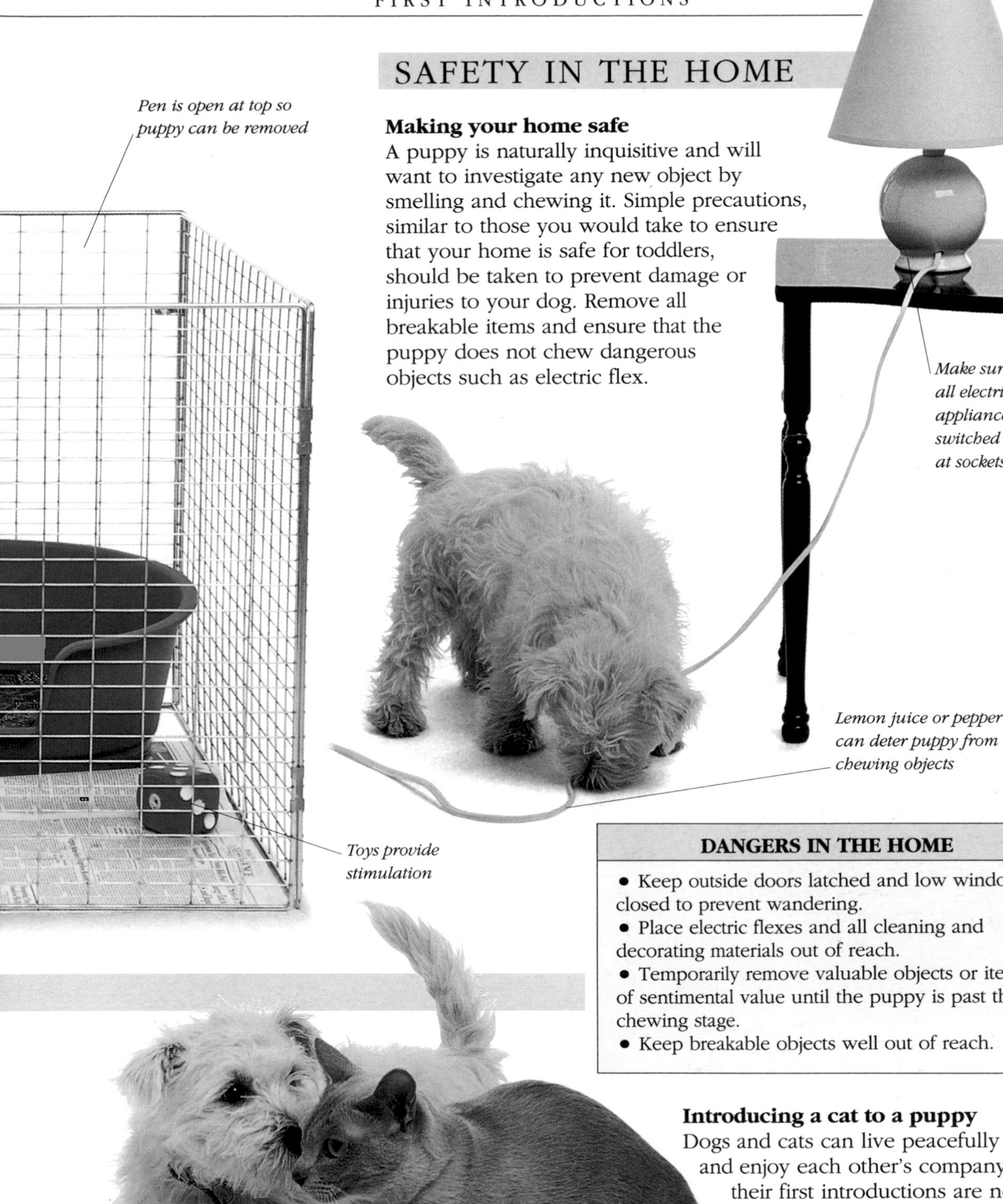

Pen is open at top so puppy can be removed

Make sure all electrical appliances are switched off at sockets

Lemon juice or pepper can deter puppy from chewing objects

Toys provide stimulation

DANGERS IN THE HOME
• Keep outside doors latched and low windows closed to prevent wandering. • Place electric flexes and all cleaning and decorating materials out of reach. • Temporarily remove valuable objects or items of sentimental value until the puppy is past the chewing stage. • Keep breakable objects well out of reach.

Introducing a cat to a puppy
Dogs and cats can live peacefully and enjoy each other's company if their first introductions are not threatening. Introduce the resident cat to the puppy when it is sleeping.

HOUSE TRAINING

Dogs are naturally clean animals that will not willingly soil their sleeping areas. They enjoy the routine of urinating in specific places. As a dog owner you can intervene and decide where these should be, initially on newspaper in the home and later on grass and in the gutter. Because canine droppings are aesthetically unpleasant and a minor health hazard, you should always clean up after your dog.

PAPER TRAINING

1 After eating, drinking, playing, or awakening are times when a dog's bladder and bowels need emptying. Young puppies must relieve themselves every few hours, so there will probably be a few accidents until a puppy is fully house trained.

2 Sniffing the ground is often the only sign the puppy will give that it needs to empty its bladder or bowels. Some puppies both sniff and race around frantically at the same time. You have only seconds in which to intervene, and place the puppy in the designated place.

Puppy sniffs to find a spot that smells right

3 Quickly pick up the puppy and place it on the paper. Newspaper is best because it is cheap, readily available, and also very absorbent. Keep a small piece of soiled newspaper along with the fresh supply to provide the puppy with its own odour and to encourage it to use the paper again.

4 Praise the puppy after it has urinated on the paper. Never discipline a puppy after it has soiled the floor, and never put its nose in the mess. Both actions are valueless and will make the puppy scared of you.

Praise puppy for using paper

Accidents
Clean up accidents in the home with an odour-eliminating disinfectant. Do not use ammonia products, since these may remind the puppy of its own urine smell.

TOILET TRAINING OUTSIDE

1 An older puppy can be trained to relieve itself outside. Learn to recognize the warning signs so that you know when it has to be let out to answer the call of nature. In time, going outside to relieve itself will become a regular habit for the puppy.

2 Encourage the puppy to use a remote area for its toilet. A puppy is more likely to urinate where it has soiled before.

3 Having found the right place, the puppy urinates. Dog urine is acidic and burns grass, leaving brown patches. Train the puppy to relieve itself when and where you want it to.

CLEANING UP DOG MESS

Always clean up after your dog. Carry a plastic bag or "pooper-scooper" with you, and place the mess in a provided dog bin. If it is in your own garden, flush it down the toilet. Roundworms and certain tapeworms can be transmitted in dog faeces, so worm your dog regularly.

HANDLING A DOG

Stroking and grooming are comforting to a dog, and at the same time teach it that humans are in control. You should handle a new dog as much as possible. If you first see a puppy while it is still with its breeder, ask that it be handled frequently by many different people until it is old enough to come home.

You should get your dog accustomed to being picked up and carried. Even large dogs must occasionally be lifted, and it is best to teach them this from a young age. Always be careful when approaching a strange dog. Even a dog that has been trained not to be hand-shy may be wary of a stranger.

CHILDREN AND DOGS

Introducing children to a dog
Even a friendly dog, such as this Golden Retriever, should be introduced to young children in the presence, and under the supervision, of an adult. While a dog may enjoy being stroked by adults, it might not be used to the more rapid and jerky movements of children.

A friendly dog enjoys being stroked on its neck and head

Sharing tasks
Children can help care for the family pet. By choosing a fun task, such as grooming, feeding, or walking a dog (always under the supervision of an adult), children will enjoy a closer relationship with their pet.

PICKING UP A LARGE DOG

1 Always talk to the dog to reassure it before trying to pick it up. You should muzzle it first if you have any doubts about its temperament. Place one arm around the dog's chest and forelimbs, and the other around its rump. Bending your knees, draw the dog in to your chest. Keep your back straight.

2 Keeping a secure grip on the dog, lift it up. A nervous dog may need to be restrained by a helper, who should gently hold its head and talk to it. A dog should be used to being picked up from an early age and should not struggle to get free. Put the dog down if it begins to panic.

PICKING UP A SMALL DOG

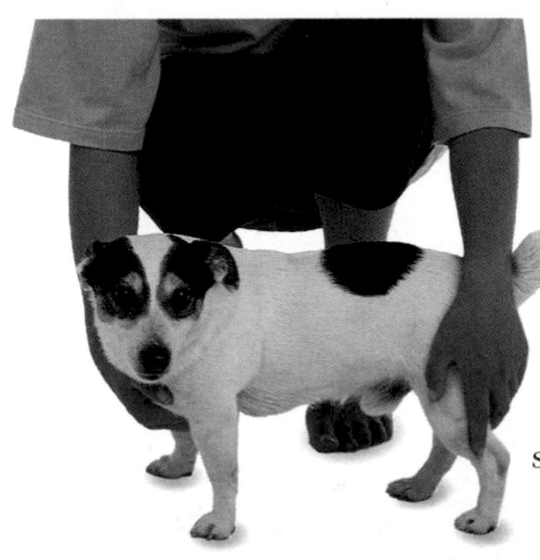

1 Reassuring the dog calmly, place one hand under its forelimbs and chest, and the other around its hind limbs and rump. This gives you firm control over the dog and helps to stop it squirming and paddling.

2 Lift the dog by supporting the chest with one hand, keeping the other under the dog's rump. This method prevents the dog from jumping out of your grasp.

Support the dog's hind legs and rump

APPROACHING A DOG

1 Approach a dog that you do not know well with caution. Do not use jerky movements. Offer a hand at face level for the dog to bend down to sniff. Avoid reaching down from above, since this is an intimidating gesture.

2 If the dog appears to be friendly and does not show any obvious sign of fear or aggression, it can now be stroked. Do not pat it on the head, which is a dominant gesture.

COLLARS AND LEADS

When you get your dog, provide it with a collar and lead. Always leave the collar on, together with the dog's identity tag. Your dog might resent it at first but this ensures identification if it accidentally strays. Choose the type of collar, head halter or harness, and length of lead that is most appropriate for you and your dog. You can protect your dog in case it strays by using a method of permanent identification like a tattoo or microchip implant.

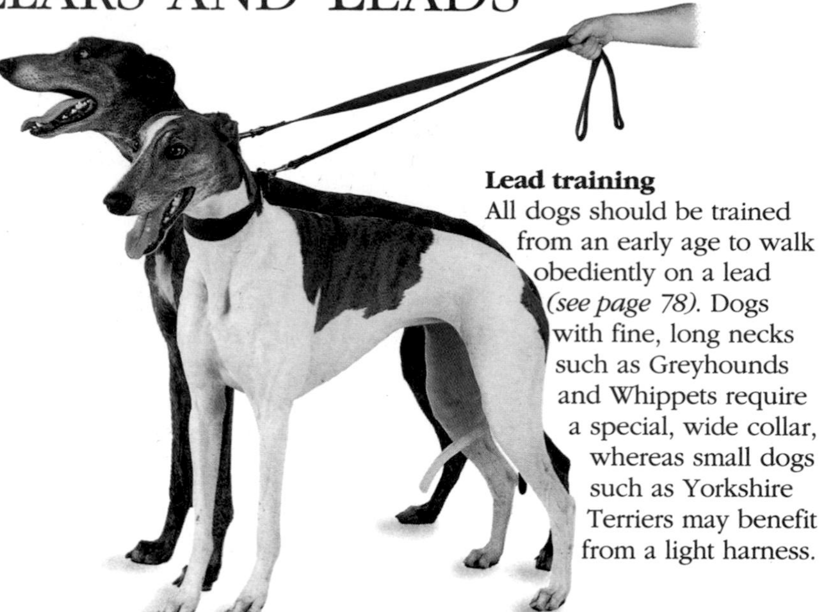

Lead training
All dogs should be trained from an early age to walk obediently on a lead *(see page 78)*. Dogs with fine, long necks such as Greyhounds and Whippets require a special, wide collar, whereas small dogs such as Yorkshire Terriers may benefit from a light harness.

TYPES OF COLLAR AND LEAD

Choosing a lead and collar
Leads and collars vary in quality, price, and usefulness. They are usually made of leather, rope, or nylon. Plaited or rolled leather is comfortable and long lasting. Meshed nylon is firm, supple, and usually less expensive. An extending lead is very practical. It allows a dog greater freedom than an ordinary lead, while the owner still retains control.

It is important to get a puppy used to wearing a collar from as young as eight weeks of age. Start by putting the collar on the puppy for short periods each day. Always remove the collar when the puppy is unsupervised in case it gets caught.

A puppy's first walks on a lead should take place in the safety of the home. This will make walking on a lead outside less traumatic and frightening. The lead should represent the fun of going for a walk. It should never be used for punishment.

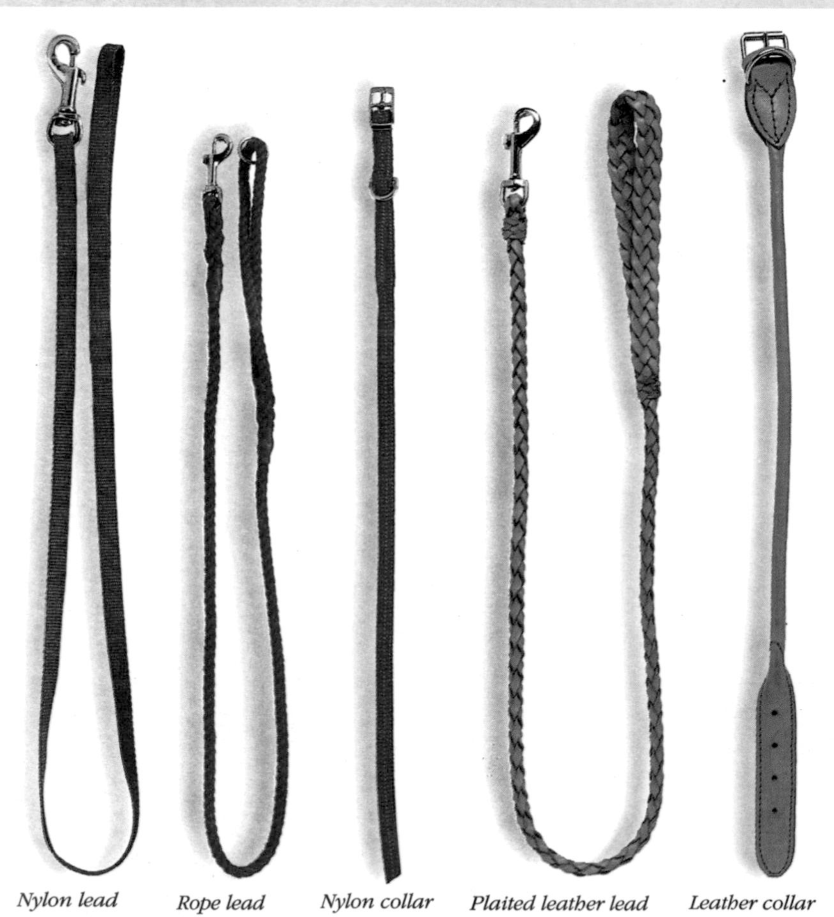

Nylon lead *Rope lead* *Nylon collar* *Plaited leather lead* *Leather collar*

PUTTING ON A COLLAR

1 Always choose the right length of collar for the dog's neck. Make sure that the collar sits comfortably and does not get caught on the fur of a longhaired dog. Do not fasten the collar too tightly.

2 You should be able to slip two fingers under a well-fitted collar. This means that it will not come off if the dog tugs backwards on its lead, but it will not cause discomfort and can be slipped off in an emergency.

Extending lead *Wide collar* *Designer collar*

HALTERS AND HARNESSES

A harness slips over the dog's body and around the chest. The lead is attached over the dog's back. This avoids collar pressure on the neck if the dog pulls or is frightened while walking on its lead. A light harness is suitable for small dogs, while a head halter is much more effective for controlling strong dogs.

Harness

Head halter

A head halter is made of strong nylon and attached to the lead under the dog's chin. If the dog pulls or lunges forward on the lead, its momentum pulls its head down and its jaws shut. This is ideal for a large dog that may be difficult for its owner to keep under control in public. A head halter is tolerated by most dogs and is a good alternative to using a check chain. Remember to choose the correct size of harness or halter for your dog.

PLAY AND EXERCISE

Dogs of every age and size enjoy playing with each other, and with humans and objects. If a dog is denied mental and physical activity, its energy may be released in destructive and unacceptable behaviour *(see pages 86–87)*. The actual amount of exercise needed varies according to a dog's breed, age, and state of health, but all obedient dogs should be let off their leads daily and allowed to run in a safe, appropriate place.

By training a dog to retrieve objects you can concentrate this necessary exercise into a shorter period of time. And by providing a dog with toys you can ensure that, even in your absence, your dog can stimulate its mind and senses.

TYPES OF EXERCISE

Exercise off the lead
All active breeds, such as this spaniel, revel in daily physical activity. When you have trained your dog in obedience and where regulations permit, you should regularly let it off its lead to enjoy vigorous exercise.

Exercise on the lead *(left)*
In addition to daily rigorous exercise, provide your dog with frequent walks. An extendable lead provides the handler with short lead control when walking among other pedestrians, and provides a dog with longer lead freedom so that it can exercise safely.

Road walking helps keep nails short

Playing games
Playing games with your dog reinforces your authority, because the dog depends upon you to throw the toy. This is also a good way to use your own time efficiently, since it concentrates the dog's activity into a short time.

Chewing toys
When a dog is provided with toys, it can exercise its mind and senses even in its owner's absence. This Standard Poodle finds chewing a toy a satisfying way of filling its time when it is not playing with humans and is restricted indoors.

Playing with each other
Just like humans, dogs enjoy playing with each other, even as adults, as these Italian Spinones are doing.

Playing together with toys
These Brittany Spaniels know each other well, and exercise their minds and bodies by playfully tugging together on a rope toy.

Tug-of-war
This mongrel delights in playing tug-of-war. However, when playing games such as this, never let your dog win, since this may make it believe it is dominant over you.

DANGEROUS TOYS

Avoid poorly made toys or small balls that can be swallowed. Do not give articles of clothing or shoes as toys, since a dog will not restrict itself only to the items offered, but will chew anything that bears its owner's scent.

Playing with a ball
Chasing games stimulate natural canine behaviour. This puppy chases a ball as it would chase prey in the wild.

DIFFERENT TYPES OF TOY

All dogs enjoy playing games with balls and frisbees. These toys help exercise your dog and teach it to chase, capture, and retrieve. Some balls and rubber toys have squeakers, and dogs enjoy "killing" them. Be sure such toys are well made. Knotted ropes and tug toys are ideal for two dogs to play with together. Specially made nylon chews can also help to keep teeth and gums healthy.

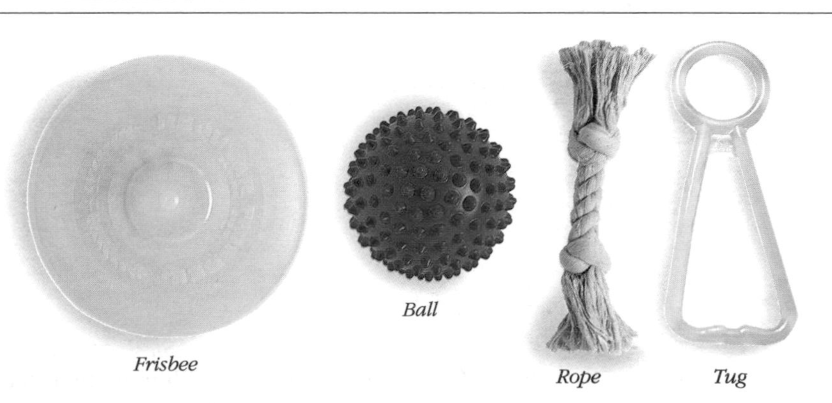

Frisbee *Ball* *Rope* *Tug*

DOG-PROOFING A GARDEN

Dogs need daily outdoor activity, preferably in the company of their owners or other dogs. Outdoor activity provides stimulation, but it can be dangerous for dogs on their own. Never let your dog roam freely, except in special areas where you can quickly regain control of it. Allowing a dog to roam around the streets is life-threatening to the dog and anti-social to your neighbours. Working dogs can be kept in a well-equipped outdoor kennel, provided that they are released regularly for physical activity.

The dog outdoors
Make sure that your garden is escape-proof and that a dog is not exposed to dangers within it. You can secure it with a high fence.

OUTDOOR KENNELS

When trained from an early age, most dogs are content to be housed in an outdoor kennel. It should contain food and water bowls, and a few chewable toys. Never leave a single dog alone in a kennel for extended periods – it is better to house two or more dogs together. The dogs must also be let out regularly and given plenty of exercise.

Garden dangers

The greatest danger for your dog in the garden is the possibility of escape. Use sturdy gates, latches, and fencing. Make sure that there are no gaps in the hedges. Fine wire mesh at ground level on gates and beneath hedges is a good additional safeguard to keep small dogs from escaping. Keep all horticultural and other chemicals locked in a garden shed or greenhouse, and put rubbish bins in a covered cupboard. Do not let your dog near a barbecue while it is being used for cooking. Avoid placing ornamental plant containers where they can be knocked over, and make sure a garden pond is kept covered. Train your dog to use a specific part of the garden, such as a sand pit or rough grass area, for its toilet. Remove and dispose of all waste. Provide your pet with a dog house in which it can be kept outside for short periods during warm weather.

TOXIC PLANTS

Many garden plants are poisonous to dogs. In particular, dogs should be prevented from eating all kinds of fungi, and kept away from laburnum trees and mistletoe berries. Keep plant bulbs such as daffodils out of reach. The following plants are potentially dangerous to dogs: columbine (*Aquilegia vulgaris*), hemlock (*Conium maculatum*), oleander (*Nerium oleander*), yew (*Taxus baccata*), lupin (*Lupinus* sp.), box (*Buxus sempervirens*), clematis (*Clematis* sp.), lily of the valley (*Convallaria majalis*), and ivy (*Hedera* sp).

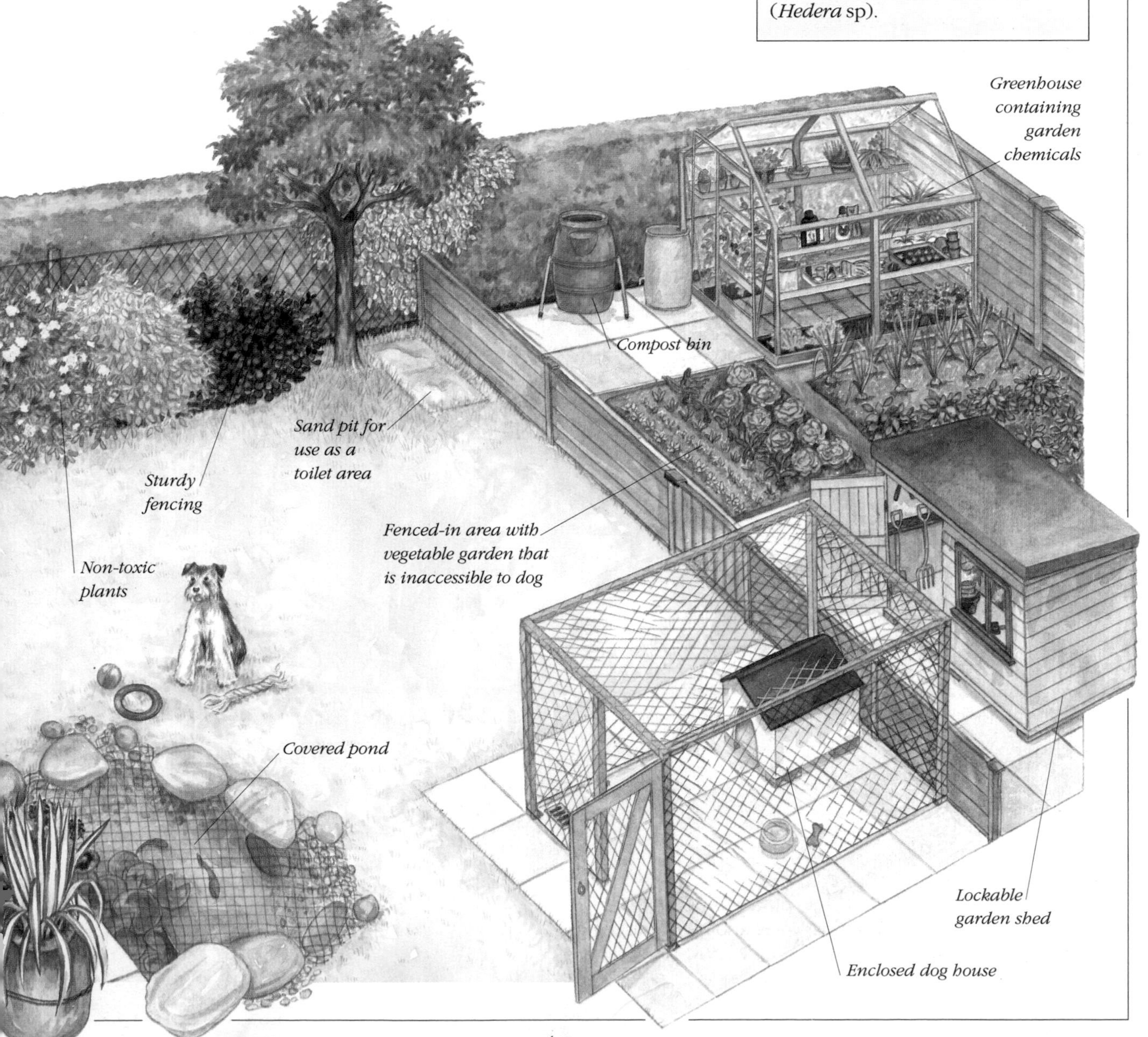

TRAVELLING AND HOLIDAYS

Travelling with your dog can be enjoyable, but it requires careful planning. If you are driving, make sure your car is well equipped. You should stop every few hours on the journey to allow your dog to exercise, drink, and relieve itself. Never leave your dog in your car in hot or sunny weather. Dogs have poor control of their body temperature and can suffer potentially fatal heatstroke much easier and faster than humans *(see page 170)*.

Obey local regulations on dog control. Remember that your dog will be excited by new sights and smells, but away from its normal territory it could easily get lost. Make sure that it carries your local telephone number on its name tag. When you arrive, find out the location of the local vet, in case of an emergency.

USING A DOG CARRIER

Travelling box
A carrier provides safety and security for a small dog when travelling by air or road.

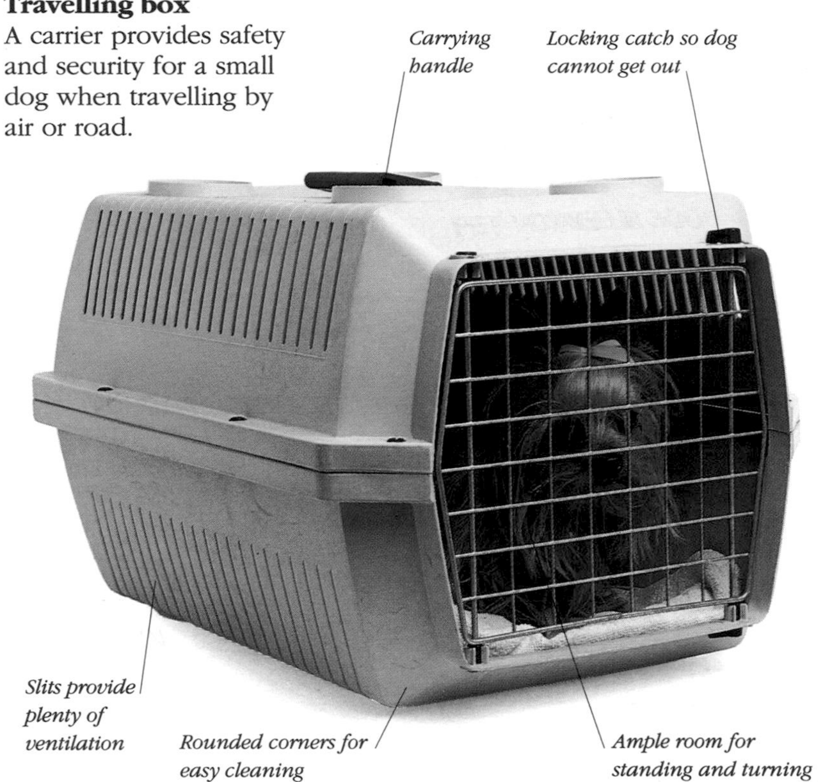

Carrying handle

Locking catch so dog cannot get out

Slits provide plenty of ventilation

Rounded corners for easy cleaning

Ample room for standing and turning

SAFETY IN A CAR

Seatbelt *(left)*
Special seatbelts can reduce the risk of a dog being injured in a car accident, and also prevent the dog from distracting the driver.

Dog grille *(right)*
A special grille restricts dogs to their own secure place in the car and prevents them from hurtling forwards in the event of a sudden stop.

THE DOG ON HOLIDAY

Backpack *(left)*
Some dogs can be trained to carry their own food and dishes in special saddlebags when out camping with their owners.

Lifejacket
Although they are excellent swimmers, dogs should always wear lifejackets when taken boating on open water a long way from the shore.

QUARANTINE KENNELS

Some rabies-free countries maintain quarantine regulations to control the import of animals from countries where this fatal disease exists *(see page 126)*. Other nations require proper identification and proof that a dog has been vaccinated against the disease before it is allowed to enter the country. If you are planning to move to a rabies-free area, make sure that you have the necessary documentation, including all veterinary certification in the country of origin. Where rabies quarantine exists, get a list of approved quarantine kennels from that country's agriculture department, and whenever possible, get someone to inspect the facility for you. Virtually all quarantine kennels permit routine visiting.

Dog sitter *(below)*
If you prefer to leave your dog in the comfort of its own home while you travel, a vet can put you in touch with an approved "dog-sitting" agency.

RESPONSIBILITIES OF A DOG OWNER

Enjoying the love, loyalty, and companionship of a canine brings obligations to maintain not only the dog's basic needs, but also the quality of life of your family, friends, and neighbours.

A dog depends upon its human owner to ensure its well being. This involves making sure that you obey the local legal requirements concerning dogs, as well as protecting your pet from injury, harm, or ill health.

Dogs are social animals and your pet should be treated as one of the family. Your dog relies on you to train it from an early age to be trusting, even-tempered, and sociable with humans and other dogs.

SOCIALIZING A DOG

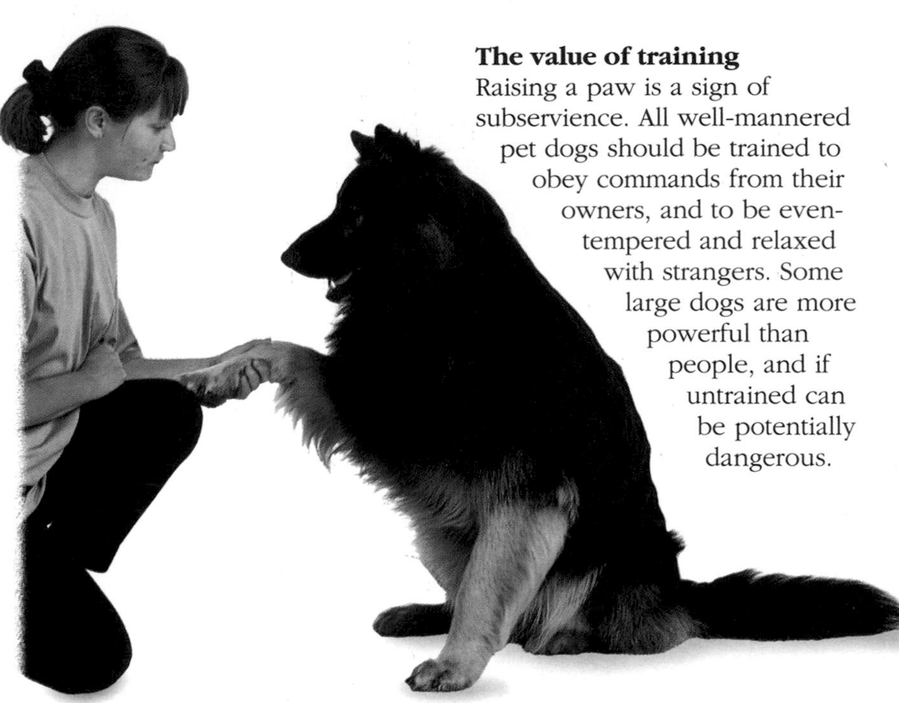

The value of training
Raising a paw is a sign of subservience. All well-mannered pet dogs should be trained to obey commands from their owners, and to be even-tempered and relaxed with strangers. Some large dogs are more powerful than people, and if untrained can be potentially dangerous.

Canine conviviality
Dogs should be trained to willingly sit together without showing any aggression. Early socialization ensures that your dog is relaxed and comfortable in the presence of other dogs. With so many dogs living in crowded urban environments where they meet other dogs daily, this type of training is essential.

CHOOSING A VET

Routine medical care
All dogs should have a routine annual veterinary examination. They should be wormed quarterly, and routinely vaccinated against infectious diseases. Choose your vet with the help of pet-owning friends.

All vets provide 24-hour emergency cover. Find out the location of your local emergency facilities and keep the telephone number close to hand. Veterinary treatment can be expensive, but health-care insurance is available to help cover some medical costs.

Vaccinations
Vaccination protects a dog from the main infectious diseases.

YOUR DOG AND THE LAW

DANGEROUS DOGS
Following public concern, it is now an offence in many countries to allow a dog to be dangerously out of control in a public place. You must always obey local muzzling laws, but only use a safe, basket-type muzzle that allows a dog to pant freely. A vet can advise you on any local legislation.

Muzzling
If you have doubts about your dog's temperament or behaviour, it is safest to keep it muzzled in public, especially in the presence of young children.

Identity tags
Every dog must always wear an identity tag on its collar. You might also consider having your dog permanently identified with a tiny microchip implant, or a number tattooed inside its ear.

Chapter 3

FEEDING

A NUTRITIOUS, well-balanced diet produces a strong-boned, well-muscled, healthy-coated canine. Just like humans, dogs love their food. Unlike humans, however, they have a poor sense of taste, and are therefore willing to eat almost anything. Many pet dogs also lead somewhat boring lives, and see mealtime as the highlight of the day. Some dogs may even bribe their owners to give them unhealthy treats they should not have, or to feed them more often than they should eat. This combination of facts explains why obesity is a problem in almost one out of three pets. Whatever you choose to feed your dog, make sure that it is part of a well-balanced diet, and that it is not given in excess of the dog's energy requirements.

DIETARY NEEDS

Each dog has its individual requirements, which will change at the various stages of its life. All dogs, however, require minimum quantities of a wide range of nutrients if they are to remain healthy. Dogs are not true carnivores, and cannot exist on meat alone. Therefore, meat, which provides protein, should never form more than half your dog's diet. Meat also provides fat, which contains essential fatty acids necessary for a variety of body functions, including good skin and coat condition. The remainder of a dog's daily calories should come from carbohydrates such as dog meal. A balanced diet has all the necessary vitamins.

THE VALUE OF NUTRIENTS

The well-fed dog
With a well-balanced diet, this Border Collie puppy will grow to have a shiny coat on a well-muscled, straight-boned body.

FEEDING EQUIPMENT

A heavy ceramic feeding bowl will not be knocked over easily by a dog. If you cook fresh meat for your dog, you can use any saucepan, but as a hygiene precaution, keep the utensils that you use in preparing your dog's meals separate from other kitchen equipment. Be sure to wash bowls and cutlery after each meal. Store partly used cans of food, covered by plastic lids, in the refrigerator for a maximum of three days, then discard.

THE NUTRITIONAL REQUIREMENTS OF AN ADULT DOG

Component	Dietary source	Function in body	Results of deficiency	Results of excess
Protein	Complete dog food, meat, fish, milk, eggs	Builds bones and repairs tissue; maintains growth	Slow growth, weak or deformed bones	Obesity, brittle bones
Fat	Animal and vegetable fats and oils	Provides energy and healthy skin; aids metabolic processes	Dull coat, delayed healing of wounds	Obesity, liver disease
Carbohydrate	Cereals, rice, pasta, dry dog meal, potatoes	Provides energy, and is source of bulk in diet	Possible fertility and whelping problems	Obesity
Minerals				
Calcium	Milk, cheese, bones, bread, and meat	Builds bones, needed for clotting and muscle function	Poor growth, rickets, convulsions	Lameness, joint problems, deformity
Phosphorus	Milk, bones, meat	Builds bones and teeth	Rickets (rare)	Bone resorption
Iron	Meat, bread, vegetables	Builds haemoglobin	Anaemia	Weight loss, anorexia
Copper	Meat, bones	Builds haemoglobin	Anaemia	—
Magnesium	Bones, fish, green vegetables, cereals	Builds bones; helps in protein synthesis	Convulsions, muscle weakness, anorexia	Diarrhoea
Zinc	Meat, cereals	Tissue repair; aids digestion	Poor growth and skin	Diarrhoea
Manganese	Cereals, nuts	Fat metabolism	Poor growth, infertility	—
Iodine	Milk, fish, vegetables	Thyroid function	Goitre, hair loss, lethargy	Heart disease
Cobalt	Milk, cheese, meat	Vitamin B_{12} production	—	—
Selenium	Fish meal, meat, cereals	Vitamin E synthesis	Muscle problems	Diarrhoea
Sulphur	Meat, eggs	Amino acid synthesis	Poor growth and coat	—
Potassium	Meat, milk	Water balance; nerve function	Kidney, heart problems	Muscle weakness
Sodium	Salt, cereals	Water balance; nerve function	Hair loss, poor growth	Thirst
Vitamins				
Vitamin A	Milk, cod liver oil	Protects skin; bone growth	Skin thickening	Bone pain, anorexia
Vitamin B_1	Peas, beans, whole grains, organ meat	Carbohydrate metabolism	Nerve decay, heart failure	—
Vitamin B_2	Milk, cheese, meat	Energy metabolism	Weight loss, anorexia	—
Niacin	Meat, cereals, legumes	Energy metabolism	Mouth ulcers, diarrhoea	—
Vitamin B_6	Meat, vegetables, cereals, eggs	Amino acid metabolism	Anorexia, convulsions, anaemia, weight loss	—
Folic acid	Green vegetables	Amino acid metabolism	Anaemia, weight loss	—
Vitamin B_{12}	Meat, eggs, milk	Amino acid metabolism	—	—
Biotin	Meat, vegetables	Amino acid metabolism	Scaly skin	—
Choline	Eggs, liver, cereals, peas and beans	Aids fat metabolism and nerve function	Fatty liver, poor clotting of blood	—
Vitamin D	Milk, cheese, eggs, meat, cod liver oil	Aids bone growth; increases calcium absorption	Rickets	Diarrhoea, symptoms of calcium deficiency
Vitamin E	Cereals, green vegetables, cheese	Aids cell membrane function and reproduction	Muscle weakness, infertility, anaemia	—
Vitamin K	Meat, cereals, green vegetables, liver	Blood clotting	Haemorrhage	—

VITAMINS AND MINERALS

Vitamin supplements
Your dog should obtain all the vitamins and minerals it needs from a well-balanced diet. However, there are occasions when it may require supplements. These include during pregnancy, lactation, and puppy growth, and when a dog is recovering from an illness. You should only give vitamin supplements under a vet's supervision, since too much can be as harmful as too little.

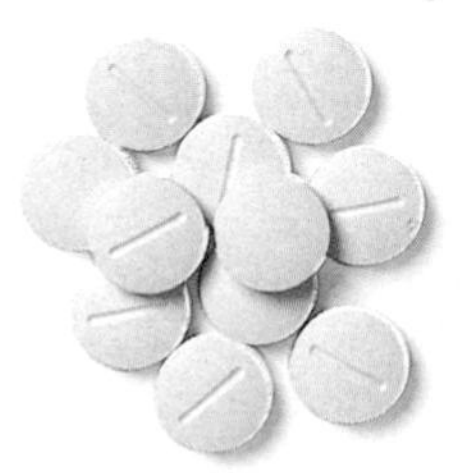

Calcium
Rapidly growing puppies and lactating bitches often need additional calcium.

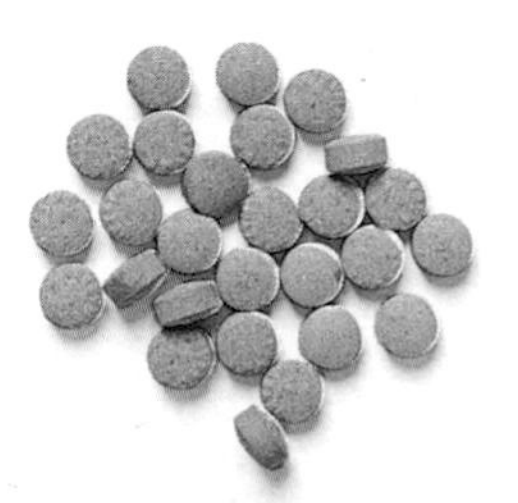

Vitamin tablets
Dogs rarely suffer from deficiencies, but tasty vitamin tablets can be used as treats.

Bonemeal
Sterilized bonemeal is a good source of calcium. Use under veterinary supervision.

Correct Feeding

In the wild, dogs gorge themselves when any kind of food is available and then live off that nourishment for several days. This food sits in the stomach, where not much digestion takes place, and is passed into the intestines a little at a time. In domestic dogs, this behaviour can lead to obesity. Some pet dogs, especially small breeds, are very fussy about what they eat. They turn up their noses at certain foods and blackmail their owners into offering them full menus from which they choose a daily selection.

Your dog should only eat what you want to feed it. The frequency of meals does not really matter, although once or twice a day is the norm. If your dog is overweight, reduce its calorie intake, or increase its consumption of calories through extra activity.

If your dog refuses to eat, seek veterinary advice about its health, then offer it food twice daily, and remove any uneaten remnants after a short period. The war of wills between you and your dog can last up to a week, but the dog will eventually eat whatever you decide to feed it.

Eating bones
Gnawing on bones massages the gums and exercises jaw muscles, but it can also damage the teeth and mouth.

GUIDELINES FOR FEEDING

General rules

1 Provide prepared foods from a reputable manufacturer.
2 Never offer spoiled or stale food to your dog.
3 A bowl of fresh water should always be available.
4 Never feed a dog cat food. It is too high in protein.
5 Always serve your dog's food at room temperature.
6 Dispose of any canned or moist food left uneaten.
7 Discard left-over dry food at the end of each day.
8 Watch your dog's weight. Do not let it get fat.
9 Never feed your dog brittle bones, for example from chicken.
10 Consult a vet for advice if your dog refuses to eat for 24 hours, since this may indicate illness.

Sharing food
Although some dogs in the same household may be happy to eat together, you should always provide separate food bowls.

CALORIE-CONTROLLED DIETS

REDUCING WEIGHT*		
Target weight	**Normal requirements**	**Dieting requirements**
2.5 kg (5.5 lb)	250 calories	150 calories
5 kg (11 lb)	450 calories	270 calories
10 kg (22 lb)	750 calories	450 calories
15 kg (33 lb)	1000 calories	600 calories
20 kg (44 lb)	1250 calories	750 calories
25 kg (55 lb)	1500 calories	900 calories
30 kg (66 lb)	1700 calories	1020 calories
35 kg (77 lb)	1880 calories	1140 calories
40 kg (88 lb)	2100 calories	1260 calories
45 kg (99 lb)	2300 calories	1380 calories
50 kg (110 lb)	2500 calories	1500 calories

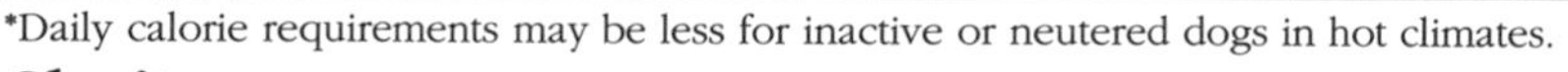

*Daily calorie requirements may be less for inactive or neutered dogs in hot climates.

Obesity

If your dog is overweight, increase its exercise, and feed it smaller meals, or a low-calorie diet available from a vet. You should feed about 60 per cent of the typical calories required for its ideal weight.

Begging for food

Food becomes an obsession for some dogs, especially if they are bored. If you keep giving in to a dog's begging you will simply reinforce this behaviour, and soon have an overweight dog.

DAILY WATER REQUIREMENTS

A dog loses water daily in urine and faeces, through panting, and to a limited extent through sweating from the pads. Dogs are as dependent upon water as humans are, and can suffer irreversible body dehydration and damage if it is unavailable for over 48 hours. Although canned dog food is usually three-quarters liquid, this is not enough to satisfy a dog's needs, as it is for cats.

You should fill your dog's bowl with fresh water to the same level each day. If you notice that it is drinking more than usual, contact a vet, since this may indicate an internal disorder.

PREPARED FOODS

It is easier to guarantee a well-balanced diet for your dog than it is for the rest of your family. You completely control what a dog eats, and by choosing from the wide array of prepared foods available from reputable pet-food manufacturers, you can provide all the nutrients necessary to satisfy your canine's feeding requirements. Through its lifetime a dog's energy needs will change. When your dog's energy demands are high, for example when working, whelping, or lactating, feed foods with more calories, and when energy demand drops, for example in old age, feed a diet specially formulated for advancing years. There are several advantages in feeding complete dry foods. These are convenient, almost odourless, and leave little indigestible residue, making it easy to clean up after your dog.

TYPES OF DOG FOOD

Dog meal *(below)*
Crunchy dog meal is an excellent source of fat, carbohydrates, and calories.

Canned foods *(left)*
Meaty, high-protein canned food is usually mixed with dog meal to provide a balanced diet.

Dehydrated variety

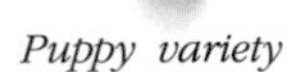

Puppy variety

High-energy variety

Complete semi-moist food
With more than three times the calories of canned food, this food is excellent for dogs, but since it has a high carbohydrate content, it should not be fed to diabetics.

Elderly dog variety

Low-calorie variety

Standard variety

Complete dry foods
These usually have over four times as many calories per gram as canned foods, and must be fed in smaller quantities. Some types of complete food must be rehydrated with water.

DAILY FEEDING GUIDE FOR ADULT DOGS*				
Dog type	**Calories required**	**Canned food/meal**	**Semi-moist food**	**Dry food**
Toy 5 kg (11 lb) e.g. Yorkshire Terrier	210 calories	105 g (4 oz) meat 35 g (1 oz) meal	70 g (2 oz)	60 g (2 oz)
Small 10 kg (22 lb) e.g. West Highland White Terrier	590 calories	300 g (11 oz) meat 100 g (4 oz) meal	190 g (7 oz)	170 g (6 oz)
Medium 20 kg (44 lb) e.g. Cocker Spaniel	900 calories	450 g (16 oz) meat 150 g (5 oz) meal	300 g (11 oz)	260 g (9 oz)
Large 40 kg (88 lb) e.g. German Shepherd Dog	1680 calories	850 g (30 oz) meat 280 g (10 oz) meal	545 g (19 oz)	480 g (17 oz)
Giant 80 kg (176 lb) e.g. Great Dane	2800 calories	1400 (49 oz) meat 460 g (16 oz) meal	900 g (32 oz)	800 g (28 oz)

* These figures are intended as an approximate guide only. Feed according to the manufacturer's instructions.

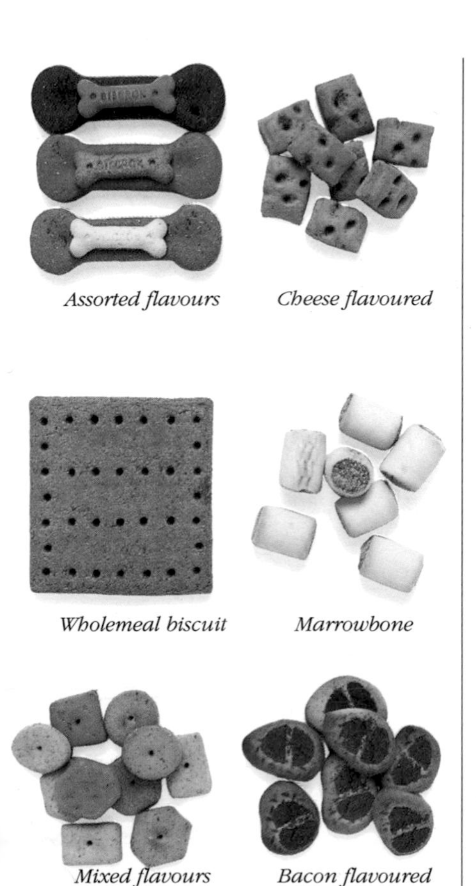

Assorted flavours · *Cheese flavoured* · *Wholemeal biscuit* · *Marrowbone* · *Mixed flavours* · *Bacon flavoured*

Biscuits
Biscuits are high in fat and carbohydrate. By weight they contain as many calories as complete foods. Remember to include these calories when calculating a dog's daily needs.

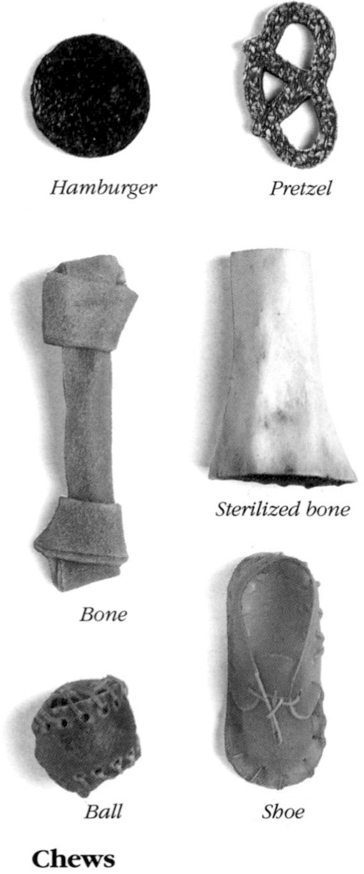

Hamburger · *Pretzel* · *Bone* · *Sterilized bone* · *Ball* · *Shoe*

Chews
These allow a dog to exercise its teeth and gums, which is necessary for good dental hygiene. They contain few calories and may help prevent destructive chewing.

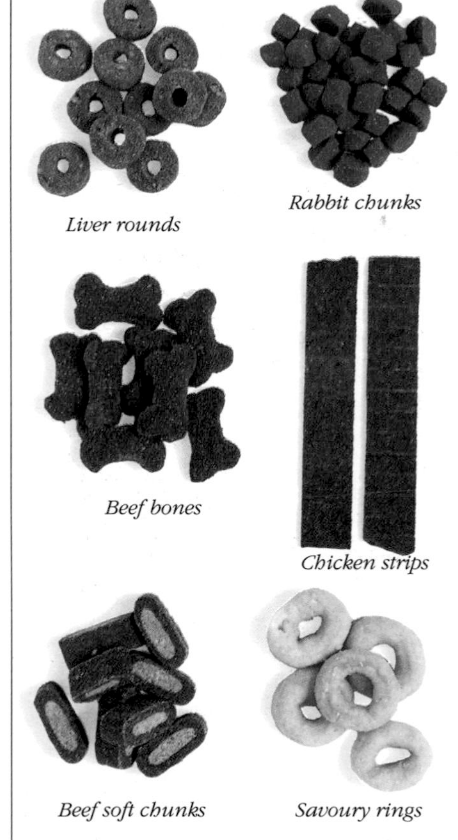

Liver rounds · *Rabbit chunks* · *Beef bones* · *Chicken strips* · *Beef soft chunks* · *Savoury rings*

Treats
These tasty snacks are good as training rewards, but they are high in calories, and must be included in any calorie count. Too many tidbits and too little exercise can lead to weight gain.

FRESH FOODS

Dogs are not complete carnivores and cannot live on meat alone. As a general rule, foods that are balanced for humans are probably balanced for your dog. If you plan to feed your pet fresh food, make sure that you provide it with all the nutritional building blocks it needs to maintain a healthy body. Mix meat or vegetable protein with vegetables, pasta, rice, cereals, or other foods to provide all the protein, carbohydrate, fat, vitamins, and minerals necessary for good health.

FEEDING A BALANCED DIET

Basic diet *(above)*
Meat and vegetables provide a dog with virtually all the ingredients it needs for a nutritious, balanced diet.

Minced meat *(above)*
The high level of fat in minced meat is not as harmful to dogs as it is to humans, but is a major source of calories.

Pasta
Pasta and noodles, good sources of carbohydrates, are rather tasteless and often need added flavouring.

Heart
Because of its fat content, heart has twice as many calories as other organs such as kidney. It should be fed in moderation.

Liver
Liver, like other meats, has a high phosphorus but low calcium content. It is also rich in vitamins A and B_1.

Raw vegetables and fruit
Uncooked vegetables and fruit, such as carrots, cabbage, and apple, are good sources of additional vitamins.

SPECIAL FEEDING FOR DELICATE STOMACHS

Chicken
Chicken and turkey are easily digested, and are lower in calories than other meats.

Fish
You should be careful to remove even the smallest bones before feeding fish to your dog.

Rice
Boiled rice is easily digested. Added to chicken, it makes a good diet for a convalescent.

VEGETARIAN FOOD

Tofu

Mixed vegetables

Unlike cats, dogs are not true carnivores. They can survive on vegetarian diets because they can convert vegetable protein and fat into the ingredients necessary for all bodily functions. Consult a vet however, if you wish to feed your dog on a vegetarian diet, since it is difficult to maintain balanced nutrition.

BREAKFAST FOODS

Cereal
Breakfast cereals with milk are good sources of vitamins, and provide a tasty light meal.

Scrambled egg
Light and nutritious, scrambled egg is ideal for puppies and dogs recovering from an illness.

ANALYSIS OF FRESH MEATS

Meat	Moisture	Protein	Fat	Calories per 100g
Tripe	88%	9%	3%	63 calories
Kidney	80%	16%	2.6%	86 calories
Chicken	74%	20%	4.3%	121 calories
Beef	74%	20%	4.6%	123 calories
Pork	72%	20%	7.1%	147 calories
Lamb	70%	20%	8.8%	162 calories
Heart	70%	14%	15.5%	197 calories

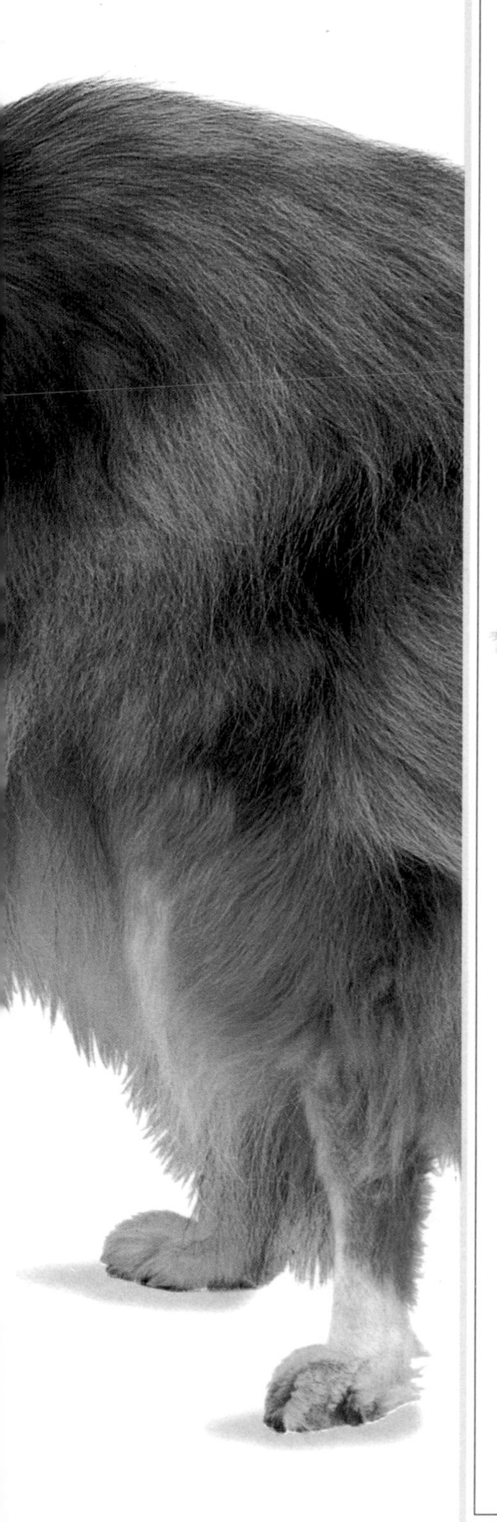

Chapter 4

GROOMING

HEALTHY DOGS are naturally good at keeping clean. They groom themselves by rolling and rubbing on the ground, scratching, chewing at matted fur, and licking their coats. Unfortunately, they also like to roll in noxious substances such as other animals' droppings, and anoint their fur with what humans consider to be unpleasant odours, and thus sometimes need help with grooming, as well as occasional bathing. Human intervention in dog breeding has led to a variety of coat textures and lengths, each with individual grooming needs. Selective breeding has also been responsible for dog coats that require frequent brushing, stripping, or clipping.

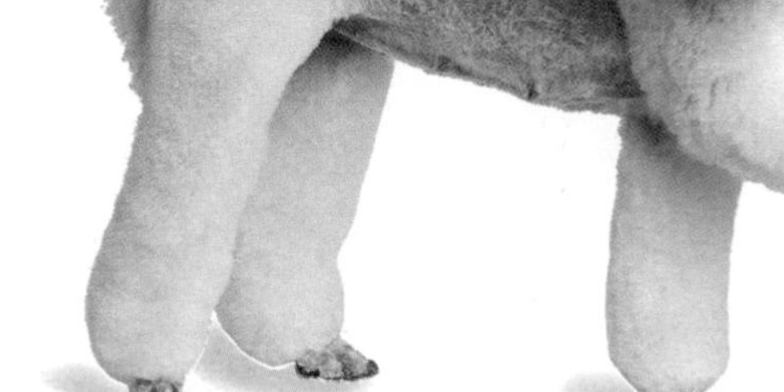

Coat Types

Having evolved in the colder regions of the northern hemisphere, the earliest breeds of dog had dense coats for protection from the cold and from predators. Then, as dogs moved into hot climates in the company of humans, their coats became shorter and thinner. The Saluki in Arabia, the Basenji in Africa, and the Australian Cattle Dog illustrate how different coats have evolved according to regional climatic conditions.

The enormous variety of coats found today is due to selective breeding of dogs by humans, who have developed breeds with specialized coats for different purposes.

GROOMING REQUIREMENTS

Short coat *(above)*
These Welsh Corgis have dense, short coats of profuse, downy, water-resistant hair close to the skin, and thick, straight surface hair. This coat should be groomed at least once a week *(see page 67)*.

Wiry coat
The wiry coat on this Airedale Terrier consists of stiff, dense hair, which needs daily grooming to prevent matting. You should never use conditioners on this type of coat, since they will soften it. Wiry coats do not moult, and require regular hand-stripping or clipping *(see page 67)*.

Curly coat *(above)*
Kerry Blue Terriers like this one have curly, non-shedding, extremely waterproof coats. Breeds with similar coats are the Portuguese Water Dog, Irish Water Spaniel, and poodles. This coat should be bathed and clipped every two months *(see pages 70–71)*.

Long coat *(below)*
This Lhasa Apso has a long, straight, coarse outer coat and a thick undercoat, which require daily grooming and regular trimming *(see page 69)*. Long coats originally offered dogs protection from the cold, but now serve purely fashionable purposes.

Long, coarse coat insulates against cold

Smooth coat
Smooth, shorthaired coats such as this Dobermann's are the easiest to maintain, but offer little protection from either dog bites or cold weather. Although short and relatively sparse, these coats are shed and require weekly brushing *(see page 66)*.

Smooth coat offers little protection

Silky coat *(below)*
Afghan Hounds have the bodies of racing dogs, but because they evolved in a cold climate, they retained heavy coats for protection against the elements. Silky coats need a lot of care, with daily grooming and regular trimming *(see page 68)*.

CANINE CLOTHING

Although dogs already have their own furry coats, there are some circumstances when items of dog clothing are useful. For example, Yorkshire Terriers have thin coats with no downy undercoat for protection against the cold. Shorthaired Chihuahuas and Dobermanns also have very little fur on their bodies. Even fairly well-furred dogs, such as this Cavalier King Charles Spaniel, can benefit from the additional protection a manufactured coat offers when they are ill or of advanced years.

Raincoat

Warm coat

First Steps in Grooming

Grooming serves two main purposes. It keeps the skin, coat, teeth, gums, and nails in a healthy state, and through routine grooming sessions you also constantly reassert your authority over your dog. You should make its daily or weekly grooming a ritual that both you and your dog enjoy and respect.

If your dog refuses to let you groom it, command it to sit and stay. Grooming should always involve a reward for your dog. In most instances, physical contact is enough, but there is no harm in occasionally giving your dog a food reward.

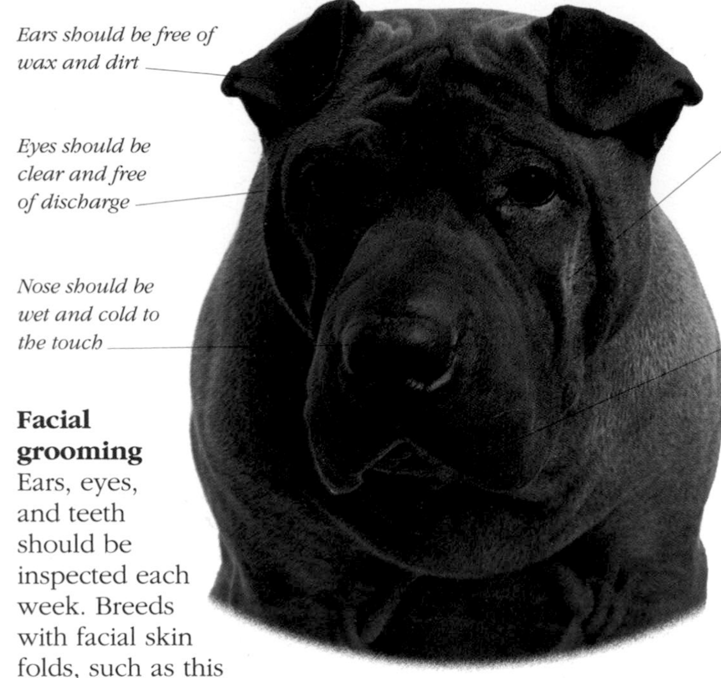

Facial grooming Ears, eyes, and teeth should be inspected each week. Breeds with facial skin folds, such as this Shar Pei, need special attention.

CLEANING THE FACE

1 Gently bathe the skin around the eyes using a fresh piece of moistened cotton wool for each one. If you notice any discharge or inflammation, you should contact a vet for advice.

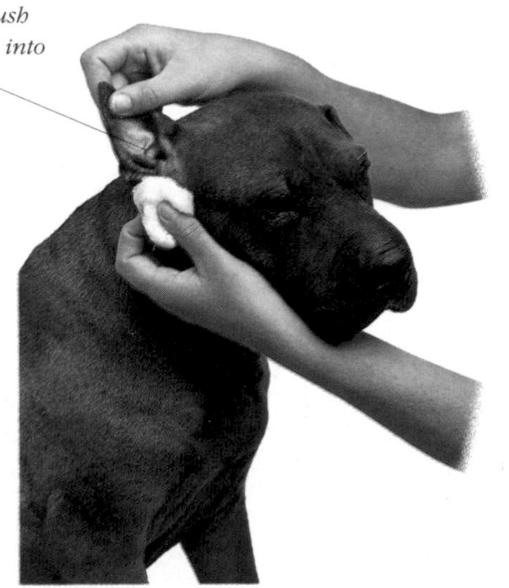

2 Hold open the ear with one hand and gently clean inside the flap with a small piece of moistened cotton wool. Use a fresh piece for each ear. Do not probe too deeply into the ears.

3 Loose facial skin must be cleaned regularly with damp cotton wool. This prevents dirt, dead skin, and bacteria from collecting in the folds and causing irritation and infection.

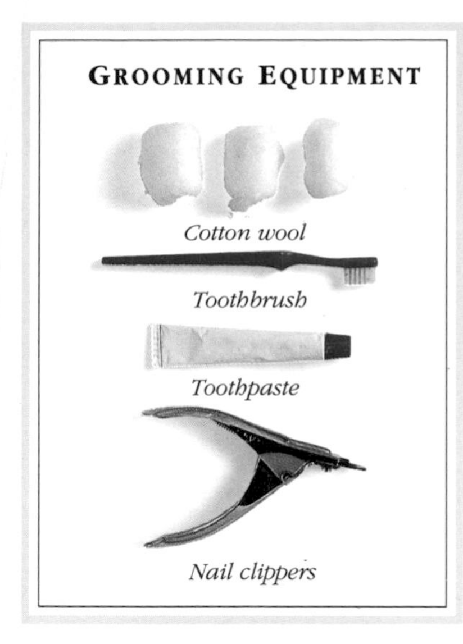

GROOMING EQUIPMENT

Cotton wool

Toothbrush

Toothpaste

Nail clippers

CLEANING THE TEETH

1 You should check a dog's teeth and gums once a week. Make sure that there is no sign of gum infection or tartar build-up on the teeth, which can lead to gingivitis and tenderness.

2 Gently brush the dog's teeth with a soft toothbrush, using either dilute salt water or a special canine toothpaste, obtainable from a vet.

DENTAL HYGIENE

A vet can provide special canine toothpaste. Never use toothpaste intended for humans.

TRIMMING THE NAILS

WHERE TO TRIM THE NAILS

The pink area inside the nail is called the nail bed, or quick, and contains the blood supply and nerves. Take care to trim the nails without cutting the quick. Ask a vet to trim the dog's nails if you are in any doubt about where to clip them.

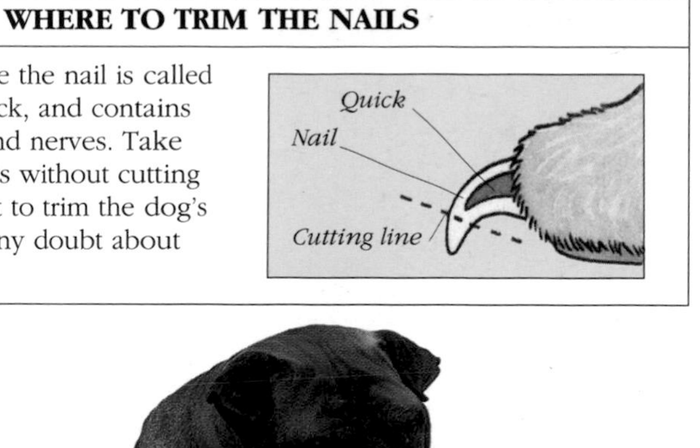

Feet are checked regularly for dirt and foreign bodies

1 Spread each of the dog's feet and inspect the area between its toes. Clean away any dirt and debris with moistened cotton wool.

2 Clip the nails carefully. You can smooth any rough edges with an emery board or nail file. Trim the dog's dew claws if it has them.

GROOMING SHORTHAIRED DOGS

Smooth and short coats are relatively self-cleaning and need less attention than other varieties of fur. Some coats, however, such as that of the Labrador Retriever, are shed heavily. Dogs kept outdoors moult twice yearly, while those housed indoors shed their hair all year round. If the hair and dandruff are to be kept under control, these dogs must be groomed almost as frequently as those with longer or more complicated coats.

Some large breeds like the Dobermann and Great Dane have smooth, sometimes thick coats, the hairs of which can act like needles and penetrate the skin at pressure points such as the elbows and hocks when the dog lies down. These susceptible areas should be treated with a conditioner to soften the hair and prevent damage to the skin.

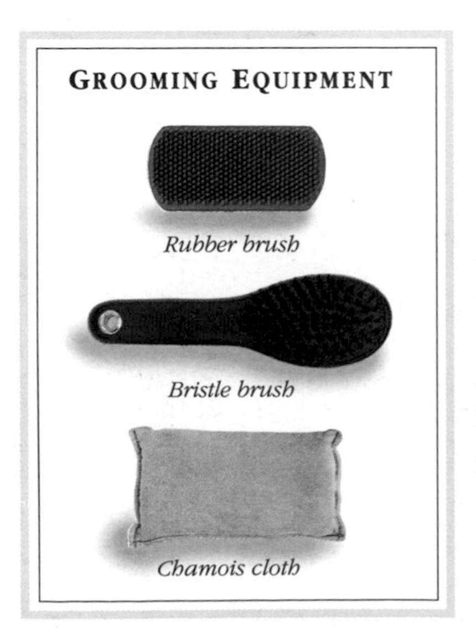

GROOMING A SMOOTH COAT

1 Smooth-coated dogs such as this Boxer do not need a lot of grooming, but they should have a regular brush once or twice a week. First use a rubber brush or hound glove, working against the lie of the fur, to loosen any dead hair and surface dirt.

Rubber brush loosens dead hair and dirt

2 Remove dead hair and skin with a bristle brush, taking care to cover the entire coat, from head to tail. A coat conditioner can be put on at this stage to give the coat a glossy sheen.

Brush vigorously with the lie of the coat to remove dead skin and hair

3 Lastly, briskly polish the coat with a chamois cloth to bring out the shine. Dogs with smooth coats are the easiest to groom, and can look immaculate with regular care and attention.

GROOMING A SHORT COAT

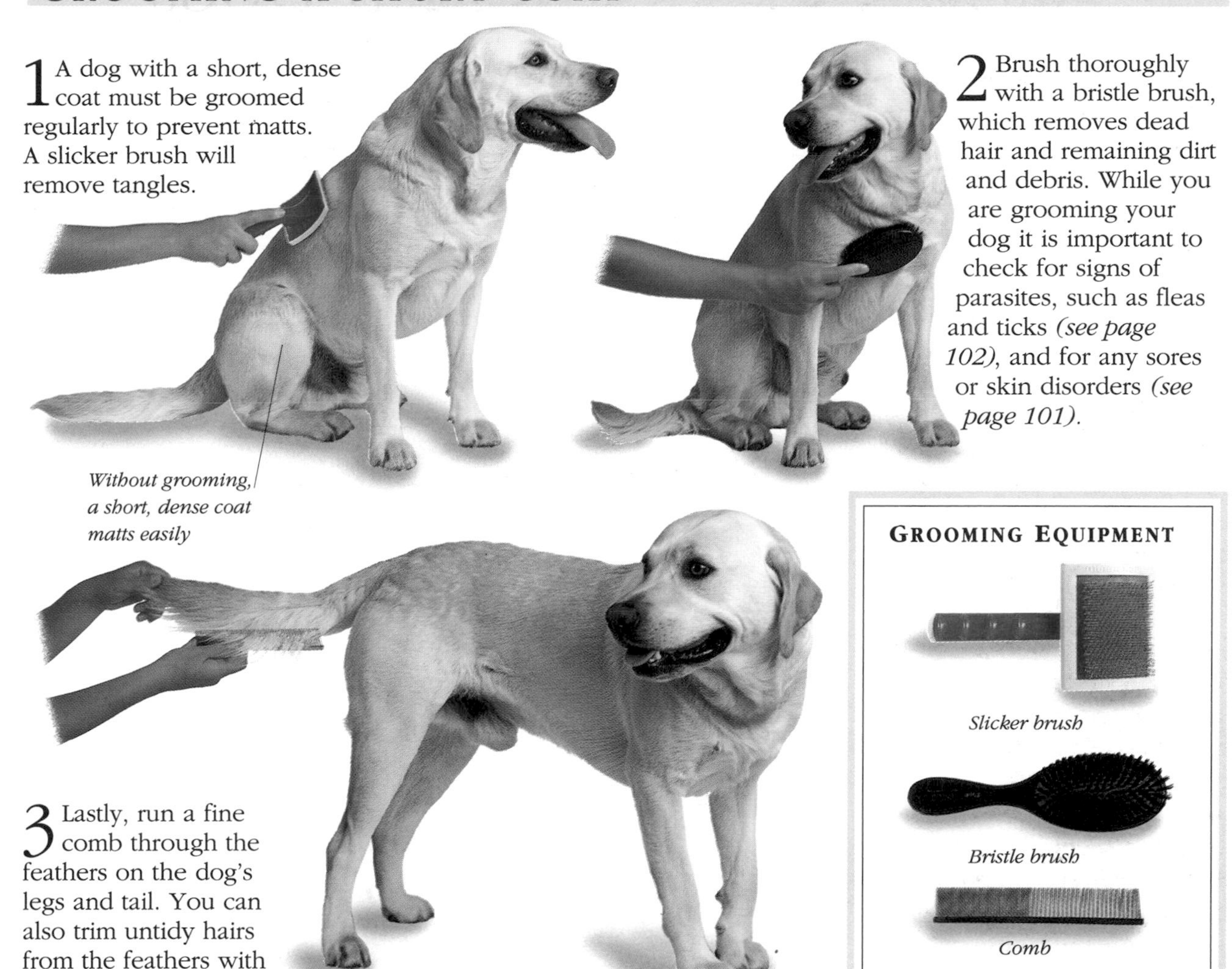

1 A dog with a short, dense coat must be groomed regularly to prevent matts. A slicker brush will remove tangles.

Without grooming, a short, dense coat matts easily

2 Brush thoroughly with a bristle brush, which removes dead hair and remaining dirt and debris. While you are grooming your dog it is important to check for signs of parasites, such as fleas and ticks *(see page 102)*, and for any sores or skin disorders *(see page 101)*.

3 Lastly, run a fine comb through the feathers on the dog's legs and tail. You can also trim untidy hairs from the feathers with scissors, if you wish.

GROOMING EQUIPMENT

Slicker brush

Bristle brush

Comb

HAND-STRIPPING A WIRY COAT

Wiry coats, such as those of terriers, schnauzers, and the Wire-haired Dachshund, must be hand-stripped every three to four months. Dead hair can be pulled out between the thumb and finger in the direction of growth. If done correctly, this should not cause the dog any discomfort. Alternatively, a stripping knife can be used. This instrument has no cutting blade, and the hair is plucked out between the thumb and the knife. If you wish, instead of stripping, the coat can be regularly machine-clipped and excess hair around the face trimmed by a professional groomer.

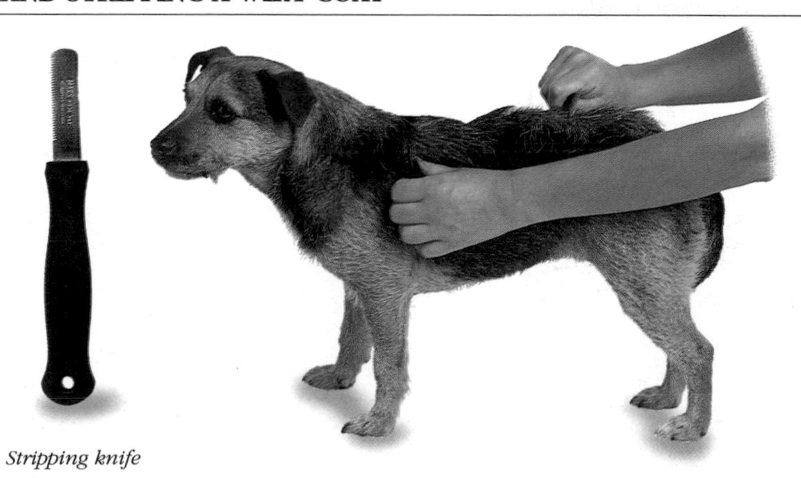

Stripping knife

Grooming Longhaired Dogs

Luxurious, long coats are elegant and insulating, but they need more attention than short coats. Breeds with silky coats like the Yorkshire Terrier have no downy undercoat, so extra care must be taken while grooming to avoid scratching or irritating the skin.

Rough Collies and Shetland Sheepdogs have long coats combined with dense, thick, protective down. This type of deep coat matts easily without thorough grooming.

Grooming a Silky Coat

1 Use a slicker brush to remove any tangles. Matts can be gently teased out. Take care not to pull on the hair and break it.

2 Brush the coat once more, using a bristle brush to bring out the shine. There should be no resistance.

Bristle brush brings out shine in coat

3 Part the long hair on the back and comb each side straight down. Any untidy ends can be carefully trimmed with scissors.

Comb hair on either side of centre parting

4 Trim around the feet and ears. The nails should also be clipped *(see page 65)*.

Carefully trim feathers around toes and feet

5 Long hair above the eyes can either be trimmed or tied with a ribbon and bow.

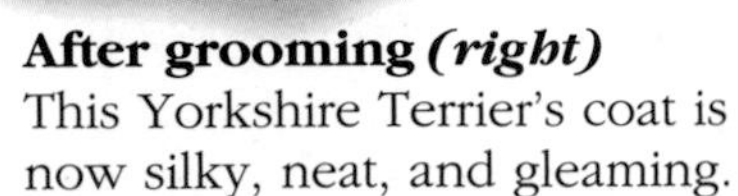

After grooming *(right)*
This Yorkshire Terrier's coat is now silky, neat, and gleaming.

Grooming Equipment

GROOMING A LONG COAT

1 Using a slicker brush, gently untangle any matted hair or knots. Be careful not to pull out the hair or cause the dog pain by brushing too vigorously.

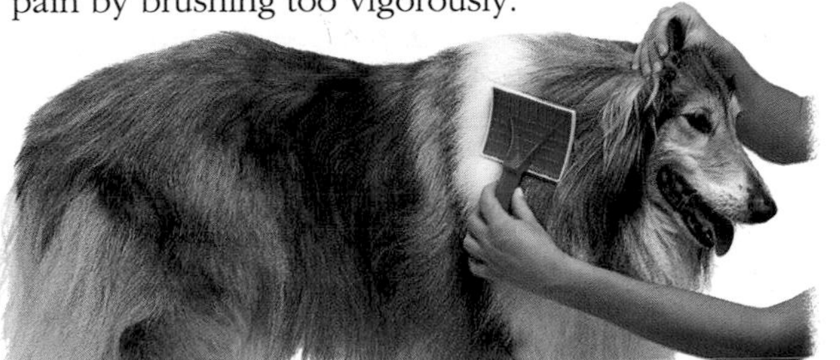

Coat should be tangle-free

2 Brush the coat again with a pin brush. You should feel no tangles as you brush through the coat.

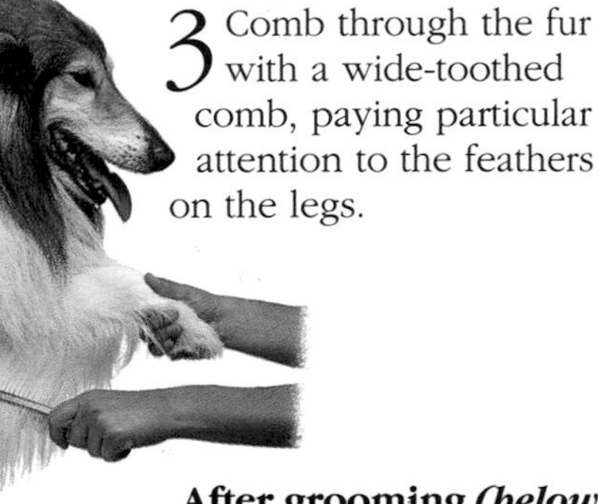

3 Comb through the fur with a wide-toothed comb, paying particular attention to the feathers on the legs.

4 Trim long hair around the feet, especially between the toes, where dirt and foreign bodies can become lodged, causing irritation.

After grooming *(below)* This Rough Collie is sleek and tidy.

5 Using sharp scissors, trim around the hocks so that the long hair does not become tangled and collect dirt and debris.

GROOMING EQUIPMENT

Slicker brush

Pin brush

Scissors

Comb

CLIPPING A DOG

Most dogs moult their coats, either constantly or in two seasonal bursts. Some breeds with curly coats, such as poodles, however, do not. The hair simply keeps growing, and is maintained through routine clipping.

Although some people like to shape their pet's coat in distinctive ways, such as the lamb clip on the Standard Poodle shown here, all that is really necessary is a regular trim, taking special care around the face and anal region.

Clipping is usually necessary about every six to eight weeks, although a dog's coat can be clipped more frequently in summer, and less often when the weather is cooler.

Most dogs enjoy having a shortened coat. Even if you do not want to completely clip your dog's coat yourself, you should be prepared to trim it to keep it from getting tangled.

CLIPPING EQUIPMENT

CLIPPING METHOD

Wax can get trapped in long hair inside ears

1 After bathing, drying, and brushing the dog with a slicker brush, pluck the long hair from inside the ears. If this hair is not plucked regularly, it can trap wax, which may cause hearing problems.

2 Holding the skin tight to avoid nicking it, carefully clip the sides of the face from the corner of the ear to the eye, and down the neck towards the body. Continue along the sides of the muzzle, cutting against the lie of the hair.

Be careful not to clip skin on face and neck

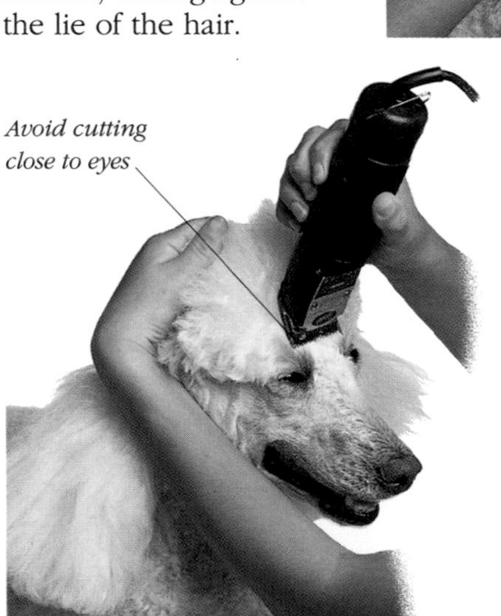

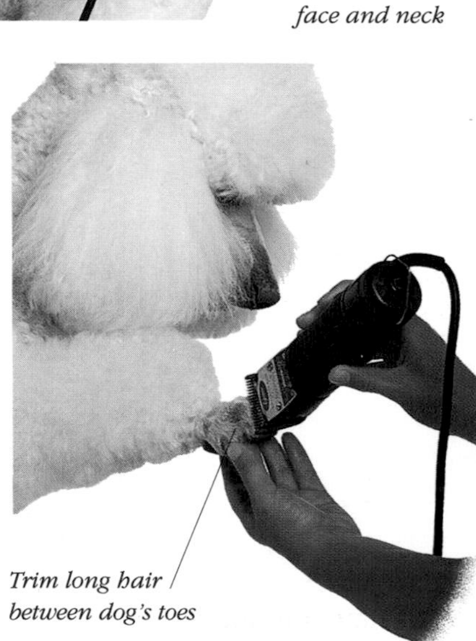

3 Finish off the muzzle by clipping down the top from the eyes to the nose. Try to keep the strokes even and parallel. Do not cut too close to the eyes.

4 Clip the feet from below the ankle bones downwards, and between the toes. Cut against the lie of the hair, taking care to avoid nicking the pads.

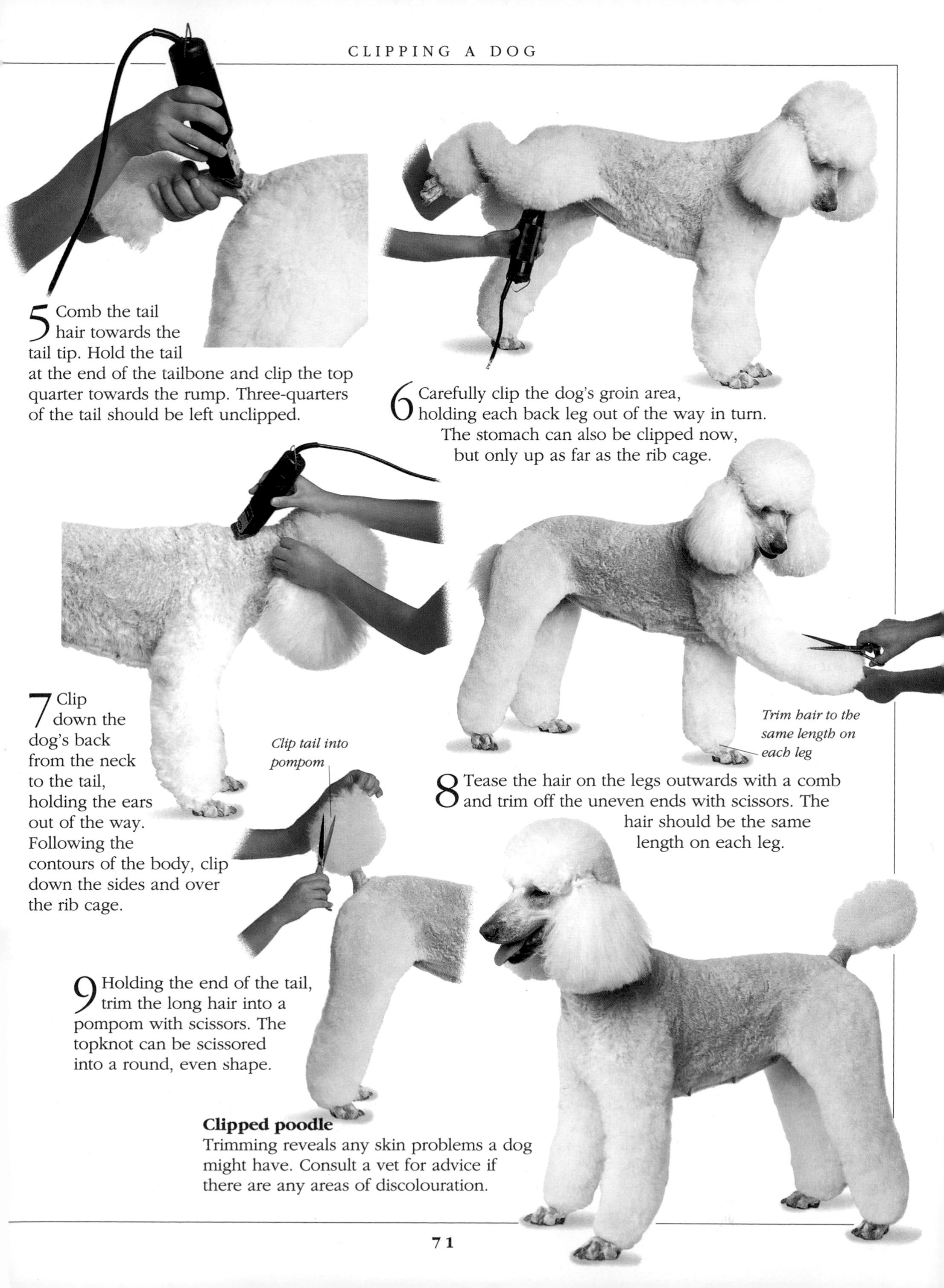

5 Comb the tail hair towards the tail tip. Hold the tail at the end of the tailbone and clip the top quarter towards the rump. Three-quarters of the tail should be left unclipped.

6 Carefully clip the dog's groin area, holding each back leg out of the way in turn. The stomach can also be clipped now, but only up as far as the rib cage.

7 Clip down the dog's back from the neck to the tail, holding the ears out of the way. Following the contours of the body, clip down the sides and over the rib cage.

8 Tease the hair on the legs outwards with a comb and trim off the uneven ends with scissors. The hair should be the same length on each leg.

9 Holding the end of the tail, trim the long hair into a pompom with scissors. The topknot can be scissored into a round, even shape.

Clipped poodle
Trimming reveals any skin problems a dog might have. Consult a vet for advice if there are any areas of discolouration.

Bathing a Dog

Routine grooming keeps a dog's coat in a healthy condition, but bathing is sometimes necessary if a dog has rolled in a malodorous substance. Bathing is also beneficial in eliminating certain skin parasites and treating a variety of dry and oily skin conditions. In some circumstances, a vet might suggest medically therapeutic shampoos and conditioners. You must always follow the manufacturer's instructions.

Rinsing is important, since any residual shampoo in the coat can irritate the skin and cause scratching. The dog may need to wear its collar in the bath, so that you can hold on to it and prevent it from jumping out. A rubber mat on the bottom of the bath will keep the dog from slipping.

Bathing Method

1 After brushing the dog and plugging its ears with cotton wool, stand it carefully in the bath on a rubber mat. Hold it tightly by the collar and pour warm water on its coat.

Rub shampoo well into coat to loosen dirt and dead skin

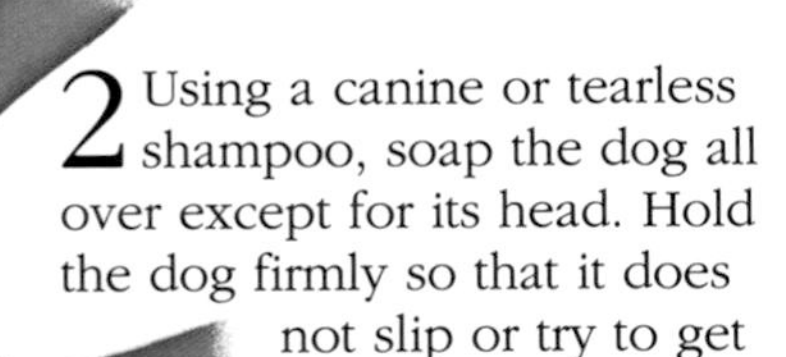

2 Using a canine or tearless shampoo, soap the dog all over except for its head. Hold the dog firmly so that it does not slip or try to get out of the bath. Work up a good lather, massaging the skin against the lie of the coat, but be careful not to splash water or soap in the dog's eyes.

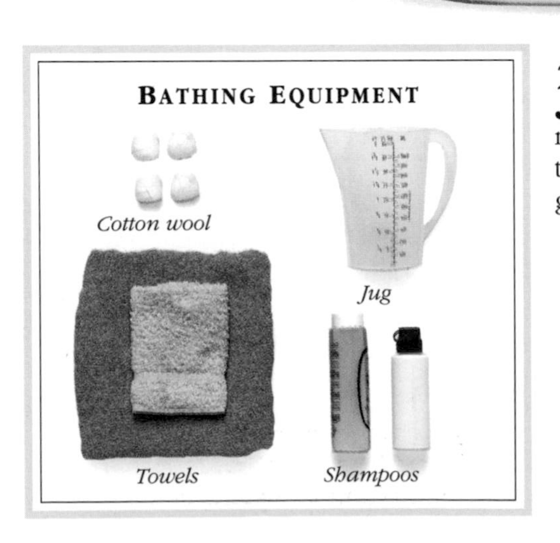

3 Lather the dog's head with a tearless shampoo poured in your hands, and massage the hair gently, being careful to avoid splashing the eyes or getting soap in the mouth.

Keep soap out of dog's eyes

4 Rinse and dry the dog's head before rinsing the body. This will help prevent it from shaking water everywhere.

5 Rinse the rest of the body in warm water, taking care to remove all the shampoo. If necessary, rub conditioner into the coat, then rinse it off.

6 Squeeze excess water from the coat, then dry the dog with a large towel. Remove the ear plugs and dry the insides of the ears.

7 A hair dryer set on warm, not hot, can be used on dogs with healthy skin, but not on dogs prone to itchiness, since heat exaggerates itch. Brush the hair straight, away from the body.

After bathing
After its bath, a dog often runs around with excitement. Take care it does not instantly roll over and try to cover itself in more natural smells.

Chapter 5

TRAINING

TRAINING IS a most important part of caring for a dog. An untrained dog is like a car with faulty brakes. It is unreliable and, until the fault is corrected, potentially dangerous. All but the most dominant dogs enjoy training because it involves mental stimulation. Training also helps prevent the dog from adopting bad habits through boredom. Prevention of bad habits is always easier than cure. If you train your dog from as early an age as possible to instantly obey your commands, walk on a lead, and play games, you are far less likely to ever have to deal with unwanted behaviour. If you do have to correct bad habits, it will be much easier if your dog has already learned basic obedience, so that it can be stopped the instant it does something wrong.

PUPPY TRAINING

Informal training should begin as soon as you bring a new puppy home at eight weeks old. Whenever it does anything you eventually want it to do on command, such as sit, say the appropriate word several times while the puppy maintains that position. It will rapidly learn to associate the word with what it is doing. At the same time, praise the puppy to let it know you are pleased with what it is doing. It quickly learns what praise words like "good dog" mean.

If the puppy does something you do not want it to, say "No!", but only when you catch it actually misbehaving. Never discipline the puppy even seconds after it has done something wrong. It will not associate your discipline with a previous action.

Early lead training *(see pages 78–79)* can be started as soon as a puppy is used to wearing a collar and lead.

THE BASIC COMMANDS

The puppy's name
This puppy sits attentively when it hears its name. Each time you play with the puppy, repeatedly say its name. Sharp, two-syllable names like "Sparky" are easiest for a dog to learn.

Puppy stops and listens when it hears its name

Sitting on command
The puppy's attention is drawn to its impending meal. Hold the food bowl above the puppy so that it will sit in order to keep its eye on the bowl. As it does so, say the word "Sit", then reward it with the meal.

Puppy's gaze is fixed on food bowl

TRAINING A PUPPY TO LIE DOWN

1 By teaching the puppy to lie down you are telling it that you are in charge. Begin with the puppy in a sitting position. Command, "Lie down", at the same time patting the ground in front of it.

2 If the puppy ignores the command, ease it to the ground by gently pressing on its body and pulling its legs forwards. Give the puppy lots of praise when it is lying down.

TRAINING A PUPPY TO COME

1 With the puppy in the sit position and wearing its collar and lead to give you greater control, command it to wait. Remain standing in front of the puppy until it is settled. Do not pull on the lead.

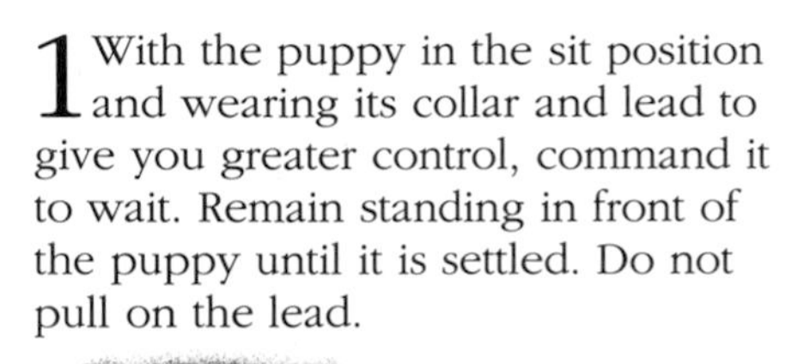

Keep the lead loose

Puppy listens to owner's voice

2 Slowly walk backwards away from the puppy to the end of the lead. Tell the puppy to "Come" and if it looks confused, give the lead a gentle tug. Continue walking and encouraging the puppy to come to you.

3 Always finish any exercise by praising the puppy. Stroking and food are powerful rewards. An encouraging, pleased tone of voice is important when praising a dog. Remember the puppy understands not what you say but the way in which you say it.

PREVENTING BAD BEHAVIOUR

Jumping up
If the puppy jumps up, gently push it down and say firmly, "No!". Command it to sit, and then greet it. A puppy must be discouraged from this type of behaviour early on *(see page 84)*.

Chewing objects
Meticulously store away any personal items the puppy might chew. Provide it with several dog toys, giving it praise when they are chewed.

WALKING A DOG

When walking with you, your dog must always be under control. For its own safety as well as a courtesy to others, this means that it should be on a lead. A simple rule of physics applies when walking your dog on a lead: for every action there is an equal and opposite reaction. If your dog strains on its lead and you pull back, all you do is provoke it to strain harder.

As a puppy your dog should have learned to accept its collar and then a trailing lead. You should keep lessons in walking to heel short, no more than fifteen minutes at a time, up to four times a day. Give basic lessons in a quiet area and do not lose patience. If your dog is not performing properly, finish off with a command you know it will follow. Lessons should be enjoyable. Always finish the training session with a game.

THE CHECK CHAIN

When used correctly, check chains help with training by applying intermittent tension on a dog's neck. They should only be used on dogs that are insensitive to touch, or have thick neck fur. Never use a check chain on a puppy or on breeds like the Chihuahua or the Yorkshire Terrier, which have fragile windpipes. You should not use a check chain on a dog with a respiratory complaint.

HEELWORK

1 Walk up to the right side of the dog and attach the lead to its collar. Without applying any tension to the lead, hold the handle in your right hand and the middle of the lead in your left hand, with a loop in between.

2 The dog should be on your left side with its shoulder just about level with your thigh. There should be no tension on the collar.

Hold lead securely, with both hands

Dog's shoulder is level with handler's thigh

4 A great deal of concentration is needed when you first begin training a dog. The dog will soon learn to walk correctly. When turning left, you should walk around the dog, and when turning right, the dog should walk around you.

3 Attract the dog's attention by speaking its name. Begin walking, keeping the dog close to your leg. If it pulls ahead or back, jerk the lead gently and say "Heel". Praise the dog when it obeys and walks correctly.

5 When you stop walking, command the dog to sit. You may have to push down its rump at first. It will eventually learn to sit automatically.

PUTTING ON A CHECK CHAIN

1 To put on the check chain correctly, hold it open in a circle as shown, then gently slip it over the dog's head until it hangs loosely around the neck.

2 When the check chain is positioned correctly, it will only tighten when tension is applied. Always keep the dog on your left side.

Incorrect method
If the check chain is put on backwards, it will cause discomfort and not loosen after it has checked the dog.

Obedience Training

Due to their differing temperaments, some dogs are easier to train than others. With proper training your dog will always be under control, both on and off its lead. While six months is a good average age to start formal obedience training, some dogs are ready earlier and others need longer to mature.

Training requires just as much patience and control from you as it does from your dog. If you have little or no experience with dogs it is best to undertake obedience training under the supervision of an experienced dog trainer recommended by a vet or your local breed club.

Training to Wait and Come

1 Using a simple hand signal, tell the dog to sit *(see page 76)*. Whenever you want to teach a dog something new, you should begin by giving the command "Sit", to ensure that you have its full attention.

2 With the dog sitting, give the command "Wait". Holding the lead, walk around the dog, making sure that it stays in the same position all the time.

3 Walk to the end of the lead. Repeat the command "Wait". If the dog moves, go back to it, and start the exercise from the beginning.

4 Call the dog using its name and the command "Come". Always make the dog sit before praising and releasing it.

Dog pays attention to voice and hand signals

Dog sits patiently, waiting for next command

TEACHING THE DOWN-STAY

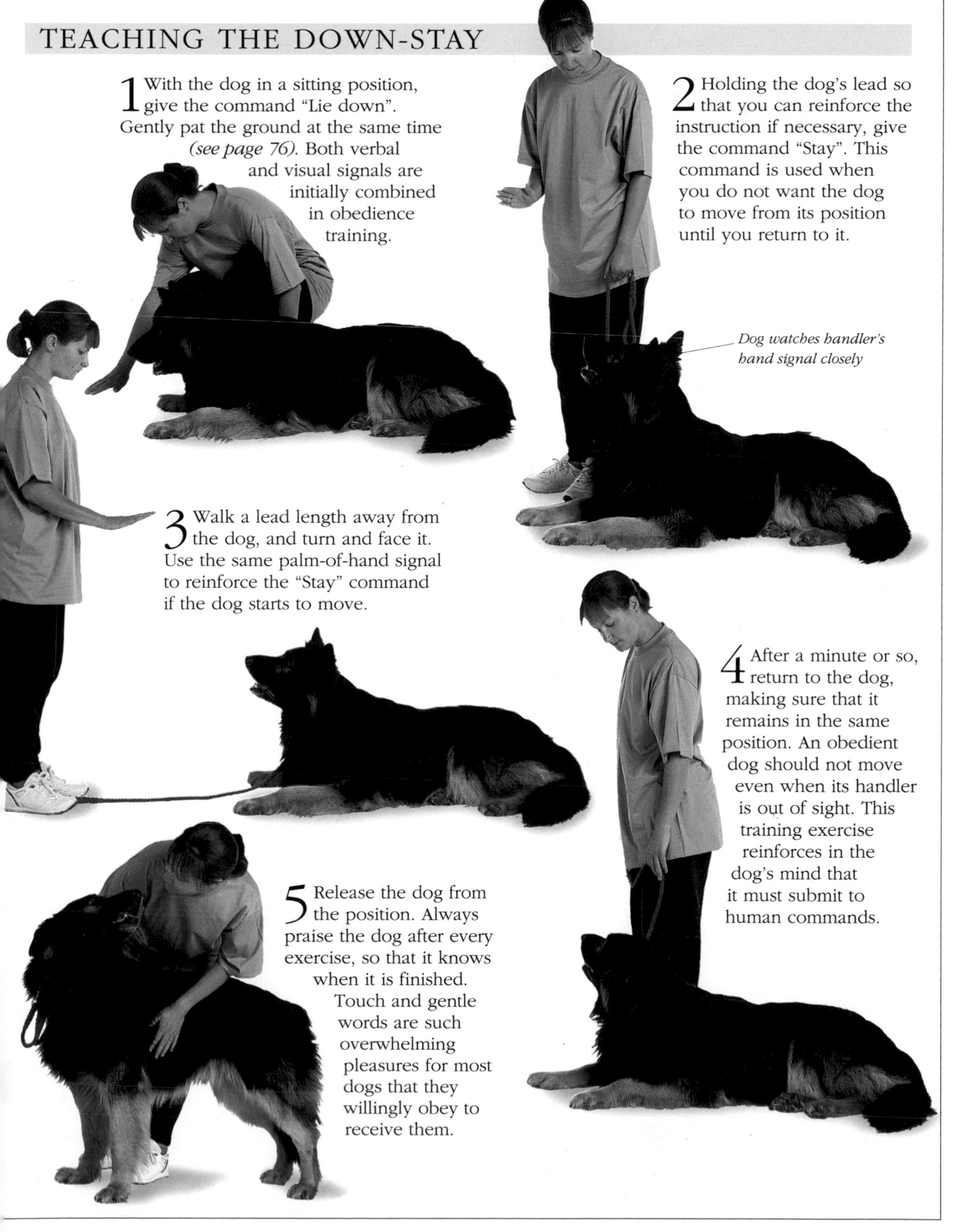

1 With the dog in a sitting position, give the command "Lie down". Gently pat the ground at the same time *(see page 76)*. Both verbal and visual signals are initially combined in obedience training.

2 Holding the dog's lead so that you can reinforce the instruction if necessary, give the command "Stay". This command is used when you do not want the dog to move from its position until you return to it.

3 Walk a lead length away from the dog, and turn and face it. Use the same palm-of-hand signal to reinforce the "Stay" command if the dog starts to move.

4 After a minute or so, return to the dog, making sure that it remains in the same position. An obedient dog should not move even when its handler is out of sight. This training exercise reinforces in the dog's mind that it must submit to human commands.

5 Release the dog from the position. Always praise the dog after every exercise, so that it knows when it is finished. Touch and gentle words are such overwhelming pleasures for most dogs that they willingly obey to receive them.

THE WELL-BEHAVED DOG

The well-behaved dog is a pleasure to its owner and to the community in which it lives. Ensure that your dog is enjoyed by training it to live in harmony with its human and animal neighbours. It should respond to your commands, be friendly to strangers and other dogs, not be scared by distractions, and be content at home without creating havoc.

THE WELL-TRAINED DOG

Sitting on command
Tell the dog to sit. By doing so you will get its attention and demonstrate that you are in charge. A well-behaved dog will sit when anyone, even a stranger, asks it to do so.

Ears pricked to listen for instructions

Staying in position
Tell the dog to stay, then gently drop its lead and walk away. If the dog has been properly trained you can turn your back and walk 5 metres (16 ft) away without it following.

Eyes watch handler closely

Walking on a loose lead *(left)*
With the dog on your left, walk with it on a loose lead. It should not pull back and refuse to move, or strain forwards to run.

THE SOCIABLE DOG

Accepting a stranger *(below)*
A well-mannered dog shows no resentment when people stop to talk to its owner. Nor does it fidget or show signs of shyness. It should sit or lie down quietly, without pulling on its lead.

Petting by a stranger
A dog should be content to be stroked by a stranger, even on the top of its head, which is a gesture of dominance. People often approach dogs like this.

Sitting for examination *(above)*
A dog should allow itself to be examined by you, a member of your family, or by a stranger. This means that a vet will always be able to examine it when necessary.

Reaction to another dog *(above)*
Ask a friend with a dog to approach while you are walking your own dog, stop, talk for a short while, and then move on. Well-behaved dogs show interest in each other but no signs of fear or aggression.

Walking through a crowd
Walk the dog along the pavement through pedestrian traffic. It can show interest in the various sights and sounds but should not strain on its lead or act shyly or aggressively.

Reacting to distractions *(right)*
When the dog is not expecting it, drop a book or heavy magazine about 3 metres (10 ft) behind it. If it has been properly trained, it will show curiosity and interest, but will not panic, bark, run away, or show aggression.

THE CONTENTED DOG

Leaving a dog alone
Leave the dog alone in either your home or garden, then listen for any howling, whining, barking, or pacing the floor. A well-behaved dog might be agitated, perhaps even a little nervous, when you leave, but should show no signs of separation anxiety *(see page 87)*. A toy may comfort the dog.

Controlling Unwanted Behaviour

Dogs sometimes get carried away by their feelings or simply by the desire to act as they please. This can often lead to overexcitement or disobedience. A submissive dog is most likely to jump up in an effort to lick its owner's face, mimicking the way it behaved as a puppy. It will also jump up to greet visitors whom it looks upon as equally dominant as its owner.

Disobedience is more likely to be found in confident and independent dogs than in submissive or shy ones. Good training prevents bad habits, but if they occur, they can be remedied with patience.

The Excitable Dog

Jumping up
Dogs often jump up to greet their owners, as this Standard Poodle is doing. In dog terms this is normal.

Remedy
1 To correct this behaviour, say "No" sharply, at the same time turning away and avoiding eye contact. Do not make a fuss of the dog.

2 Command the dog to sit. If it has been trained properly, it will obey at once *(see pages 76–83)*.

Dog watches owner for instructions

3 Now you can greet the dog on your own terms. Praise it for obeying you. It will soon realize that it must not jump up to greet you.

Owner praises and greets dog as it is sitting

THE DISOBEDIENT DOG

DISCIPLINARY EQUIPMENT

Plant sprays, water pistols, and high-pitched alarms are useful as distractions. Toys can be used to attract a dog's attention or as rewards. Do not physically punish a dog for bad behaviour.

Dog runs away from owner when called to be put back on lead

Not coming when called *(above)*
Your dog may sometimes refuse to come back when called, especially if you only call it to put it back on its lead. It should not associate coming to you with an unpleasant event or a reprimand. However, if you chase it, the dog may think you are playing a game.

Remedy
Use a favourite toy to attract your dog's attention, then have a game with it before taking it home. Do not let it associate you or the toy with being restrained on a lead. When it comes to you, command it to sit, and praise it.

Favourite toy is used to attract dog's attention

Correcting Bad Habits

Even the most delightful dog is likely to develop habits that you find annoying or unpleasant in the restricted environment of your home. Obedience training from an early age can prevent many of these behavioural problems, and prevention is always easier than cure. If your dog behaves at home in ways that you find antisocial, you must go back to basics and use common sense to develop a correction method based on its willingness to obey. Remember that a dog does not misbehave to punish its owner: retribution is a trait in primates like humans, but not in dogs.

THE DESTRUCTIVE DOG

Chewing objects
Dogs left on their own, especially puppies, may sometimes chew objects through frustration at being alone, and to relieve boredom.

Remedy *(left)*
Restrict the dog to a small area of its own where it cannot do any damage, such as a special dog crate. This helps a dog to feel more secure, especially if it has a selection of toys to chew and play with, and a radio or television as background noise. A dog should only be confined to a crate for short periods and must also be given plenty of exercise and personal attention from its owner.

THE GREEDY DOG

Stealing food *(right)*
Dogs are natural scavengers, and will eat most food they find. Success reinforces this bad behaviour, producing a chronic canine thief.

Remedy *(left)*
Teach the dog to sit before feeding it, and only give it food in its own bowl, not on a plate or from the table. Once it knows it must obey you before eating, it will not steal food in your absence. As a precaution, do not leave tempting food within its reach.

THE OVERSEXED DOG

Hypersexuality
Denied a more natural outlet for its sexual energy, a young, unneutered male dog may mount a human leg or furniture. This occurs most frequently in dogs between one and two years old, although females in season may behave in a similar manner.

Remedy
Distract the dog by spraying it with water from a plant spray or water pistol. Any discipline must be carried out immediately so that the dog associates this with its bad behaviour. Neutering may prevent this behaviour.

THE LONELY DOG

Separation anxiety *(left)*
Left alone in the house, a nervous dog may bark or howl. This is especially common in dogs that have not been properly socialized during puppyhood, or that have known several homes.

Remedy *(above)*
Before leaving, provide the dog with a special treat, such as a favourite toy that you have rubbed in your hands, or a succulent marrowbone. Do not make a fuss when you leave. The dog may feel more secure in a dog crate *(see opposite)*.

Controlling Aggressive Behaviour

The most serious problem a dog can develop is to show aggression. A dog can become aggressive to other animals, to strangers, or even to its owner. To prevent this behaviour, you must assert your pack leadership. Train your dog to always obey your commands, and reinforce your dominance over it through routine exercises.

AGGRESSION TO OWNER

Possessive aggression
A dominant dog may challenge its owner for possession of favourite objects. Food, old bones, resting places, and toys are all possessions that a dog may aggressively defend.

Remedy
Command the dog to lie down. When it does so, it automatically becomes subservient to the person above it. You could also lift its hind leg to symbolize your dominance, if it has not done so itself. The dog must be taught that it is the lowest-ranking member of the human pack.

Alternative remedy
An alternative exercise to reassert authority over an aggressive dog is to command it to stay, then stand over it and lift its front legs off the ground. The dog may find this loss of control intimidating and it may struggle. However, it will soon accept that you are in charge.

AGGRESSION TO VISITORS

Territorial aggression
A resident dog may bark at a visitor to its home, bravely defending its territory and its owner, whom it considers a member of its pack. By standing over the dog and bending down to stroke it, the visitor appears to be acting in a threatening way. A dog may be especially frightened of strangers if it has not been handled during puppyhood.

AGGRESSION TO OTHER DOGS

Dominant aggression
A dominant dog, or one that has not been properly socialized with other canines when it was young, may bark aggressively at, or even try to fight with, other dogs that it meets.

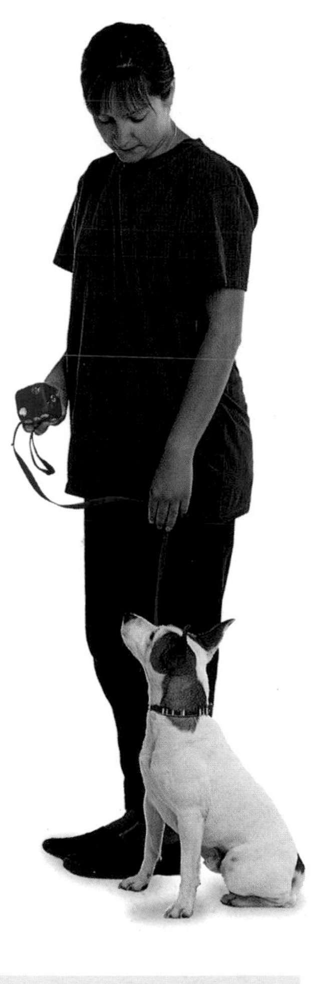

Remedy *(right)*
To remedy this type of aggression, command the dog to sit. Since you are the dog's pack leader, it will realize that you are unconcerned about the strange dog, and that it is no threat. Always praise good behaviour with other dogs.

CONTROLLING AGGRESSION
Aggression takes a variety of forms and responds to different methods of control. Obedience training is of paramount importance in preventing this behaviour. Seek professional advice from a vet, an experienced trainer, or a dog-training club if your pet shows any signs of not always being under your control.

Remedy
Introduce the dog to new people gradually and offer it rewards for good behaviour. The visitor should initially avoid direct eye contact with the dog. By sitting down and offering the dog food or a toy as it is restrained on its lead, the visitor will appear less intimidating. Do not allow visitors to force themselves on a shy dog, but allow the dog to set the pace.

Chapter 6

YOUR DOG'S HEALTH

DOGS CAN suffer from almost all the physical diseases and ailments that afflict humans. In addition, selective breeding by humans has intensified the incidence of some canine health disorders. Fortunately, modern veterinary care provides a vast array of diagnostic aids, treatments, and remedies. When a dog is not well, it relies upon its owner to notice and take appropriate action. Many dogs may try to hide their discomfort and want to please their owners so much that they attempt to behave normally. Whenever you notice any changes in your dog's routines, demeanour, or behaviour, contact your local veterinary practice for advice.

THE HEALTHY DOG

The healthy dog is vibrant, alert, and almost always enthusiastic about living. Although happy to snooze and relax for most of the day, a fit dog is constantly observing humans, and is always ready for exercise and entertainment of any kind.

Assessing your dog's health soon becomes natural. Once you understand its daily routines and behaviour, any deviation from the norm becomes obvious. Dogs are creatures of habit with finely tuned biological clocks. If your dog does not get up when it usually does, is reluctant to play, moves slower, eats less, or behaves in an abnormal way, contact a vet for advice.

As well as observing your dog's behaviour, check its health when you groom it. There should be no unpleasant or new odours or discharges from the mouth, nose, eyes, ears, body, or urinary or anogenital regions. The dog should move with natural grace, showing no signs of difficulty when getting up or down. Breathing, appetite, thirst, and frequency of emptying the bowels and bladder should be routine.

If you notice any change in the colour, consistency, or quantity of droppings, contact your veterinary clinic for advice. The nursing staff can often answer your questions over the telephone, and an appointment is unnecessary.

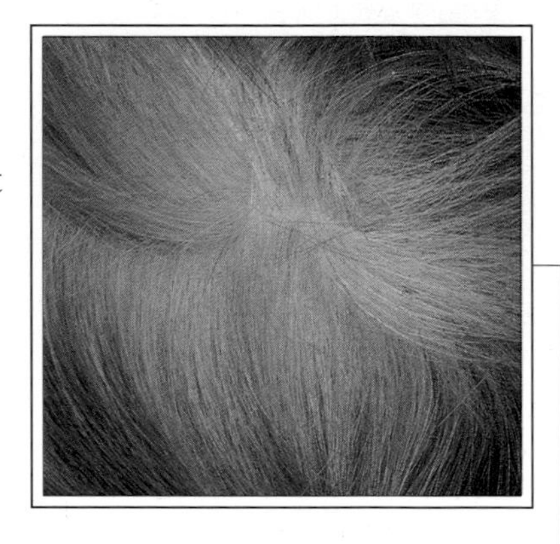

Skin
Normal skin is resilient, clean, and has no dry flakes, odour, or grease. Healthy fur glistens and does not come out when pulled except during moulting. According to the breed, the hair should lie evenly on all parts of the body. There should be no sign of parasites, flea dirt, dandruff, sores, baldness, itchiness, or strong odour.

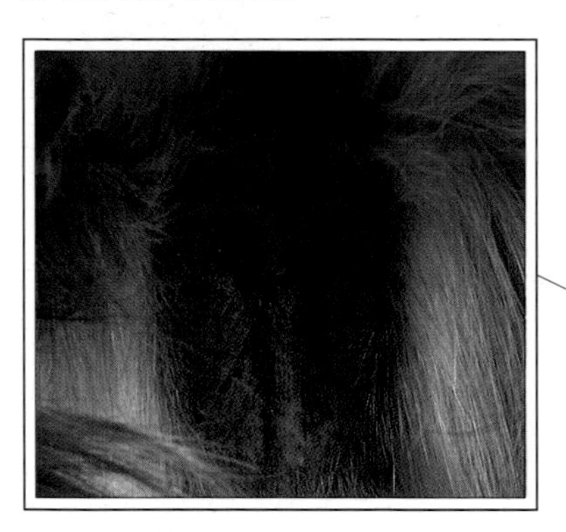

Anal region
The anal region should be clean with no signs of inflammation, lumpy growths, or dried faeces. Excess licking or dragging of the rear along carpet or grass means irritation, most frequently caused by blocked anal glands.

Canine fitness
Healthy dogs are clean, robust, and full of spirit. They enjoy the company of humans and do not resent being touched. Even slight changes from normal behaviour can signify illness.

Eyes
A dog's eyes should be bright, clean, and free of discharge. There should be no redness, squinting, or vision impairment.

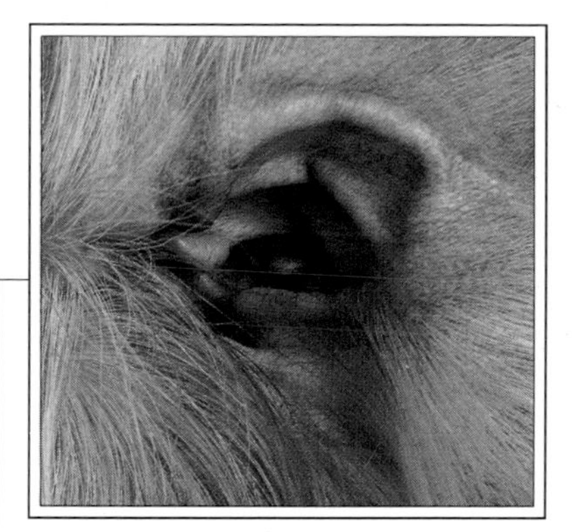

Ears
The insides of the ears should be dull pink and free of discharge and odour. The flaps should hang symmetrically. Occasional head shaking is normal, especially when a dog wakes up from a snooze.

Mouth
Dogs have whiter teeth than do humans. The gums and tongue should be pink, sometimes mottled with black pigment. Gums should form a clean margin with the teeth, with no recesses in which food can get trapped, causing bad breath.

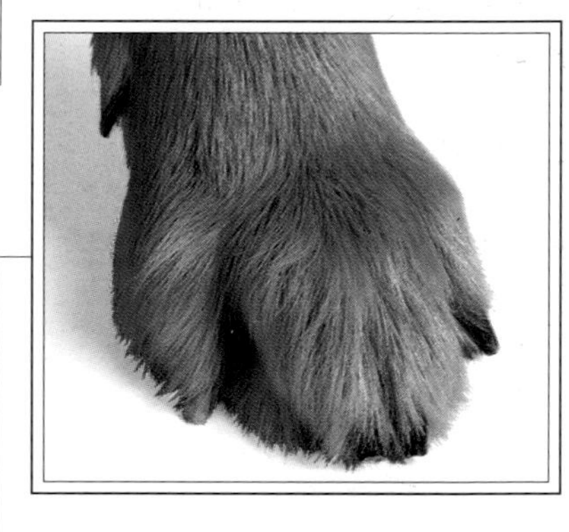

Paws
Paws should be neat, clean, and symmetrical. Check the pads for cuts or burns, and the nails for breaks or damage, and always check between the toes for grass seeds that can easily penetrate the skin, causing swollen, painful abscesses.

Signs of Ill Health

Because your dog enjoys human companionship, it will often try to behave normally even when it is unwell. For example, if your dog refuses to eat unless you feed it by hand, it may be ill but eating just to please you. It may be experiencing pain or discomfort even if it does not cry or yelp. Most dogs are stoic individuals and suffer their pain silently. You can help the vet make an accurate diagnosis by keeping a record of exactly when you notice any signs of ill health.

Be prepared
Keep the telephone number of your local veterinary clinic handy and always give it to anyone looking after your dog. Contact the clinic immediately if your dog appears unwell or is injured.

NERVOUS DISORDERS
(see page 121)
- Fits, convulsions, or seizures
- Staggering gait
- Partial or complete paralysis
- Behavioural changes
- Loss of balance

DIGESTIVE DISORDERS
(see page 111)
- Projectile, bloody, or painful vomiting
- Persistent, bloody, or explosive diarrhoea
- Constipation
- Weight loss or excessive weight gain
- Listlessness and abdominal discomfort

SKIN AND COAT DISORDERS
(see page 101)
- Persistent scratching
- Sudden chewing or licking
- Redness or inflammation
- Increased hair loss

REPRODUCTIVE DISORDERS
(see page 117)
- Any unusual genital discharges
- Swelling in the mammary glands
- Swelling in the testicles
- Failure to conceive
- Difficulties at birth

URINARY DISORDERS
(see page 119)
- Straining to pass urine
- Blood in the urine
- Incontinence
- Increased urination
- Increased thirst

INTERNAL PARASITES
(see page 113)
- Visible worms in the faeces
- Pot-bellied appearance
- Persistent or bloody diarrhoea
- White grains on rear
- Loss of weight

RESPIRATORY DISORDERS
(see page 109)
- Nasal discharge
- Persistent sneezing
- Coughing, gagging
- Excessive snoring
- Laboured breathing

EYE DISORDERS
(see page 105)
- Discharges from the eyes
- Failing vision
- Squinting
- Bloodshot inflammation
- Blue-grey cloudiness

EAR DISORDERS
(see page 107)
- Head shaking
- Discharges from the ear canal
- Swelling of the ear flap
- Difficulty in hearing
- Loss of balance

MOUTH AND TOOTH DISORDERS
(see page 115)
- Bad breath
- Dribbling saliva
- Reluctance to eat
- Inflamed gums
- Loose or broken teeth

EXTERNAL PARASITES
(see page 103)
- Scratching
- Excessive licking
- Dandruff
- Hair loss
- Visible parasites

BLOOD AND HEART DISORDERS
(see page 123)
- Non-productive coughing
- Reluctance to exercise
- Reduced stamina
- Fainting

BONE, MUSCLE, AND JOINT DISORDERS
(see page 99)
- Lameness and limping
- Swelling around affected area
- Paralysis
- Tenderness when limb is touched

DIAGNOSIS CHART

Use common sense when assessing the seriousness of any medical condition. By asking yourself a series of questions you can determine whether veterinary attention is necessary immediately, later the same day, or can wait 24 hours. You are responsible for your dog's health.

START

Does your dog have diarrhoea, or is it vomiting? — YES: go to the next question. NO: go to "Is your dog scratching or licking?"

- Is there blood present, or a repellent odour to vomit or faeces? — YES: **CONSULT A VET** It may have a serious digestive disorder, p.111. NO: go to the next question.
- Are there any signs of acute pain or abdominal swelling? — YES: **CONSULT A VET** It may have a serious internal disorder, p.111. NO: go to the next question.
- Does it seem dull and lethargic, as well? — YES: **CONSULT A VET** This may be a sign of a major illness. NO: go to the next question.
- Does it have watery diarrhoea, or has it vomited only once? — YES: Withhold food for 24 hours. Consult a vet if there is no improvement. NO: go to the next question.
- Apart from the vomiting and diarrhoea, does it seem normal? — YES: Withhold food for 24 hours. Consult a vet if there is no improvement.

Is your dog scratching or licking? — YES: go to the next question. NO: go to "Is your dog bleeding?"

- Is it scratching suddenly and violently, or biting itself? — YES: **CONSULT A VET** It may have an allergic skin disease, p.101. NO: go to the next question.
- Is there inflammation, damaged skin, or hair loss? — YES: **CONSULT A VET** It may have a severe allergy or infection. NO: go to the next question.
- Apart from occasional scratching, does it seem normal? — YES: Examine the coat for parasites and treat accordingly, p.103. NO: **CONSULT A VET** Seek veterinary treatment at the first sign of illness.

Is your dog bleeding? — YES: go to the next question. NO: the chart continues on the next page.

- Is the bleeding excessive? — YES: **CONSULT A VET** Meanwhile, give first aid to stop bleeding, p.168. NO: go to the next question.
- Is it pregnant and bleeding from the vulva? — YES: **CONSULT A VET** It may be having a miscarriage, p.117. NO: go to the next question.
- Is it bleeding from the penis or anus? — YES: **CONSULT A VET** This may be a sign of a serious disease. NO: go to the next question.
- It is bleeding from the eye, ear, mouth, or any limb? — YES: **CONSULT A VET** Meanwhile, give first aid to stop bleeding, p.168.

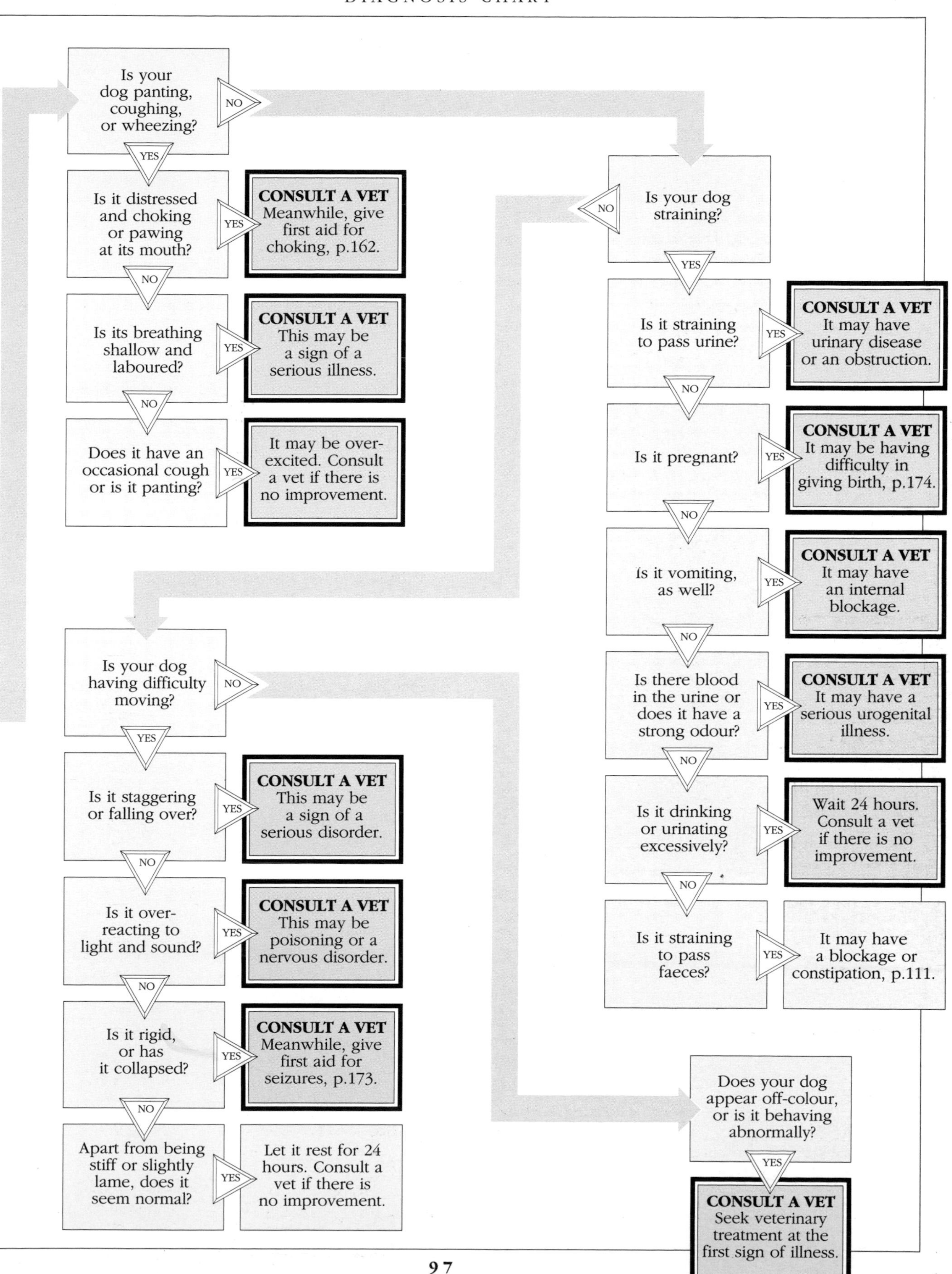
Is your dog panting, coughing, or wheezing?
NO
YES
Is it distressed and choking or pawing at its mouth?
YES
CONSULT A VET Meanwhile, give first aid for choking, p.162.
NO
Is its breathing shallow and laboured?
YES
CONSULT A VET This may be a sign of a serious illness.
NO
Does it have an occasional cough or is it panting?
YES
It may be over-excited. Consult a vet if there is no improvement.
Is your dog straining?
NO
YES
Is it straining to pass urine?
YES
CONSULT A VET It may have urinary disease or an obstruction.
NO
Is it pregnant?
YES
CONSULT A VET It may be having difficulty in giving birth, p.174.
NO
Is it vomiting, as well?
YES
CONSULT A VET It may have an internal blockage.
NO
Is there blood in the urine or does it have a strong odour?
YES
CONSULT A VET It may have a serious urogenital illness.
NO
Is it drinking or urinating excessively?
YES
Wait 24 hours. Consult a vet if there is no improvement.
NO
Is it straining to pass faeces?
YES
It may have a blockage or constipation, p.111.
Is your dog having difficulty moving?
NO
YES
Is it staggering or falling over?
YES
CONSULT A VET This may be a sign of a serious disorder.
NO
Is it over-reacting to light and sound?
YES
CONSULT A VET This may be poisoning or a nervous disorder.
NO
Is it rigid, or has it collapsed?
YES
CONSULT A VET Meanwhile, give first aid for seizures, p.173.
NO
Apart from being stiff or slightly lame, does it seem normal?
YES
Let it rest for 24 hours. Consult a vet if there is no improvement.
Does your dog appear off-colour, or is it behaving abnormally?
YES
CONSULT A VET Seek veterinary treatment at the first sign of illness.

BONE, MUSCLE, AND JOINT DISORDERS

Endurance and agility are important attributes of the natural hunter, and a dog's body is built to enhance these characteristics. The front legs are attached to the rest of the body by muscles, and there is no collarbone, which gives maximum flexibility. The hind legs have massive muscles to power instant acceleration and to maintain speed.

All this superb equipment is susceptible to injury and damage by misuse, especially in breeds whose bone structure has been much altered through selective breeding. Lameness is a common problem in dogs and requires rest. Examine the dog for signs of injury to the limbs, such as swelling or tenderness to touch. Determining the cause of lameness can be difficult and often requires veterinary help.

Fractures
When a fracture is simple and the bones remain straight, healing is assisted with a cast or bandage.

THE DOG'S SKELETON

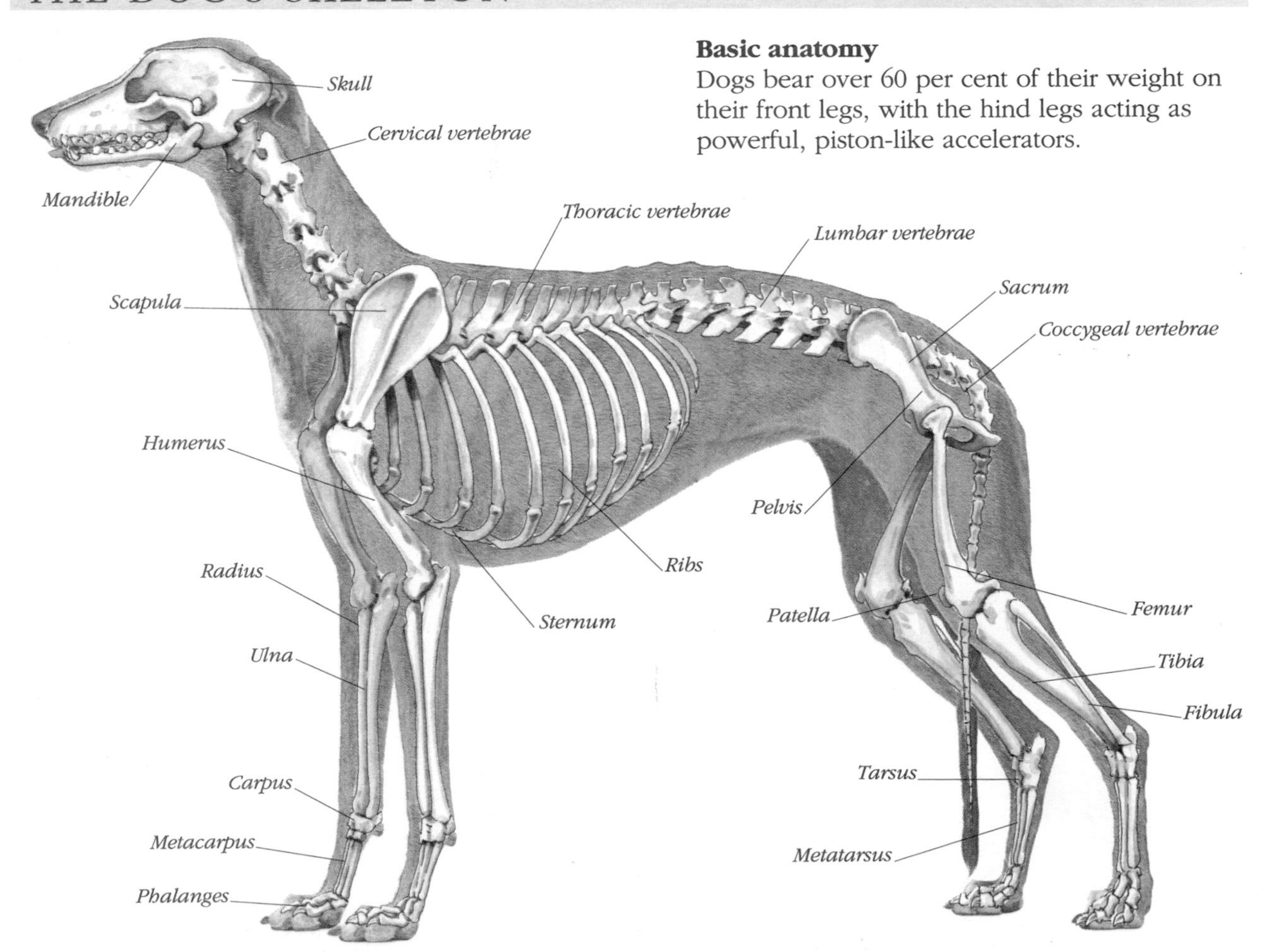

Basic anatomy
Dogs bear over 60 per cent of their weight on their front legs, with the hind legs acting as powerful, piston-like accelerators.

BONE, MUSCLE, AND JOINT DISORDERS

Signs and disorders	Description	Action
Front leg lameness Fractured bones Dislocated joints Torn ligaments and tendons Bruised muscles Osteochondrosis (OCD) Elbow dysplasia Bone infection	With simple fractures there may be a little swelling, but more complex breaks involve substantial damage to the surrounding tissue. Hip, shoulder, and knee joints are most frequently injured or dislocated in traffic accidents. Torn ligaments and tendons are less painful than fractures, but cause considerable lameness, with or without swelling. Bruised muscles are tender to the touch, although deep bruising is not always apparent from looking at the skin. In OCD, small pieces of cartilage break off the ball of the humerus in the shoulder joint and float around in the joint fluid, causing pain. The dog's head bobs down on the side of the affected shoulder, but otherwise it seems normal. Elbow pain and lameness are caused by injuries or an ununited anconeal process (elbow dysplasia), in which an elbow bone does not meet the ulna properly, leaving a loose piece of bone that can eventually cause arthritis. Bone infections usually occur after a penetrating injury such as a dog bite.	If a dog is injured in a road accident, carry out emergency first aid *(see page 158)* and get the dog to a vet. Some fractured bones heal well by being splinted or cast, while others require internal fixation with pins, plates, or screws. Dislocated joints are manipulated back into position, or may require surgical repair. Torn ligaments and tendons often need surgical repair, while bruised or strained ligaments, tendons, and muscles respond to professional bandaging, rest, and painkillers. A vet can diagnose OCD according to the history of the dog, its breed, an examination, and X-rays. Sometimes only medication is necessary, but when pain and lameness are severe, the floating pieces of cartilage are surgically removed from the joint. Elbow injuries are treated with drugs, or by surgical correction with screws, while bone infection needs antibiotics that concentrate in bone tissue.
Hind leg lameness Hip dysplasia Perthe's disease Luxating patella Ruptured cruciate ligament Fractures, dislocations, torn ligaments, bruised muscles *(see above)*	Hip dysplasia causes pain and lameness to one or both hind legs. The pain is exaggerated when the leg is flexed, and occurs most frequently in large breeds. A similar pain occurs when the head of the femur loses its blood supply and "dies" (Perthe's disease, or avascular necrosis). This cause of hip pain is most common in small dogs. Small breeds are also more prone to luxating patellas (slipped kneecaps), while all breeds can suffer from ruptured cruciate ligaments. In both instances weight is not carried on the affected hind leg, but there is no pain associated with either problem other than at the time when the ligament tears.	Contact a vet to determine the cause of lameness. Some cases of mild hip dysplasia respond well to medication, while more severe problems require surgical correction. Surgery is the only treatment for Perthe's disease. The "dead" head of the femur is removed. Luxating patellas can be surgically corrected but, like hip dysplasia, this is an inherited defect. Cruciate ligaments are most likely to rupture in overweight, mature dogs, although young, lean dogs of some breeds, like Boxers, can also tear these ligaments. Weight reduction, rest, and surgical repair are all necessary.
Paralysis Slipped discs	Mildly slipped discs cause intense pain, and the dog is reluctant to move. Greater slippage causes a partial or even complete paralysis *(see page 121)*, eliminating movement and also the dog's perception of pain.	If the slippage is severe the dog needs immediate surgery to reduce the damage to the spinal cord. Absolute rest is most important for slipped discs.
Joint pain Arthritis	Osteoarthritis can occur in any joint, and usually affects older dogs. It can be either hereditary, or caused by disease, poor nutrition, or congenital abnormalities. Polyarthritis also causes pain in many joints. It can be caused by infection, autoimmune conditions in which the body destroys its own tissues, or as a reaction to certain drugs. Some giant breeds can develop arthritis in later life as a result of injuries or sprains during their critical period of growth.	Chronic arthritis is controlled with steroid and non-steroid anti-inflammatories. Giant breeds should have controlled exercise while growing. Polyarthritis can be permanently damaging. A vet may take a blood sample to determine the cause and might use antibiotics, anti-inflammatories, and painkillers. It is important to alleviate the dog's pain, since there is no definitive cure for arthritis.
Bone weakness Osteoporosis Hyperparathyroidism	Osteoporosis is usually a direct consequence of a meat-only diet, and can cause stunted growth and bowed legs. A poor ratio of calcium to phosphorus stimulates the parathyroid gland into overactivity (hyperparathyroidism). Affected dogs move slowly and feel discomfort when touched. An excess of vitamins during a puppy's growth stage can produce similar problems, with constant discomfort in the joints.	Feed only a well-balanced diet to avoid osteoporosis. Calcium supplements are often necessary for fast-growing dogs, but never give more than the amount recommended by a vet, since too much can be as harmful as too little.

Skin and Coat Disorders

Irritating skin conditions are among the most common medical problems that dogs can suffer. Scratching usually begins mildly, and is most frequently caused by parasites such as fleas. Continued scratching damages the skin, allowing bacteria to multiply. The consequent inflammation stimulates the skin glands into producing excess discharge and odour. Routine grooming and parasite control prevent these complications from occurring. As a consequence of selective breeding, some breeds, such as the Cocker Spaniel, Golden Retriever, and West Highland White Terrier, have a higher-than-average incidence of skin and coat disorders *(see page 125)*, while others, such as poodles, have a very low incidence.

Rhythmic scratching
If a dog scratches in a classic fashion, suspect fleas even if you see no sign of them.

ANATOMY OF THE SKIN

Protective layers
Thick, outer guard hairs and smaller, softer accessory hairs provide good insulation from the cold. Glandular secretions add shine to the coat, and, more importantly, make it waterproof. The surface of the skin consists of multiple tough layers of dead cells, which are constantly being replaced at their base. Beneath this is an insulating layer of fat.

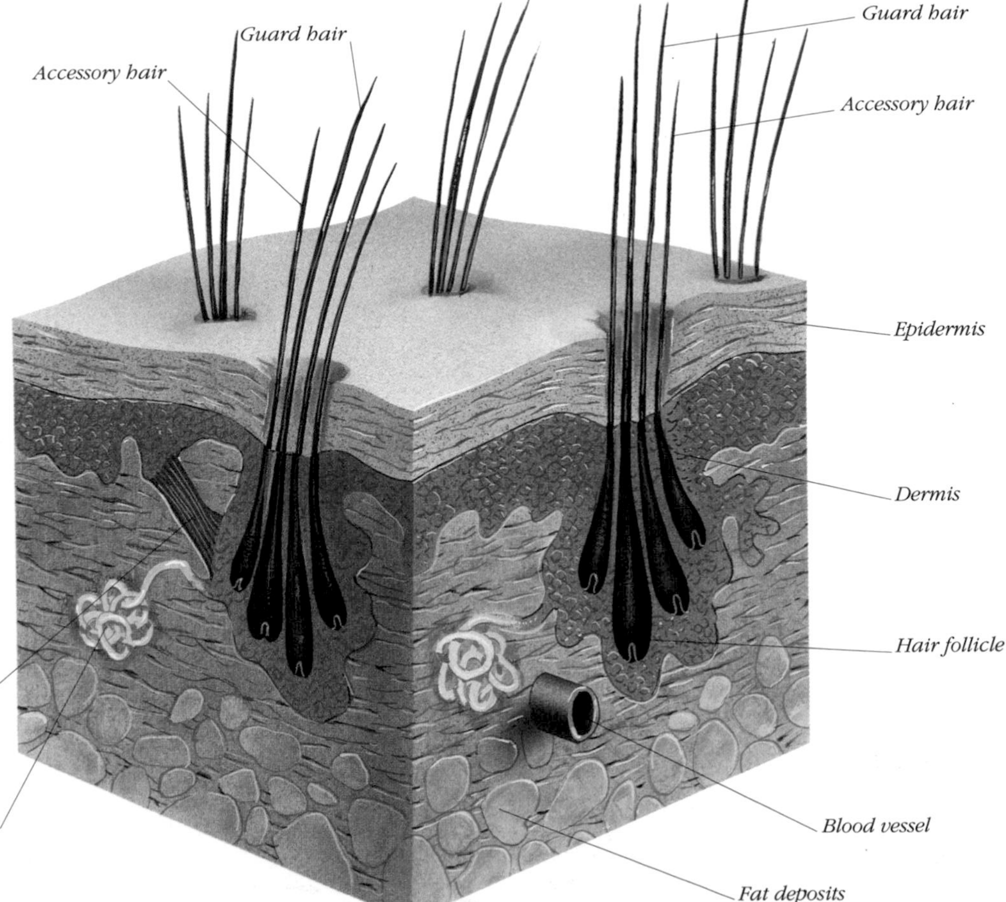

SKIN AND COAT DISORDERS		
Signs and disorders	**Description**	**Action**
Scratching External parasites (p. 103) Allergies Irritation Internal disorders	Scratching and chewing sometimes occur with or without accompanying inflammation. Parasites such as fleas account for most itchiness, although a dog could be scratching an allergic rash caused by inhaling pollen or dust; as a reaction to a contact irritant, such as shampoo or certain plants; or because its coat has just been clipped. Disorders of the kidneys and liver can also cause skin irritation.	Eliminating the source of the irritation or allergy is the ultimate goal, although this can be difficult to determine in some instances. In the meantime, a vet can control self-mutilation with anti-inflammatory medication. Elizabethan collars are sometimes necessary to keep a dog from scratching or chewing itself *(see page 139)*. Always consult a vet before treating a dog for any skin problems, since the condition could be caused by an internal disorder.
Inflammation Allergies Sunburn Foreign body (p. 163) Abscesses Skin infections	Inflammation can be due to allergy, sunburn, or to foreign bodies lodged in the skin, such as grass seeds between the toes, which cause abscesses. With skin infections (pyoderma), bacteria invade the skin surface, which becomes red and sometimes moist and oozing (acute moist dermatitis). Bacteria sometimes breed between folds of skin and produce lesions (skin-fold pyoderma). Puppies can sometimes suffer from juvenile pyoderma, in which their faces swell up. Deep infections, such as cellulitis, produce hot, painful swellings.	Accurate diagnosis of the underlying cause of inflammation is essential. A vet can treat the inflammation with an appropriate antibiotic or antifungal medication. In hot, sunny countries avoidance of strong sunlight and the use of a high-factor sunblock may prevent sunburn. Bathe abscesses twice daily in tepid salt water.
Skin changes Seborrhea Acanthosis nigricans	Due to an inadequate diet, hormonal imbalance, parasites, or yeast infections, a dog's skin can sometimes become flaky, or its coat can look dull or greasy. Dry seborrhea looks like dandruff, while oily seborrhea is the over-production of oil by the skin. The disease acanthosis nigricans results in thickened, black skin, most commonly in dachshunds. It may be due to hormonal imbalance or allergic reaction.	Skin conditions can be treated with special shampoos and medication, but accurate diagnosis is necessary for complete control of the condition.
Lumps Cysts Warts Tumours Abscesses *(see above)*	Cysts feel like hard, volcanic eruptions just under the skin. Warts are most common in elderly dogs. They are often pink, mottled, and crusty around their roots, but they can also be pigmented. Melanomas are pigmented, highly malignant skin tumours that occur most frequently in Boxers. Slow-growing, soft, fluctuating, egg-shaped masses under the skin in older dogs are usually benign tumours.	An accurate diagnosis is essential, since warts, cysts, and tumours require removal by a vet.
Hair loss Ringworm External parasites (p. 103) Collie nose Hormonal imbalance Calluses	Local hair loss can be caused by fungal infections like ringworm, and parasites such as mange mites. Local hair loss on the nose of collie breeds can occur due to sunburn (collie nose). Generalized, especially symmetrical, hair loss often has hormonal origins in the thyroid, adrenal, or pituitary glands, or in the ovaries or testicles. Hair loss on the elbows of heavy dogs is caused by excess pressure on a hard surface causing calluses of the skin.	Ringworm responds to antifungal ointments and oral antibiotics. Mange mites must be treated with an insecticidal shampoo. Collie nose may be prevented by use of a high-factor sunblock. Hormonal imbalances can be diagnosed through blood tests and corrected with appropriate medicines. A skin cream will keep skin supple and prevent calluses, but the dog should also be provided with soft bedding.
Excess licking Lick dermatitis Blocked anal glands (p. 111) External parasites (p. 103)	Dogs lick their skin to clean wounds and remove debris from their fur, but obsessive licking of any part of the body, especially the forepaws, can be a sign of a serious disorder. Excessive licking can be psychological and result in damage to a dog's skin (lick dermatitis).	Obssessive licking is difficult to control, although it responds to drugs. A vet can treat the skin sores of lick dermatitis with antibiotic medication.

EXTERNAL PARASITES

Regardless of how careful you are in keeping your dog's coat clean and healthy, skin parasites are common, and whenever possible will hop on to a canine for a meal. Cat fleas in particular are happy to use dogs (and humans) as hosts, while dog fleas and even human fleas create considerable problems, especially in warm climates. Look for tell-tale sooty, black specks of flea droppings in your dog's coat and bedding.

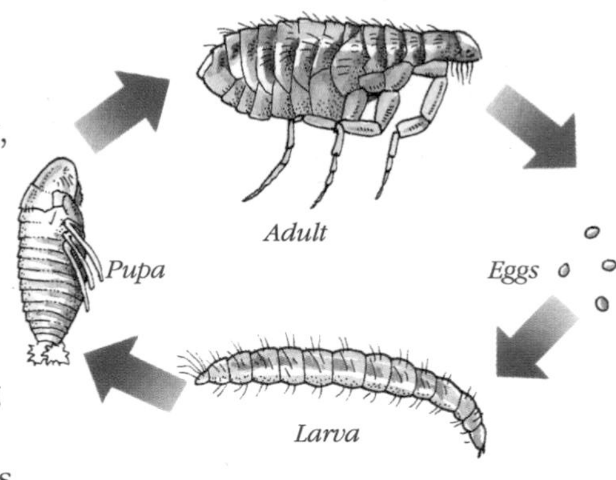

The flea life cycle
Flea eggs can remain viable for up to a year before hatching into larvae, then emerging as adults.

Mange mites and lice are usually transmitted through direct contact with other dogs, although wild animals such as foxes and wolves are also sources of these parasites. Ticks can be a problem, especially in areas where they transmit serious infections. Wildlife and sheep are sources of these blood-sucking parasites. Most parasites prefer dogs to humans, but mange mites can cause an irritating skin rash.

COMMON EXTERNAL PARASITES

Examining a dog for parasites
Persistent scratching is a common sign of parasite infestation. Check the skin for signs of dandruff or parasites, and the hair for lice, especially in warm weather.

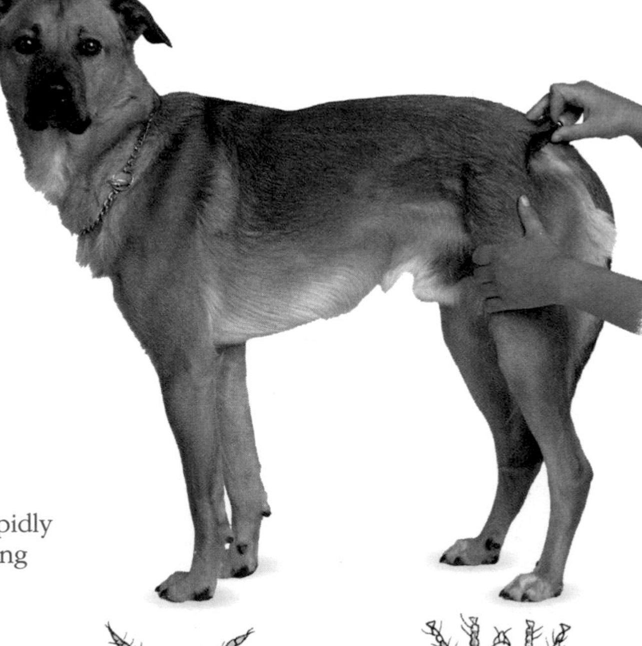

Sarcoptes* mite *(above)
Preferring the ear tips and elbows, this mite causes severe itching.

Flea *(above)*
This tiny insect moves rapidly through the coat, preferring puppies to older dogs.

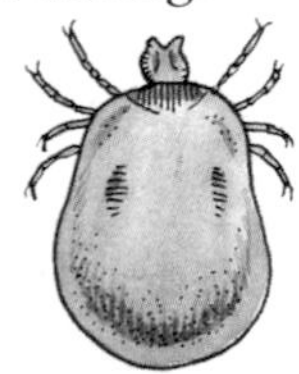

Tick *(above)*
This parasite swells to the size of a small pea when feeding on blood.

***Demodex* mite**
Only visible through a microscope, this mite lives inside hair follicles.

Harvest mite
Known as a "chigger", this mite is visible in autumn as a red dot.

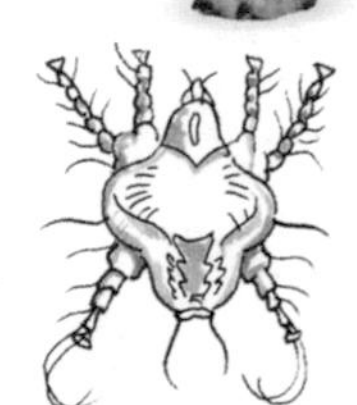

***Cheyletiella* mite**
Highly contagious, this mite resembles a flake of moving dandruff.

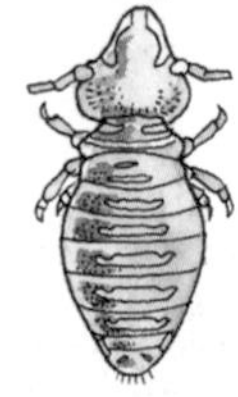

Louse
Visible as it feeds on the skin, the louse glues its eggs on to the hair.

EXTERNAL PARASITES

Parasite	Description and signs	Action
Fleas *Ctenocephalides* sp. *Ceratophylus* sp.	Mahogany-coloured, long-legged fleas spend most of their lives in carpets and upholstered chairs, only hopping into a dog's fur for a meal. Some dogs are allergic to the saliva left in the bite wound and scratch intensively. Others are irritated as fleas walk around biting them. Dogs also pick up their most common tapeworm *(see page 113)* from flea infestation. Fleas often leave shiny black droppings in the fur.	Place black, hard dirt from the dog's coat on moistened tissue. If blood leeches out and stains the paper red, this confirms the presence of fleas. Treat the affected dog with a suitable insecticide, obtainable from a vet. It is also important to vacuum the dog's environment and treat its bedding with a biological spray that prevents flea eggs from hatching.
***Sarcoptes* mange mites**	These microscopic mites burrow into the skin, favouring the tips of the ears, which become scabby, crusty, and itchy, and the elbows. They cause intense irritation, frantic scratching and subsequent hair loss, and body sores. Humans can sometimes be temporarily affected with itchy pimples like mosquito bites, especially around the waist *(see page 127)*.	Bathe the affected dog weekly for at least four weeks with a veterinary insecticidal shampoo that kills sarcoptic mites. Thoroughly clean or destroy the dog's bedding, since these mites can survive for a short period of time off the dog.
***Demodex* mange mites**	These parasites normally inhabit canine hair follicles, but for unknown reasons they sometimes multiply excessively in either young, shorthaired dogs, or elderly, debilitated ones. There is seldom any itching, but nasty pustules develop as a result of secondary infection.	Examination of a skin scraping under a microscope readily reveals these tiny, cigar-shaped mites. Weekly bathing in a prescription insecticide is necessary until the mites are no longer seen in the scrapings.
***Cheyletiella* mites**	*Cheyletiella* mites are just visible to the eye and produce copious dandruff over the back, a condition known as "walking dandruff". Heavy infestations cause skin scaling but only limited itching. These mites can cause an irritating rash in humans *(see page 127)*.	These mites are easily destroyed with insecticidal shampoos, obtainable from a vet. Since the parasite has a long life cycle, shampoo all dogs with which the affected dog comes into contact, and thoroughly clean their bedding.
Harvest mites *Trombicula autumnalis*	The small, red, barely visible larvae of these free-living autumn parasites usually infest field mice, but also irritate dogs. They especially affect a dog's toes and cause it to lick its feet.	Veterinary insecticidal shampoos destroy these mites, but dogs sometimes need treatment with anti-inflammatory medicines, as well.
Lice *Trichodectes canis* *Linognathus setosus*	Visible to the eye, biting lice walk around on the skin and glue their glistening white eggs, called "nits", to the fur. They are intensely irritating and are usually spread by direct contact.	Because their complete life cycle is on the dog, treatment consists of appropriate veterinary insecticidal shampoos, and combing nits out of the fur.
Ticks *Ixodes* sp. *Dermacentor* sp.	Sheep and deer ticks leap into dogs' fur and bury their mouthpieces in the skin. They swell with blood, and become engorged, brownish-white, and pea sized. Some ticks in Australia and North America can cause paralysis. Lyme disease can also be transmitted by ticks *(see page 127)*.	Swab the tick and surrounding tissue with surgical spirit. Using tweezers, grasp the tick and "unscrew" its mouthpiece from the skin with a rotating action. Treat the area with an insecticide.
Blowfly maggots	Fly strike is a seasonal problem, most common in longhaired and poorly groomed dogs. Blowflies lay eggs in hair that is matted or contaminated with blood, pus, or faeces, especially around the anus. These eggs then hatch into maggots that damage the skin.	Consult a vet urgently. Maggots can be flushed out with hydrogen peroxide, and the area cleansed with antiseptic. Routinely cut the hair around the anus of a longhaired dog to prevent faeces from adhering and attracting flies.
Hookworm larvae *Uncinaria stenocephala* *Ancylostoma caninum*	These microscopic larvae live in damp hay and burrow into a dog's chest and feet, causing bumps and "damp hay itch". The dog scratches vigorously, often damaging its skin. This parasite is mainly found in dogs that are housed in outdoor kennels *(see page 113)*.	Consult a vet, who can treat the affected area with insecticide. The condition can be prevented by using shredded paper or bark for a dog's bedding instead of hay. The bedding should be changed regularly.

EYE DISORDERS

Because dogs communicate so well with humans with their eyes, any changes due to injury, disease, or infection are usually noticeable. The most common problems are discharges and inflammation. A dog may paw at its eyes because of irritation. This can cause accidental damage to the surface of the eye, the cornea, especially in breeds with protruding eyes, such as the Pekingese. More difficult to notice are changes inside the eye. Some of these, such as progressive retinal atrophy, are inherited, and can lead to blindness. Other internal changes are indicators of disease elsewhere in the body. Consult a vet at once if you notice any eye abnormality.

Eye inspection
A vet can examine the interior of a dog's eye with an ophthalmoscope.

THE STRUCTURE OF THE EYE

Producing an image
Light passes through the surface of the eye, the cornea, and then through the lens within, which focuses the rays on the light-sensitive cells of the retina. This stimulates impulses that travel to the brain via the optic nerve, producing the image that the dog sees. Extra cells in the retina help dogs to see well in dim light.

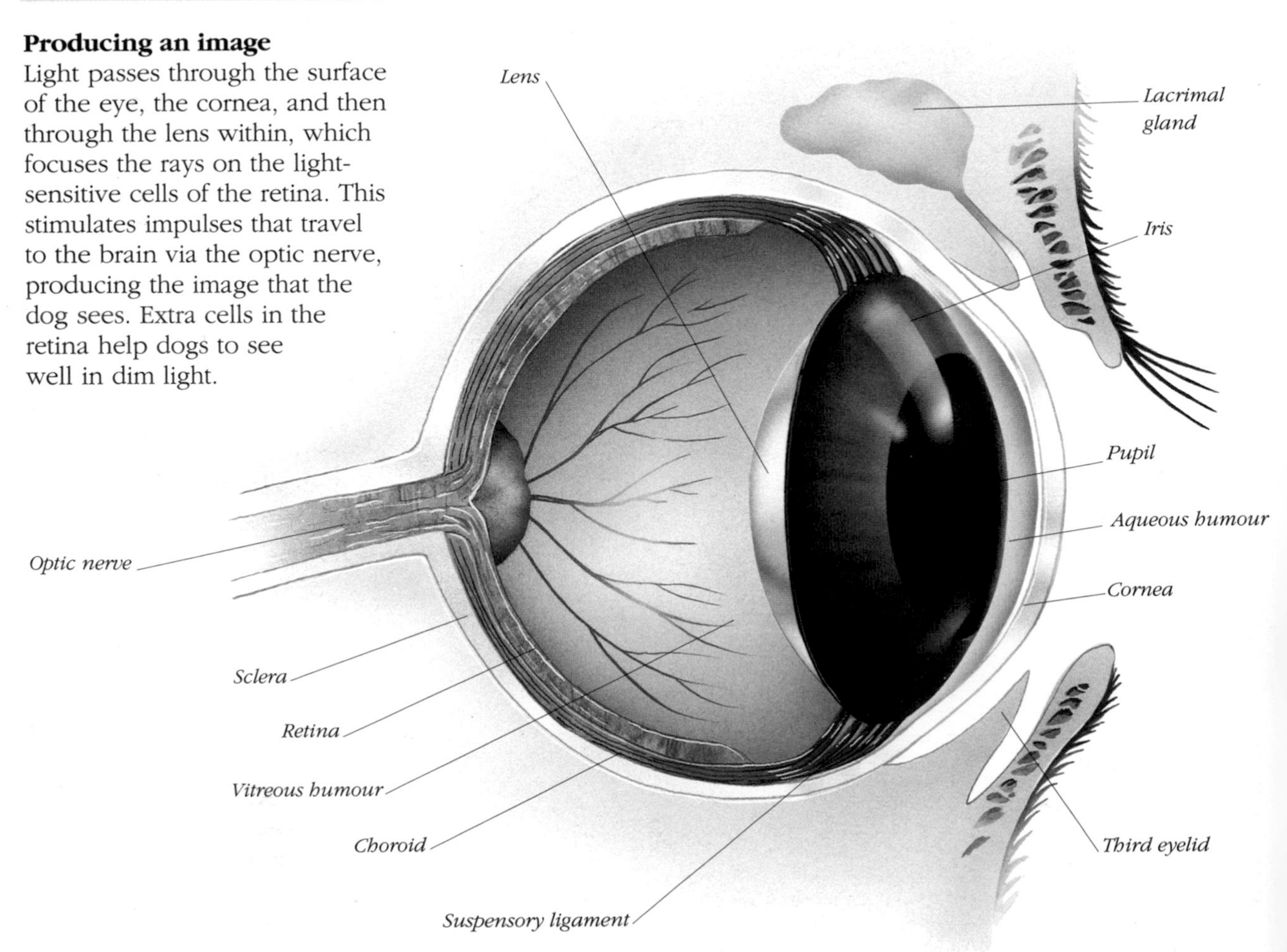

EYE DISORDERS

Signs and disorders	Description	Action
Clear discharge Infection Irritation Allergy Poodle eye	Tears usually drain down a canal to the back of the nose. If mucus or inflammation from infection plugs the tear ducts, tears overflow down the face. Excess tears are sometimes produced to wash away irritants, or as a reaction to an allergy. Continuous tear overflow can stain the face brown (poodle eye).	Consult a vet immediately, since excess tears are often a sign of other, more important problems. A vet can flush out tear ducts to unblock them, and treat infections with antibiotics.
Purulent discharge Dry eye	If the tear glands fail to produce enough tears, the eyeball initially looks dull and lustreless. Then bacteria invade, causing a tenacious yellow discharge. This disorder is most common in older dogs, and is a serious problem.	Consult a vet immediately, since a lack of lubrication can lead to infection and blindness. Dry eye can be treated with antibiotics and artificial tears, although correction by surgically transferring a saliva duct up to the eye is sometimes necessary.
Inflammation Conjunctivitis Allergy Distichiasis Entropion/Ectropion Injuries Infected third eyelid gland Glaucoma Foreign body (p. 163)	Conjunctivitis, allergies, or physical irritation from dust, wind, pollen, or shampoo all cause eye inflammation. So do inherited conditions such as distichiasis (ingrown eyelashes) or excessively tight or loose eyelids (entropion and ectropion). Inflammation is also caused by injuries, infection of the third eyelid gland, and glaucoma, an increase in fluid pressure inside the eye due to injury or disease.	Veterinary treatment is urgently needed. If the eye is uninjured, anti-inflammatories can be used in conjunction with other treatments. Inherited problems may require surgical correction, as does an excessively inflamed third eyelid gland. Glaucoma needs pressure-reducing treatment for life, although if the pain is too great it is best that the eye is surgically removed.
Clouding (keratitis) Corneal injury or infection Cataract Lens problems Ageing Blue eye	When the cornea is damaged through injury or disease it retains fluid and becomes cloudy and blue-grey in colour (keratitis). A similar colour change occurs in the lens when a cataract forms, which can lead to blindness, or if the lens drops out of its normal position (luxation). Ageing produces a gradual clouding of the lens (sclerosis), usually in dogs over ten years old. Blue eye is a clouding of the eye due to a deep inflammation of the cornea, sometimes connected with infectious hepatitis.	Corneal injuries are serious, and an accurate and immediate veterinary diagnosis is necessary. The results of treatment are often excellent, but depend upon the extent of the damage. Cataracts and luxated lenses are only surgically removed when the surgery will result in improved vision. Sometimes, using microsurgical techniques, a vet can insert plastic internal lenses into the affected eye.
Bleeding Injuries Prolapse of the eyeball	Eyelids are most frequently damaged in dog fights. Bleeding in the eye occurs after severe trauma from fights or traffic accidents. Breeds with bulging eyes like the Pekingese are prone to prolapse of the eyeball, a condition in which the eyeball is pushed out of its socket.	Immediate veterinary attention is necessary. Wounds should be cleaned and sutured. A prolapsed eye can be returned to its socket and the eyelids sewn together for a week to keep it in place. Topical and oral medicines reduce swelling and infection.
Failing vision Progressive retinal atrophy (PRA) Stroke (p. 121) Collie eye anomaly (CEA) Retinal dysplasia Ageing *(see above)*	Progressive retinal atrophy, an inherited disorder in which the retina deteriorates, is not outwardly apparent, except for the affected dog becoming confused in strange surroundings and bumping into objects. It can be difficult to spot damage to vision from strokes and also from an inherited retinal disease of collie breeds known as collie eye anomaly. Retinal dysplasia is a congenital defect involving folding or displacement of the retina, and can cause blindness.	A vet can examine the inside of the eye with an ophthalmoscope. Because PRA, CEA, and retinal dysplasia are inherited eye disorders, affected dogs and their close relatives should not be used for breeding purposes. Some affected dogs continue to see despite their eye condition. If blindness develops slowly many dogs cope well.
Lumps Eyelid tumours Cysts Tumours in the eye	Eyelid tumours appear as brown or black protruding growths on the edge of the lid. They are most common in dogs over six years old. If the tumour rubs on the eye surface it can cause a watery discharge and may damage the cornea. Cysts can also develop but these look like swellings in the lid. Tumours in the eye initially cause bulging and associated inflammation.	Eyelid tumours are almost always benign, and can be successfully removed with surgery. Cysts should also be removed if they provoke irritation. The only treatment for rare tumours inside the eye is total eye removal. With the edges removed the eyelids are sewn together, producing a good cosmetic result.

EAR DISORDERS

Ear complaints are a regular reason for a visit to a vet. Head shaking, ear scratching, and pungent discharges are the most common conditions, and when these occur, ear mites should be considered as a possible cause. Dogs with pendulous, well-furred ear flaps, such as spaniels, are more likely to suffer from ear disorders than breeds with erect ears such as the German Shepherd Dog. Deafness can be hereditary in some breeds and is often associated with a white coat. Impaired hearing and eventual deafness is a condition often associated with elderly dogs, especially retrievers. Loss of balance relating to hearing disorders can occur at any age and is usually caused by an infection arriving in the inner ear from the ear canal or the throat.

Examining the ears
A magnifying auriscope permits a vet to gently examine the ear canal for parasites and debris.

THE STRUCTURE OF THE EAR

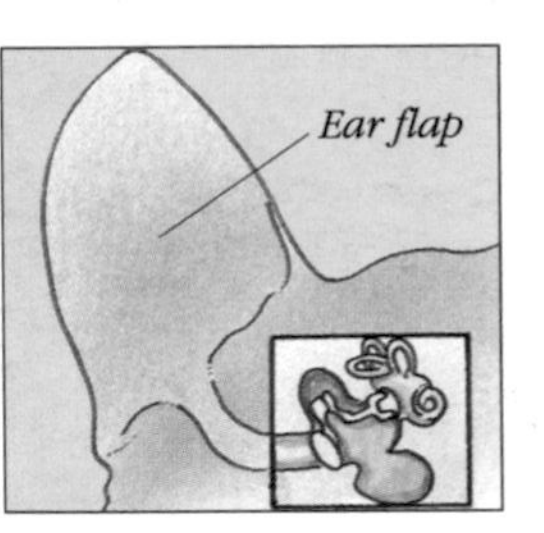

The outer ear
Sound waves are gathered by the large outer ear and channelled to the ear drum.

The inner ear
Sound waves arriving at the ear drum cause vibrations that are transmitted to the ossicles of the middle ear, and then on to the inner ear. These sounds are translated into electrical impulses and conveyed to the brain.

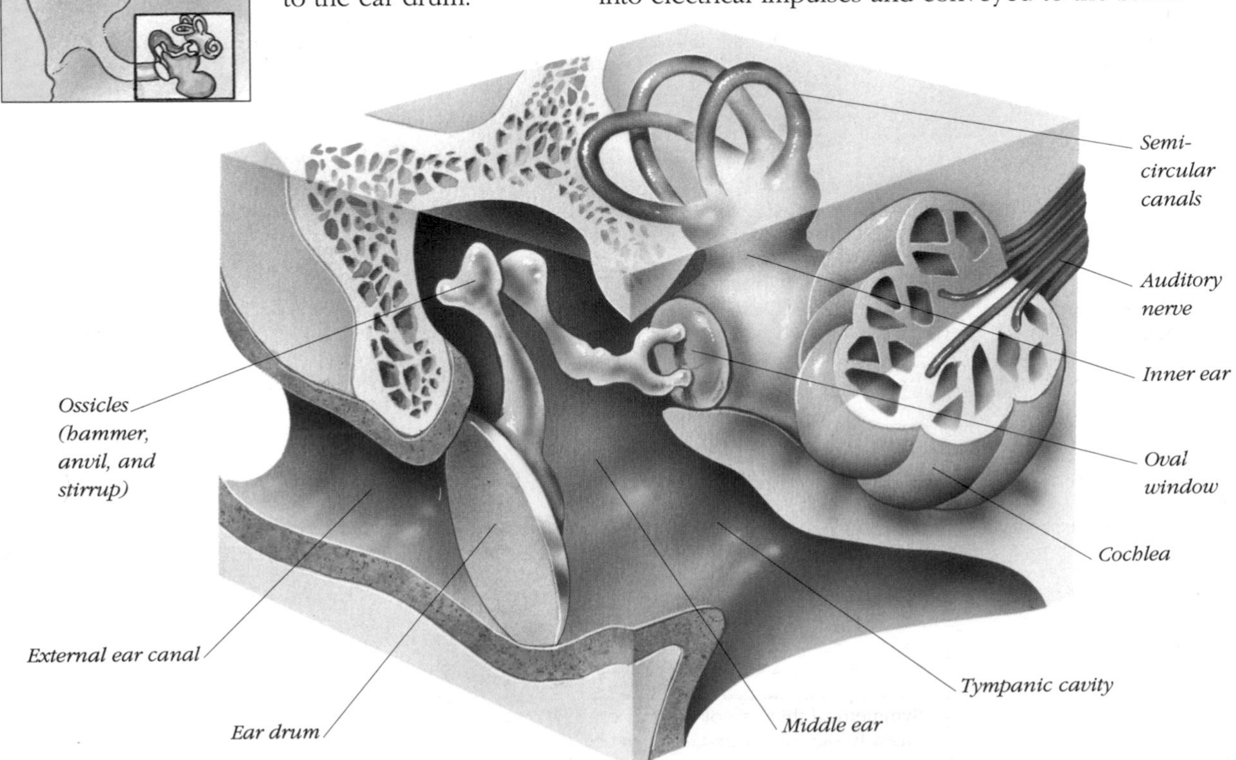

EAR DISORDERS

Signs and disorders	Description	Action
Head shaking and ear scratching Ear mites Foreign body (p. 163) Allergy Infection *(see below)*	Ear mites are common in puppies and spread easily within a litter. They irritate the lining of the ear canal, stimulating wax production, and are just visible to the naked eye. Foreign bodies such as grass seeds in the ears cause sudden, violent head shaking. The ear is quite painful when touched. If a dog has an allergy or an infection, the inside of the ear flap and the ear canal will be inflamed and sensitive.	Consult a vet, who can prescribe insecticidal ear drops to eliminate ear mites. All contact dogs and cats should be treated, since these mites can easily be transmitted to other animals. Because mites can live outside the ear, insecticidal shampoos are also beneficial. A vet can remove a foreign object with special forceps. The cause of an allergic reaction should be determined and eliminated, if possible, or else the ears can be treated with anti-inflammatory drops under veterinary supervision.
Discharge Bacterial or yeast infections Ear mites *(see above)*	Infection of the outer ear (otitis externa) often produces discharges. These can be due to bacteria (thick, yellow discharge), yeast (black and runny), or mites (black and gritty). If left untreated, otitis externa can lead to middle ear infection (otitis media), which can result in severe conditions such as a ruptured ear drum.	A vet can treat discharges with antibiotics and anti-inflammatories. It is best to prevent middle ear infection by treating infections of the outer ear, since severe cases of otitis media can only be cured by surgically removing the affected parts of the ear canal.
Loss of balance Inner ear infection	Infection can reach the inner ear from the external ear, through the Eustachian tube from the throat, or via the bloodstream. This causes the dog to tilt its head in the direction of the affected ear. The eyes often flick in the same direction. Since the semi-circular canals in the inner ear control balance, any infection there will make a dog unsteady on its feet.	Confine the dog to prevent it from injuring itself while its balance is impaired. A vet can control possible nausea and treat the dog with high levels of antibiotics by mouth. Surgical drainage of the inner ear is sometimes necessary.
Deafness Excess wax production Seborrhea Tumour Blocked ear canal Ageing	Temporary deafness can be due to the excess production of wax, or to seborrhea *(see also page 101)*, which produces a yellow, malodorous substance that builds up in the ear. This is common in dogs with narrow ear canals, such as poodles. A tumour inside the ear makes the skin appear thickened and dark. The ear canal can also be blocked by the hair inside the ears in some breeds like poodles and Yorkshire Terriers. Wax catches in this hair, forming a plug of material and an ideal environment for bacterial multiplication. Some hearing loss is natural in old age.	To eliminate wax or seborrhea, the ear must be cleaned daily with a purpose-made liquid, which can be obtained from a vet. Dry the ear thoroughly after cleaning. Tumours must be removed surgically. A vet can remove hair blocking the ear and treat infections with antibiotics.
Swelling on ear flap Haematoma (blood blister) Physical damage	Chronic head shaking – for whatever reason – can cause internal bleeding, especially in older dogs. The ear swells, forming a warm, egg-like structure (haematoma). The tips of the ears bleed easily and are prone to damage from dog bites and other injuries.	Consult a vet. A haematoma can be surgically drained and stitched. In the case of physical damage to the ear, stop bleeding and prevent infection by cleaning the wound thoroughly and bandaging the ear to the head *(see page 168)* before seeking veterinary advice.
Hair loss Genetic predisposition *Sarcoptes* mange mites (p. 103) Ringworm (p. 101) Hormonal imbalance (p. 101)	In certain lines of some breeds, such as the Yorkshire Terrier, all the hair on the ears drops off when the dog is mature, leaving only dry, leathery ear flaps. A similar loss occurs on the nose. *Sarcoptes* mange mites often infest the tips of the ears in all breeds, causing itchy, crusty lesions and hair loss. The fungal infection ringworm also favours the ears, causing hair loss but frequently no itch or inflammation. Symmetrical thinning of the hair on both ears is an early sign of hormonal imbalance.	A veterinary examination can determine the cause of local hair loss. Genetic hair loss from the ears cannot be arrested, but selective breeding can reduce this condition. Blood samples can ascertain hormonal imbalances. Treatments are specific to the exact cause of hair loss.

RESPIRATORY DISORDERS

The dog has a very robust respiratory system and suffers from few common breathing disorders. Kennel cough, a bacterial infection of the voice box and windpipe, is the most frequent infectious cause of coughing, while allergy is probably the next most usual reason. Coughing related to heart disease is common in older dogs or in young members of breeds like the Cavalier King Charles Spaniel, which are prone to hereditary heart problems *(see page 125)*. Internal parasites, infections, foreign bodies, and systemic illnesses all cause respiratory disorders that can include abnormal breathing, whether shallow, deep, rapid or laboured. Always seek prompt veterinary attention if your dog shows any signs of respiratory abnormality.

Listening to breathing
Using a stethoscope, a vet can listen to breathing. Radiographs also help with the diagnosis.

THE RESPIRATORY SYSTEM

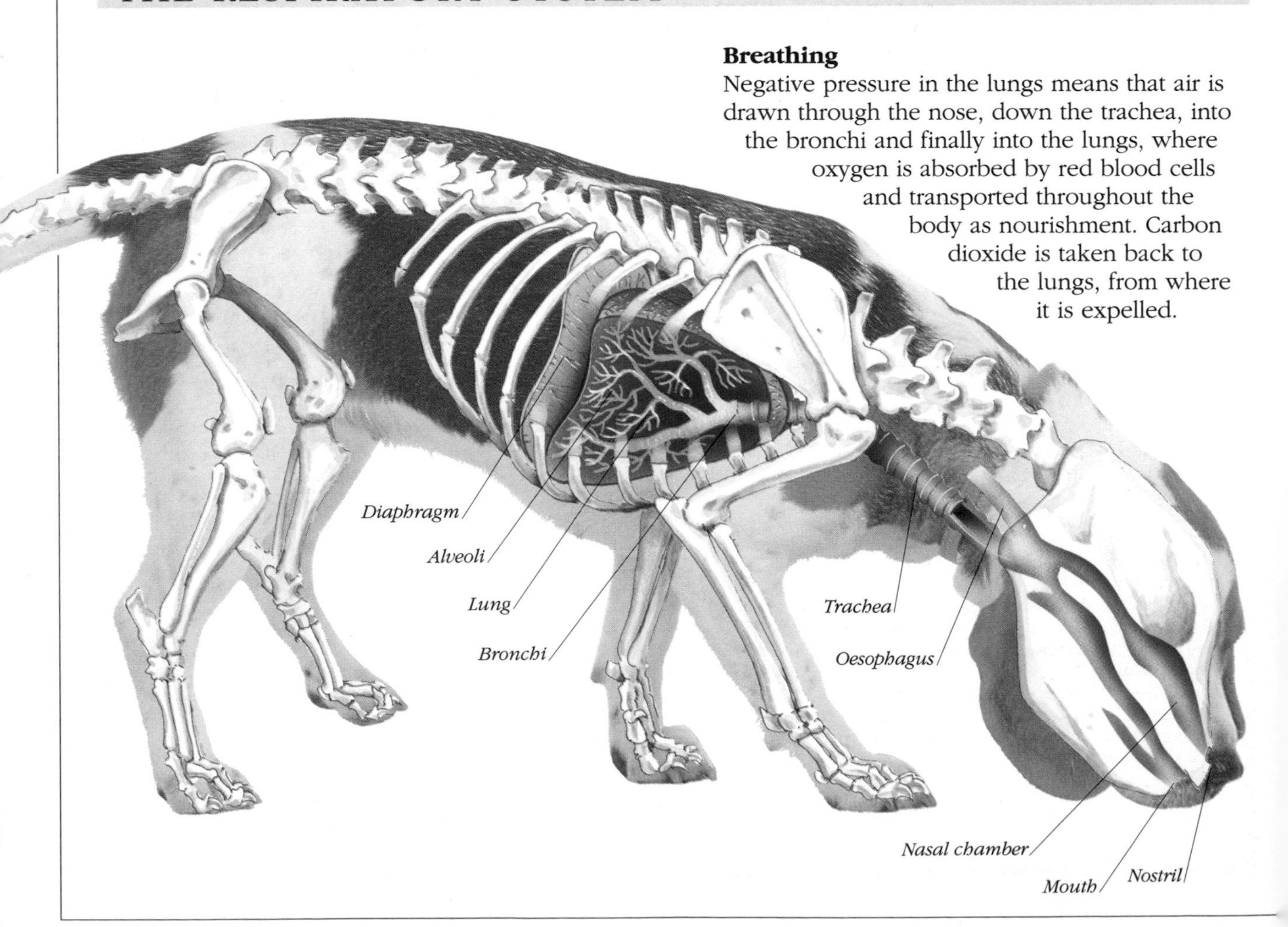

Breathing
Negative pressure in the lungs means that air is drawn through the nose, down the trachea, into the bronchi and finally into the lungs, where oxygen is absorbed by red blood cells and transported throughout the body as nourishment. Carbon dioxide is taken back to the lungs, from where it is expelled.

RESPIRATORY DISORDERS

Signs and disorders	Description	Action
Nasal discharge or sneezing Allergy Infection Tumour Foreign body Cleft palate (p. 115)	All dogs sneeze occasionally, especially when they wake. Allergic sneezing is usually non-productive, occurring in paroxysms, while infections often produce pus. A purulent or bloody discharge from a single nostril indicates a tumour, or a foreign body such as a grass seed.	Consult a vet for correct diagnosis. Allergic sneezing can be reduced by antihistamines, although eliminating the cause is best. Infections can be viral, bacterial, or fungal and are treated with medication. Tumours can be surgically removed, while foreign bodies are often sneezed forwards until they can be extracted by a vet.
Acute coughing or gagging Kennel cough Tonsil, pharynx, or larynx infection Acute bronchitis Inhalation pneumonia Foreign body in the airway	Kennel cough is contracted from another dog and causes inflammation to the voice box and windpipe. Other bacterial and viral diseases inflame the tonsils, pharynx, or larynx, causing the dog to stretch its neck forwards, gag, and cough. Bacterial or allergic inflammation to the bronchi in the lungs, causing acute bronchitis or inhalation pneumonia, and foreign bodies in the airways all stimulate acute coughing.	Kennel cough is highly contagious, so isolate the dog and contact a vet immediately if you suspect this ailment. A vet can treat infections with medication, and remove foreign bodies with special forceps. Cough suppressants can make a dog more comfortable, although in most circumstances these are not actual cures. These medicines reduce the unpleasant side effects of disease, allowing the respiratory system to return to normal.
Persistent coughing or gagging Poor heart function Collapsed windpipe Chronic bronchitis Lungworms Heartworms (p. 123) Roundworms (p. 113)	A night-time cough can mean poor heart function *(see page 123)*. Fluid builds up in the lungs, causing a non-productive gag. As time progresses the cough becomes pronounced, especially after exercise. A collapsed windpipe, a congenital defect of some toy breeds, causes a distressing cough, and even light exercise induces a coughing spasm. Chronic bronchitis occurs in older dogs, causing a persistent cough, especially when they are excited or after exercise. Lungworms, heartworms, and migrating roundworm larvae all cause light coughing.	Consult a vet as soon as possible, since a persistent cough is a sign of serious disease. Improvement to cardiac function controls heart-related coughing. A collapsed windpipe is potentially life-threatening, and when this occurs in a young dog an artificial windpipe can be surgically inserted. Chronic bronchitis improves with appropriate medication. Lungworm infestation can be treated with appropriate medication, although internal damage sometimes requires surgical repair.
Snoring Elongated soft palate Allergy Ageing Narrow nostrils and larynx	Many breeds, especially those with compressed faces, have elongated soft palates that hang at the back of the throat. The soft palate interferes with the larnyx, producing a snore. This also happens when there is allergic inflammation in the throat or simply when the soft palate loses elasticity with age. Narrow nostrils and larynx exacerbate snoring.	In some breeds like the Pekingese and Pug snoring is a sign of potential heart and breathing problems in the future, so it is best to consult a vet. Surgical reduction of the length of the soft palate lessens or eliminates the condition. Allergic snoring can be treated with appropriate medication, while narrow nostrils and larynx can be enlarged with simple surgery.
Breathing abnormalities Pleural effusions Injury to the ribs Lung disease Heart failure (p. 123) Kidney disease (p. 119) Heatstroke (p. 170) Poisoning (p. 164)	Distressed or unusual breathing can be a sign of a potentially life-threatening problem. Pleural effusions of blood, pus, and other fluids can sometimes cause a persistent cough, as well as breathing difficulties and an unwillingness to exercise. Shallow breathing may indicate an injury to the ribs that makes breathing painful. Rapid breathing may denote lung, heart, or kidney disease.	Immediate veterinary attention is needed, especially if you suspect that the dog has an injury causing painful breathing. Pleural effusions are surgically tapped and drained to reduce pressure on the lungs.
Voice changes Injury to the larynx Allergy Laryngeal tumour Laryngeal paralysis	A dog's bark is altered when its larynx is damaged. Allergic reactions, typically from bee and wasp stings, cause laryngeal swelling. Tumours can develop in old dogs, although they are rare. Laryngeal paralysis occurs particularly in elderly Labrador Retrievers and German Shepherd Dogs, turning their bark into a roar.	Consult a vet. Antihistamines or anti-inflammatories can reduce allergic swelling, while tumours are sometimes surgically removed. Surgery to correct laryngeal paralysis is often unsatisfactory. A safe alternative is the surgical creation of a permanent opening in the windpipe in the neck, bypassing the blocked larynx. This dramatically improves breathing.

DIGESTIVE DISORDERS

The dog is a scavenger and opportunist feeder. Many dogs will deliberately overeat whenever food is available. It is not surprising, therefore, that vomiting is more common in dogs than in many other kinds of mammal. Regurgitation is also the normal way a wild bitch feeds her puppies until they can hunt for themselves. Constant or projectile vomiting, however, are signs of a serious disorder, as is vomiting blood or bile. Similarly, persistent or explosive diarrhoea requires immediate veterinary attention. Constipation can be a serious problem, and even a lack of appetite can sometimes be a sign of illness or internal disorder.

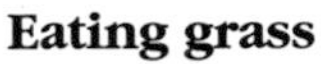

Eating grass
Some dogs enjoy eating grass on a regular basis, while others only do so when they feel abdominal discomfort, since it induces vomiting.

THE DIGESTIVE SYSTEM

Digestion
The dog has a large stomach and a relatively short intestinal tract, an ideal arrangement for an opportunist hunter and scavenger. Food breakdown starts in the stomach, but almost all the digestion occurs in the intestines. The liver detoxifies unwanted products, while indigestible material and waste travel to the large intestine and are excreted.

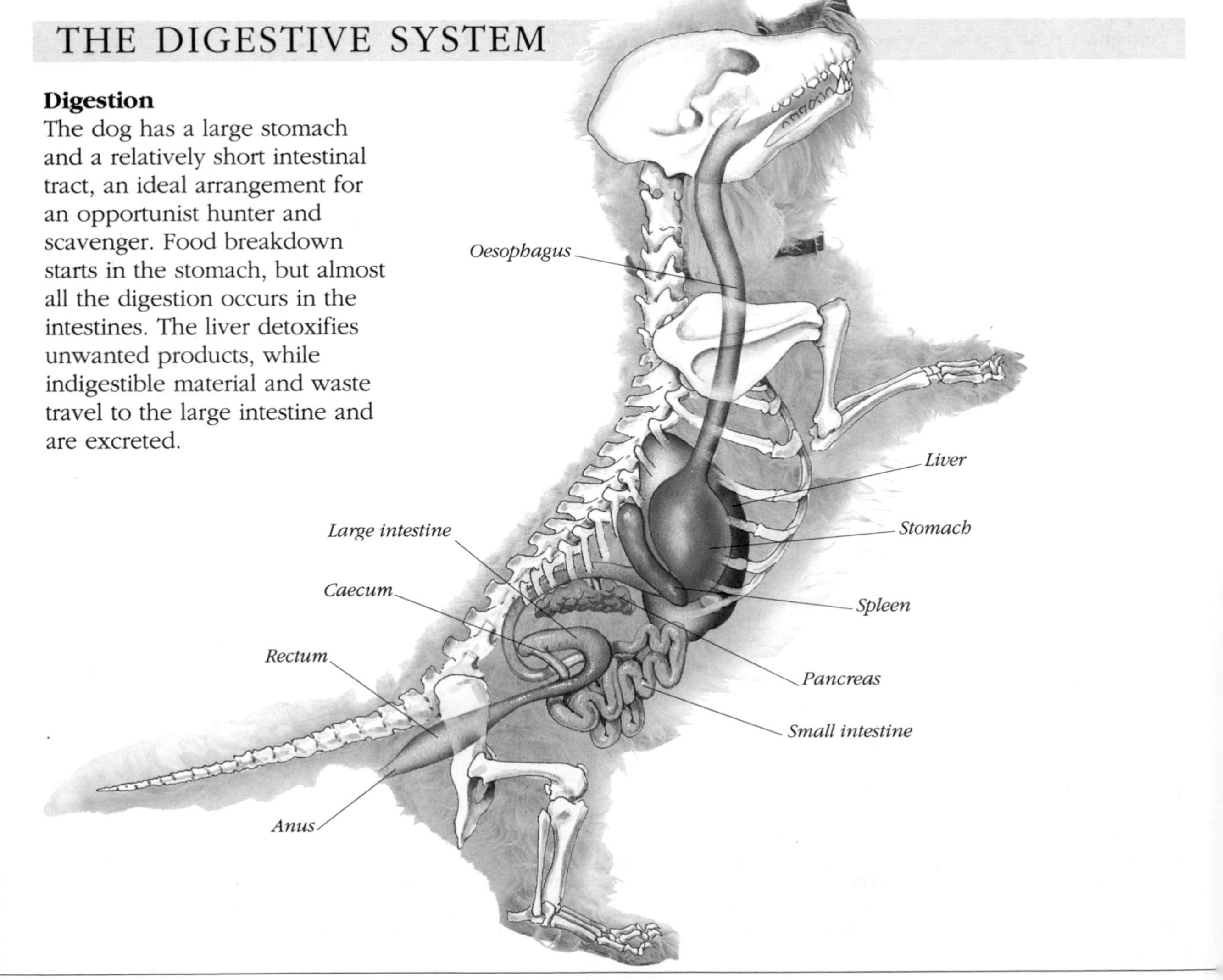

DIGESTIVE DISORDERS

Signs and disorders	Description	Action
Occasional vomiting Overeating Eating grass Allergy Travel sickness Nervousness Enlarged oesophagus	Simple vomiting is common and usually unassociated with discomfort. Through overeating, consuming unusual foods like grass, eating things to which it is allergic, or as a result of car travel or nervousness, a dog might vomit but otherwise appear normal. An enlarged oesophagus, especially in puppies, can also cause simple vomiting.	Withdraw the dog's food for up to 24 hours, and as long as there is no dehydration, ration its water to small amounts of soda water, or occasional ice cubes, for eight hours. If vomiting continues, seek veterinary advice.
Persistent vomiting or vomiting blood Gastric torsion Infection Acute pancreatitis Colitis Poisoning (p. 164)	Vomiting blood and persistent vomiting are very serious. Gastric torsion (bloat), most common in deep-chested breeds, causes painful vomiting and sudden swelling of the abdomen *(see page 173)*. Infections such as parvovirus, distemper, leptospirosis, and hepatitis all cause listlessness, and sometimes involve bloody or projectile vomiting, in which the stomach contents are ejected with great force. Inflammation of the pancreas (acute pancreatitis) or colon (colitis) both cause pain and vomiting.	Severe vomiting requires immediate veterinary attention. Gastric torsion is a life-threatening emergency requiring immediate surgical correction. Preventative vaccination protects against many of the infectious viral diseases such as parvovirus, while bacterial diseases are treated with appropriate antibiotics. Vomiting associated with acute pancreatitis and colitis, especially in small dogs, can be controlled by specific drugs.
Diarrhoea Milk intolerance Allergy Chronic pancreatitis Roundworms (p. 113) Emotional upset Infections Poisoning (p. 164)	Food intolerance, especially to milk, allergies, underactive pancreas function (chronic pancreatitis), roundworms, and emotional upsets can all cause mild diarrhoea with little or no discomfort. Bacterial and viral infections like salmonella, parvovirus, or hepatitis can cause more explosive, watery diarrhoea, sometimes with blood and accompanying lethargy.	Dogs with simple diarrhoea should fast for 24 hours, and then eat a bland meal such as chicken and rice. Once determined, the cause of diarrhoea should be avoided or eliminated. Consult a vet if diarrhoea continues for over two days. Explosive, bloody, or painful diarrhoea requires immediate veterinary attention.
Overeating or weight gain Diabetes Pancreatic hypoplasia Hypothyroidism Competition Boredom	Sugar diabetes produces a voracious appetite, increased thirst, and weight loss. Dogs that do not produce enough digestive enzymes (pancreatic hypoplasia) are effectively starving, although they may eat voraciously. An underactive thyroid gland (hypothyroidism) slows down a dog's metabolism, resulting in weight gain on a standard diet, often associated with some lethargy and hair loss. Because of their pack mentality, dogs compete for food and eat more when fed together. Boredom can also cause a dog to eat more, since mealtime is the most exciting event of its day.	Consult a vet. Diabetes is usually treated with daily insulin injections. Pancreatic hypoplasia can be diagnosed through blood tests or stool samples, and treated with enzyme supplements. Similarly, thyroid gland activity can be analyzed with blood tests, and deficiencies corrected with medication. If these tests prove normal, then boredom or competition between dogs must be considered as a cause of weight gain. In these circumstances, feed fewer calories under veterinary supervision.
Constipation Blocked anal glands Abscessed anal glands Swallowed bones Enlarged prostate gland Pelvic fracture Bowel nerve damage Perineal hernia Atresia ani	If the anal glands on either side of the anal opening become blocked or infected and abscessed, they cause discomfort. The dog licks or drags its rear on the ground, and may be unwilling to empty its bowels. Swallowed bones in the large intestine, an enlarged prostate pressing upon and narrowing the colon, pelvic fractures, and nerve damage are all more serious conditions. A bulge on either side of the anus might be a perineal hernia impacted with faeces. Some puppies are born with imperfect anal openings and cannot pass a stool (atresia ani).	Consult a vet. Anal glands can be manually squeezed empty *(see page 133)*, but require syringing with antibiotics when infected or abscessed. Bony impactions require enemas and sometimes anaesthesia and manual evacuation of impacted stool, while prostate enlargement can be treated with antibiotics and hormones. Pelvic fractures can be surgically repaired, but nerve damage is often irreversible. Surgical correction is necessary for a perineal hernia and for atresia ani.
Loss of appetite Pain or discomfort in mouth (p. 115) Nausea Anxiety	When a dog asks for food but does not eat it, it might be suffering from discomfort in its mouth. If pain is elsewhere or associated with nausea, the dog may be reluctant to even ask for food. When excited, nervous, or worried some dogs simply lose their appetites.	A lack of appetite is often a very important general sign that a dog is unwell, especially in those that routinely enjoy their food. A veterinary examination will determine the seriousness of the condition.

INTERNAL PARASITES

Intestinal parasites seldom cause much inconvenience to dogs, but since the most common, the roundworm, is a potential health hazard to humans, you must ensure that your dog is routinely wormed. Dogs can also act as intermediate hosts for certain tapeworms that can be passed to humans. In addition to roundworms and tapeworms, dogs can become infested with the more serious intestinal hookworms and whipworms, or by microscopic parasites that cause diarrhoea.

Bitch infected by eating contaminated faeces

Puppy passes eggs in faeces

Adult worms inside bitch

Puppies acquire larvae from mother's milk

Ticks can transmit a single-celled parasite called *Babesia*, which causes lethargy and anaemia. Dogs can also contract the disease toxoplasmosis from eating contaminated animals or faeces.

Puppy infection
Puppies become infected with larvae either before birth, from the larvae passing from the bitch, or after birth from their mother's milk. The puppies pass eggs in their faeces, which the bitch consumes, completing the cycle.

COMMON INTERNAL PARASITES

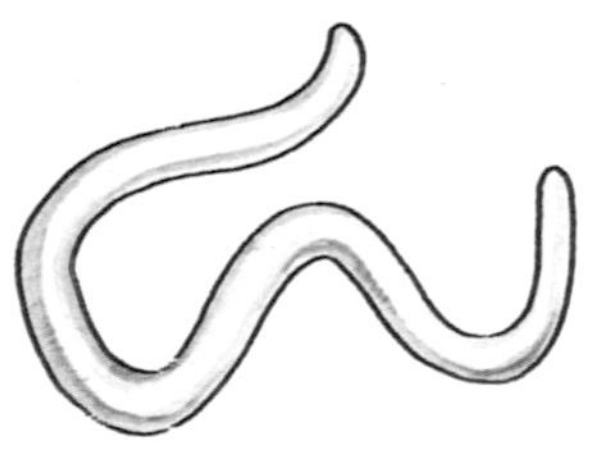

Roundworm *(above)*
Looking like a pale earthworm, this parasite lives in the stomach or intestines and reaches about 10 cm (4 in) in length.

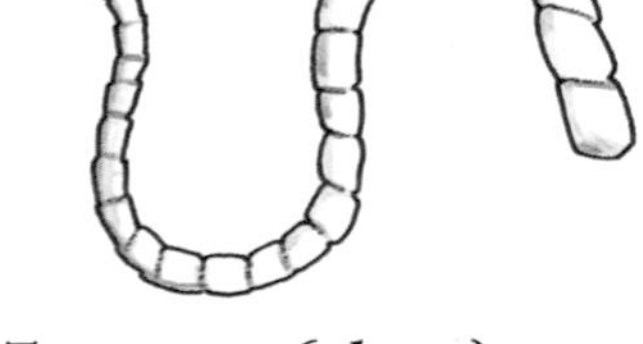

Tapeworm *(above)*
Flat and segmented, the tapeworm attaches itself by its mouth to the intestinal wall.

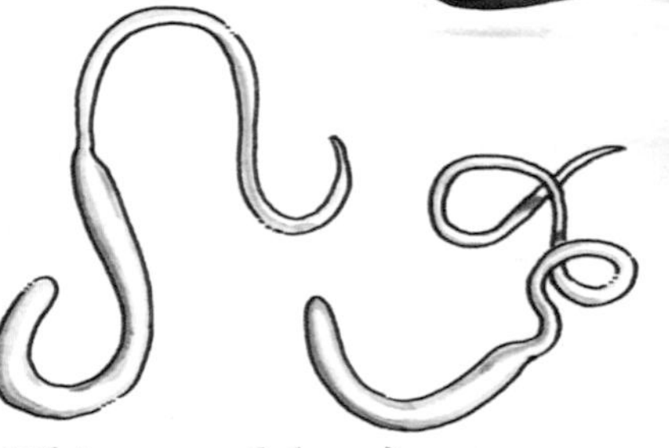

Whipworm *(above)*
Up to 7 cm (2½ in) long, this worm lives in the intestines. Its eggs can be seen with a microscope.

Signs of infestation
Licking the anal region or dragging the rear are common signs of worm infestation. Check for signs of tapeworm egg sacs in the hair around the anal region. Impacted anal glands are just as frequent a cause of excessive anal grooming. Always check that they are not causing discomfort *(see page 111)*.

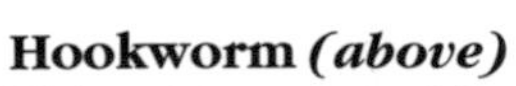

Hookworm *(above)*
This microscopic, blood-sucking worm lives in the intestines. It can cause serious bleeding.

INTERNAL PARASITES

Parasite	Description and signs	Action
Roundworms *Toxocara canis* *Toxascaris leonina*	Roundworms may cause mild vomiting and diarrhoea, with curled, round, pink-white worms being passed. Puppies may acquire this worm while still in the mother's womb, and have mature worms in their intestines by the time they are only two weeks old. If a puppy inherits a heavy load of *T. canis* worms, it will have a pot-belled appearance and a dull coat, and either gain weight poorly or suffer weight loss. It might cough, hiccough and, in rare instances, suffer from convulsions. *T. leonina* is acquired by a dog swallowing microscopic eggs.	All puppies should be routinely wormed from two weeks of age. Pregnant bitches should be wormed under veterinary supervision. Only worming medicines that destroy all stages of the life cycle are effective. Even healthy-looking dogs can have roundworms. Adult dogs should be wormed every three months to prevent roundworm infestation.
Tapeworms *Dipylidium caninum* *Echinococcus granulosus* *Taenia* sp.	Tapeworms seldom cause clinical signs. The abdomen can become distended, but the most common finding is small, dried egg sacs like rice grains in the hair around the anus. The worms can also be seen moving in the faeces. *Dipylidium caninum* is acquired by the dog eating a flea containing a worm egg. Other tapeworms are acquired by a dog eating carcasses or offal from animals such as sheep that contain cysts produced by tapeworms.	Prevent tapeworms by controlling fleas *(see page 103)*, and when possible stop a dog from eating animal carcasses and offal. *Echinococcus* is of particular importance because it can affect humans *(see page 127)*. This is of most concern in countries or regions with large sheep populations. Worm a dog regularly with a preparation approved by a vet.
Whipworms *Trichuris vulpis*	Whipworms can cause diarrhoea with sufficient bleeding to produce anaemia. They usually occur in young dogs kept in unhygienic conditions, and are most common in warm climates. The worms can be up to 7 cm (2½ in) long. They cause irritation, making a dog drag its rear along the ground.	Consult a vet, since whipworm eggs shed on grass can remain infectious for over a year. Diagnosis is based on a veterinary faecal flotation test. Because this worm is resistant to many drugs, special medicines are needed.
Hookworms *Uncinaria stenocephala* *Ancylostoma caninum*	Hookworms are almost microscopic, living off blood in the small intestine. They can cause severe anaemia and diarrhoea. When dogs lie on damp, unhygenic bedding, the larval stage of this parasite can cause skin irritation, especially between the toes *(see page 103)*.	Hygiene should be improved and the dog should be wormed with special medication supplied by a vet.
Giardia canis	*Giardia* is a microscopic parasite. Dogs and humans *(see page 127)* can become infected by drinking contaminated water. The parasite causes diarrhoea, which is often bloody and accompanied by mucus. Some dogs can contract this parasite by eating droppings from contaminated animals such as beavers.	Take a fresh sample of the affected dog's faeces to a vet, who can carry out lab tests and then treat the condition with an appropriate course of medication. *Giardia* is not destroyed by routine drugs.
Babesia	*Babesia* is a microscopic, single-celled parasite, and is transmitted through tick bites. It attacks red blood cells, causing anaemia, lethargy, vomiting, and liver problems.	Consult a vet, who can carry out a simple blood test to diagnose the condition. It is best controlled by preventing tick infestation *(see page 103)*.
Coccidia	*Coccidia* is a microscopic protozoan that causes diarrhoea, especially in young dogs kept in crowded conditions.	Take a sample of the affected dog's faeces to a vet, who can carry out a microscopic examination. *Coccidia* responds to treatment with sulpha drugs.
Toxoplasma gondii	Toxoplasmosis can, in rare circumstances, cause diarrhoea, muscle weakness, and breathing difficulties. Dogs become infected by eating other animals that contain cysts of the single-celled protozoan *Toxoplasma*, or from ingesting contaminated cat faeces.	Diagnosis is based upon blood tests. Treatment is difficult, although there is some response to certain drugs. Reduce the risk of infection by clearing cat litter trays of faeces daily. Toxoplasmosis is also a public health hazard.

MOUTH AND TOOTH DISORDERS

Because they no longer use their teeth to catch and kill prey, over 70 per cent of domestic dogs show signs of gum disease by the time they are four years old. Bad breath is often the first sign of mouth trouble. This is caused by bacteria multiplying in food trapped between the teeth, or by infection of the gums.

Small dogs such as poodles and Yorkshire Terriers, in which the teeth are closely packed, are more prone to gum disease than are larger breeds such as retrievers.

Certain breeds, such as the Boxer and bull terriers, can suffer from proliferative gum growth, while other dogs with overshot or undershot jaws are also prone to gum disease. Untreated gum disease leads to tooth decay. Chip fractures from chewing bones and stones also damage teeth and lead to infection. Without early veterinary treatment, removal is often the best option.

Examining teeth
Ensure that your dog's teeth and gums are examined by a vet at least once a year.

A DOG'S TEETH

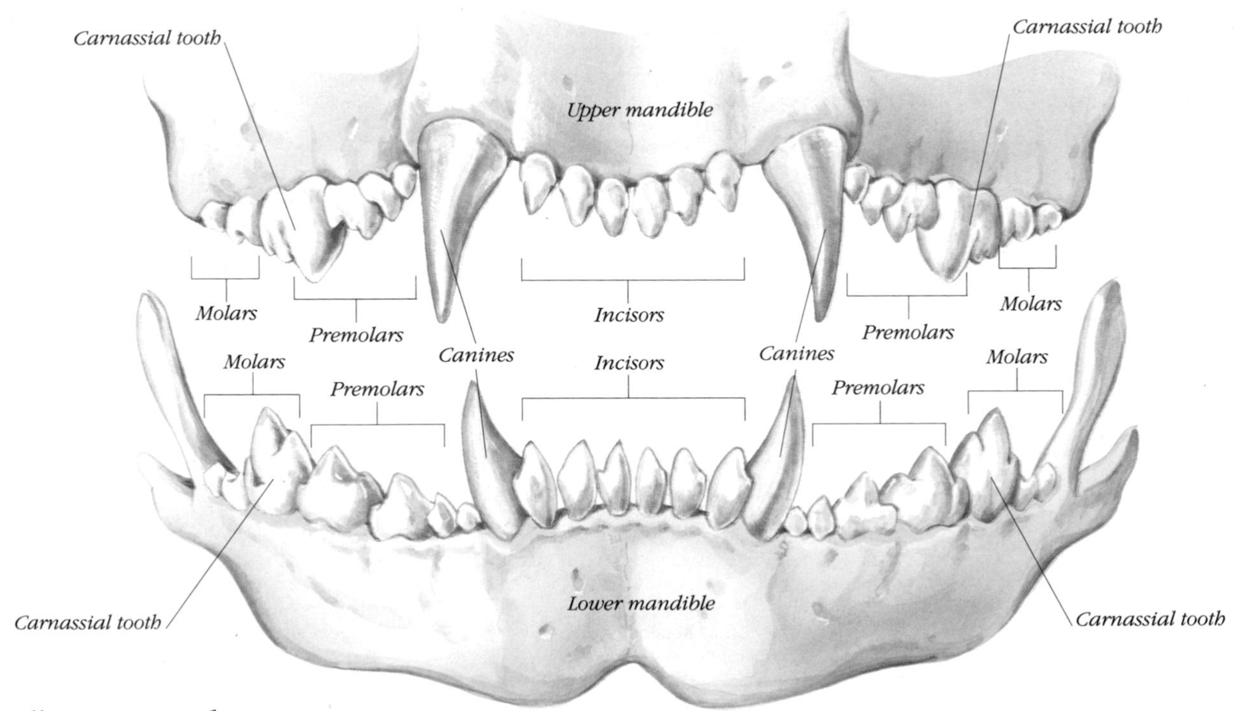

All-purpose teeth
Dogs first develop milk teeth that drop out by 20 weeks of age and are replaced with adult teeth. The canines are adapted for tearing, the molars for crushing, and the tiny incisors for scraping. These activities keep the teeth and gums clean and healthy. The carnassial teeth shear food into small pieces.

MOUTH AND TOOTH DISORDERS

Signs and disorders	Description	Action
Halitosis (bad breath) Tartar Gingivitis (gum infection) Tumours Proliferating gum disease	Sensitive, inflamed gums are common in all dogs, but especially in small breeds. Tartar builds up on the teeth, food particles catch between it and the gums, and gum infection ensues. Tumours appear as lumps in the gums. Proliferating gum disease is an inherited condition, common to Boxers and bull terriers, in which the gum grows up to cover the teeth. If left untreated by a vet, this condition can lead to gum infection.	Seek veterinary advice for correct diagnosis. Routine brushing of a dog's teeth will slow or prevent the development of tartar and gingivitis. If tartar has formed, the teeth must be scaled and polished by a vet. Some mouth tumours are malignant and life-threatening, and must be surgically removed. Infection caused by proliferating gums can be treated with antibiotics, but greatly enlarged gums must be surgically removed under anaesthesia.
Drooling Salivary cyst Periodontal disease Tongue injuries Foreign body (p. 162)	Salivary cysts look like large, fluid-filled blisters when they occur under the tongue, but can also develop under the skin in the neck by the corners of the jaw, creating fluctuating masses. Periodontal disease destroys the cement that holds the teeth in place, so that they move when touched. Tongue wounds can be self-inflicted or occur in fights with other dogs. Bites are most common to the tip, while burns occur further back and are difficult to see.	Salivary cysts require drainage and the damaged saliva gland must be removed as well, so consult a vet if this is suspected. Once periodontal disease has become so severe that the teeth are loose they must be removed. Bites and burns also need veterinary attention. Because eating is painful it is sometimes best to feed small, soft, chunky pieces of food that do not need to be chewed.
Reluctance to chew Tooth cavity Tooth root abscess Fractured tooth Distemper teeth	Large cavities are visible as damage to the tooth enamel, and often occur at the gum margin. Root abscesses are sometimes more difficult to see. A crack might appear in a tooth or a skin swelling develop. This sometimes affects tear drainage if an upper molar is affected, causing tears to run down the face. Fractures are common in molars, while the canines get chipped during play. Contact with the distemper virus while a dog is still a puppy can cause the adult teeth to erupt looking severely eroded, stained, and mottled, and these often decay.	Although it is often most practical for a vet to remove the tooth that is causing pain, routine tooth decay can be treated with fillings, while abscesses and fractures usually require root canal work. Tooth damage from the distemper virus is permanent, and severely decayed teeth should be removed by a vet.
Misaligned bite (malocclusion) Undershot jaw Overshot jaw	The upper and lower teeth should mesh perfectly when a dog closes its mouth, but sometimes the lower jaw is longer than the upper one, causing an undershot bite. This is normal in breeds with pushed-in faces, like the Pekingese and Bulldog, but is a defect in others. If the lower jaw is shorter than the upper the bite is overshot. This is a defect in any breed, but is most likely to occur in long-nosed breeds such as the Dobermann and collies.	No action is necessary unless the misaligned bite causes discomfort. This is most likely to occur in overshot dogs. With a narrow, overshot jaw the lower canines press into the hard palate each time the dog closes its mouth. A vet can fit a removable appliance over the upper front teeth and hard palate. After a few months the lower canines should have moved into a more correct and less painful position.
Abnormalities Hairlip Cleft palate Retained milk teeth No adult teeth	During foetal development, both sides of the body develop symmetrically and then join up in the middle. If the final join is not perfect, a hairlip or cleft palate develops. Puppies born with cleft palates have difficulty suckling. The palate is also prone to damage at the midline, in which there is an obvious tear down the centre of the hard palate, causing affected dogs to sneeze when they drink. Retained milk teeth are common in small breeds, especially the Yorkshire Terrier. In this case, once the adult teeth have erupted there are commonly eight canines instead of four. Rarely, adult teeth do not appear at all, and a mature dog retains only tiny milk teeth.	Hairlips look unusual but rarely need surgical correction, but cleft palates require veterinary treatment. Sometimes waterproof plasters can be temporarily applied over the damage until the puppy is larger and better able to cope with the trauma of major surgery. In most instances, surgical repair is the only effective solution. All milk teeth should loosen and drop out just before adult teeth erupt. If the adult teeth have broken through but the milk teeth are still firmly rooted, the baby teeth should be removed under anaesthesia by a vet to provide the proper spaces into which the adult teeth can grow. This reduces the likelihood of future gum disease.

Reproductive Disorders

Early neutering eliminates the possibility of most of the more serious reproductive disorders. If, for example, a bitch is spayed before her first season, she has virtually no risk of developing mammary cancer. If, however, the bitch continues to cycle until she is over two years old, her risk of developing this most common of all canine tumours has already reached a maximum. Similarly, the longer a bitch cycles, the more at risk she becomes of developing a life-threatening womb infection. All breeding dogs, especially males, should be routinely examined for sexually transmitted diseases. When problems of infertility occur, a vet can check for metabolic conditions that affect fertility.

Mother love
Maternal behaviour is hormonally induced in a bitch after each season.

THE REPRODUCTIVE SYSTEM

Mating
The male's testes produce sperm that is passed to the bitch during mating. The sperm meets the released eggs in the Fallopian tube, where union occurs. The fertilized eggs then position themselves along the length of each horn of the uterus, where they develop over the following two months.

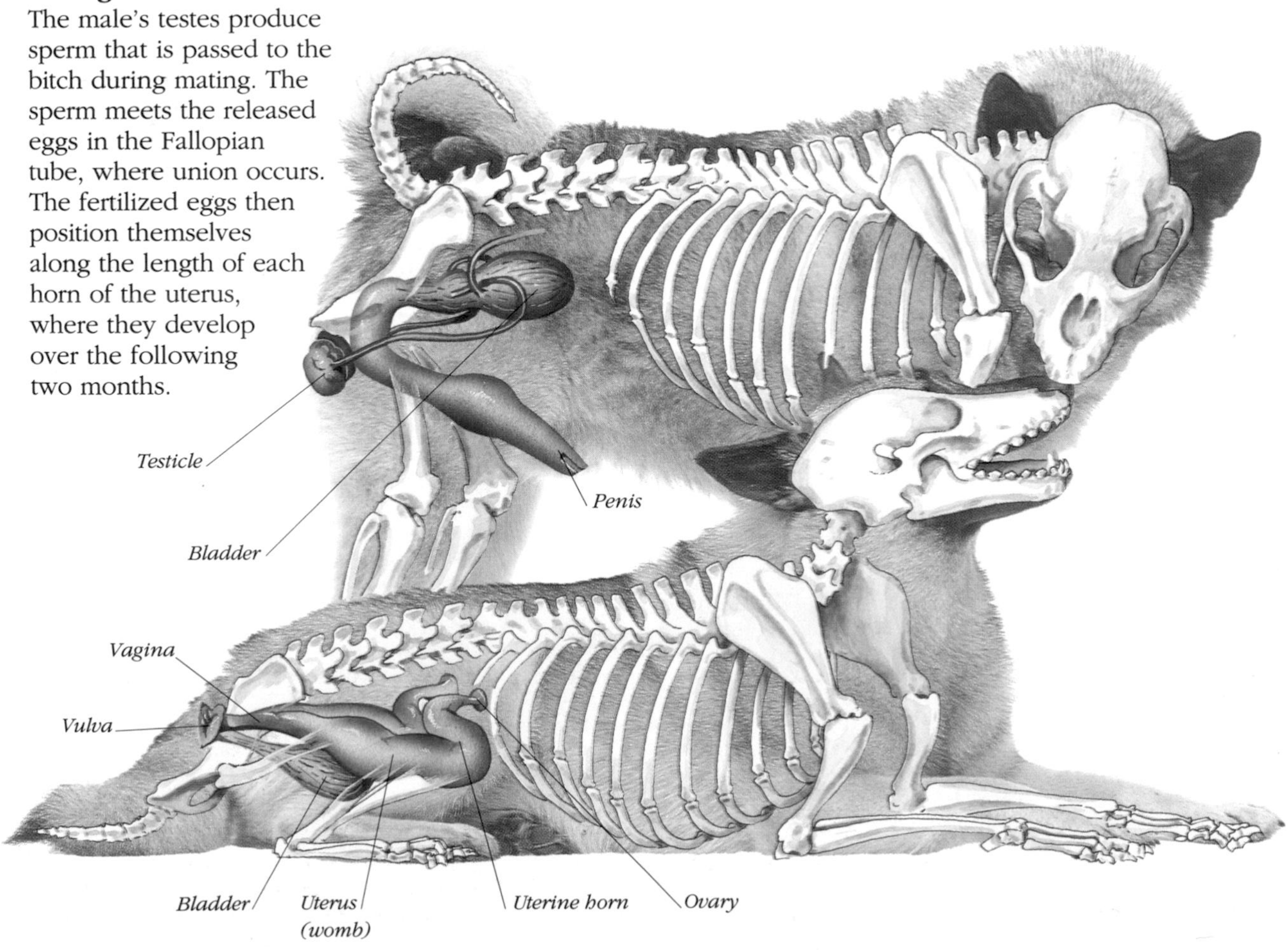

REPRODUCTIVE DISORDERS

Signs and disorders	Description	Action
Female infertility Infection Metritis Ovarian cyst Hypothyroidism (p. 111) Hypoestrogenism Physical abnormalities	Sexually transmitted infections such as brucellosis are a major cause of infertility in some countries. Carriers may have a high temperature or swollen joints. Metritis (womb infection) prevents the fertilized eggs from implanting, while ovarian cysts prevent ovulation. Hypothyroidism causes abnormal heat cycles, while hypoestrogenism, under-development of the ovaries, results in low oestrogen levels and no heat cycle. Physical problems such as a narrow vagina cause the bitch pain, and the bitch may refuse to mate.	A veterinary examination before mating can determine whether there are any infections in the reproductive system. These can usually be treated effectively with antibiotics. Laboratory tests on a blood sample help to determine whether a bitch has an ovarian cyst, which may be treated with hormones, or removed surgically. A vet may also suggest a hysterectomy. There is no treatment for hypoestrogenism. Physical abnormalities can be corrected surgically.
Male infertility Prostatitis Balanitis Orchitis Physical abnormalities Tumours	Infections that result in an enlarged prostate (prostatitis), and sheath infections (balanitis) can reduce a male dog's fertility, as can inflammation of the testicle (orchitis), due to injury or a disease such as brucellosis. Physical abnormalities can also affect a dog's fertility. With phimosis the sheath has a narrow opening that prevents the dog from extruding its penis, while in paraphimosis, the penis cannot be withdrawn into the sheath and is constricted. A monorchid dog has only one descended testicle, while a cryptorchid has neither testicle descended. Testicular tumours can produce female hormones, resulting in hair loss and enlarged mammary glands.	Stud dogs should be examined by a vet every three months. An enlarged prostate can be treated with hormones, while surgery may be necessary to correct physical defects. In the case of the latter, you can ease the dog's swelling and discomfort until it can be treated by a vet by placing ice packs on the penis and lubricating it with petroleum jelly. Undescended testicles should be removed, since they can lead to cancer. You should never breed from a monorchid dog, since the condition is inherited. Tumours may respond to hormonal treatment, although malignant ones may be surgically removed.
Discharge during pregnancy Miscarriage Pyometra Mucometra	Bloody discharges may mean miscarriage, caused by infection, injury, foetal abnormalities, poor nutrition, and perhaps stress. A discharge of pus may mean pyometra, infection of the womb. Sometimes excess mucus is discharged (mucometra), which is another sign of impending problems.	Contact a vet if there are any vaginal discharges during pregnancy. If the vet determines that the cervix is dilated, medication can be given to help clear up the infection and evacuate the aborted foetuses. If the cervix is closed, the bitch's life is in danger and the only safe option is an immediate hysterectomy.
Extended pregnancy Phantom pregnancy Resorption	Sometimes a bitch may appear pregnant but not produce puppies. This can mean a phantom pregnancy, in which the dog shows all the symptoms of a real pregnancy *(see page 146)*. Miscarriage without infection may lead to the foetuses being resorbed.	Phantom pregnancies can be treated with drugs that stop the bitch coming into heat, or by spaying *(see page 145)*. There is no treatment for resorption.
Painful or swollen teats Mastitis Mammary tumours Mammary cysts	Infection can sometimes move up the teat canal, causing a hot, hard swelling of the mammary gland (mastitis). This is painful when touched, while mammary tumours are not. These are most likely to appear in old dogs, and can be firm and mobile or soft and invasive. Mammary cysts feel hard, are fluid filled, and occur most often in old females that have lactated.	Consult a vet, who can treat mastitis with antibiotics. Puppies should be prevented from suckling from the affected gland, and since antibiotic passes into the milk, it is often best that they are bottle fed. Lumpectomies or a complete mastectomy are usually performed on mammary tumours. Cysts can be drained or left alone.
Panting or whining Eclampsia	If a female pants intensely after the birth, whines, and appears unsettled, she could be suffering from eclampsia, or a lack of calcium. This condition is most common in toy breeds, and with bitches that have had large litters.	Consult a vet urgently if eclampsia is suspected, since the bitch will die if not treated soon enough. Eclampsia may be prevented by proper nutrition during pregnancy, given under veterinary advice.
Cannibalism	Some breeds, especially bull terriers, lick their puppies obsessively and sometimes eat them.	Breeds that are prone to cannibalism must be watched 24 hours a day until the puppies' umbilical cords have dropped off.

URINARY DISORDERS

Changes in a dog's normal urinary function warrant immediate investigation by a vet. Straining to urinate can be caused by an infection, mineral sediment in the urine, or bladder stones lodged like plugs in the urethra. As well as being very painful, this can be life threatening. Increased frequency of passing urine or increases in amounts passed can mean a urinary infection or a serious metabolic illness, such as diabetes or hormonal imbalances. Incontinence is common in elderly dogs, but can also occur for a variety of reasons in young ones. Contact a vet if you notice changes in the colour or consistency of a dog's urine.

Excess drinking
This can be a sign of kidney or liver disease, or adrenal or pituitary gland malfunction.

THE URINARY SYSTEM

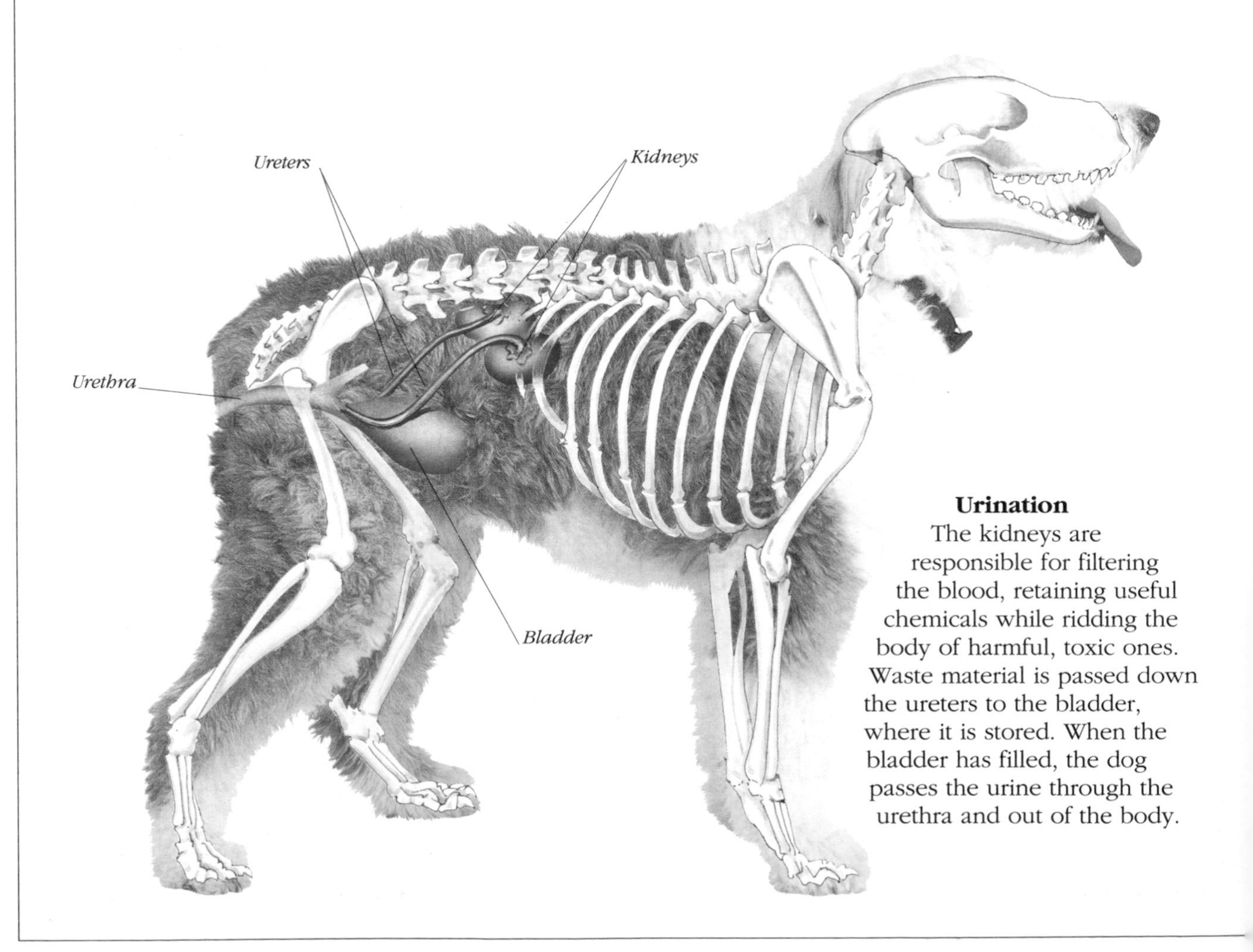

Urination
The kidneys are responsible for filtering the blood, retaining useful chemicals while ridding the body of harmful, toxic ones. Waste material is passed down the ureters to the bladder, where it is stored. When the bladder has filled, the dog passes the urine through the urethra and out of the body.

URINARY DISORDERS

Signs and disorders	Description	Action
Straining to urinate Infections Prostatitis (p. 117) Bladder or urethra stones	Infections of the bladder and urethra cause inflammation and an increased need to urinate even when the bladder is empty. Male dogs can experience the same need when the prostate gland is enlarged or infected, or the penis inflamed. Urine is often clouded with pus and discoloured by blood. Vaginal infections can cause females to strain in a similar fashion. Straining is more serious and more painful when caused by mineral stones that develop in the bladder. The male dog has a narrow urethra, and stones sometimes lodge in it just behind the bone in the penis, causing non-productive straining and pain.	Veterinary assistance is vital, since a dog can die in a couple of days if it is unable to urinate. When possible, take a fresh urine sample from the dog to a vet. When an infection is the cause of straining, urinary acidifiers may be prescribed in addition to a course of antibiotics, since bacteria often thrive in an alkaline environment. If there is a severe blockage, a urinary catheter can be used to relieve pressure and pain. Bladder stones are commonly diagnosed with X-rays. Treatment usually involves significant diet changes.
Incontinence Hormonal imbalance Bladder displacement Injury to the spine Urinary tract infection Ageing	Incontinent dogs are unaware that they are dribbling urine. It might occur when they are lying down, when they get excited, or simply when getting up and down. Incontinence should not be confused with urinating as a sign of subservience. It occurs most frequently in females, especially in spayed Dobermanns, Springer Spaniels, and Old English Sheepdogs, and is associated with a hormonal imbalance, or with an anatomical displacement of the bladder. Injuries to the spine affecting the nerve supply to the bladder, or damage to the sphincter muscles due to chronic urinary tract infection, also cause incontinence. With old age there can be a natural deterioration of bladder control.	Only some forms of incontinence can be controlled. A dog should be examined by a vet for any sign of physical injury or infection. Female hormones are often prescribed for incontinent spayed females, while male hormones are sometimes used for incontinent male dogs. Contrast X-rays of the bladder may also be taken. If these show that the bladder is sitting abnormally high on the pelvic bone, the condition can be corrected by surgically moving the bladder to a more normal position. A vet can treat infections with antibiotics, while anabolic hormones can improve sphincter muscle tone and control in ageing dogs.
Increased urination Kidney or bladder infections Nephrosis Liver disease Diabetes Cushing's disease	Kidney and bladder infections cause dogs to urinate more frequently. Poor kidney filtration, common in old dogs (chronic nephrosis) and in young dogs of certain breeds (juvenile nephrosis), results in increased amounts of dilute urine being passed. Thirst is also increased. Certain liver diseases, as well as sugar diabetes and diabetes insipidus, a condition in which the body cannot concentrate urine properly *(see page 111)*, all result in increased thirst and larger quantities of urine. There are similar signs when the adrenal gland produces too much cortisone (Cushing's disease) or when a dog is being treated with cortisone.	Take a sample of the urine to a vet, where it will be checked for sugar, liver waste products, protein, and concentration. Infections can be treated with antibiotics. If filtration has been impaired, resulting in nephrosis, treatment means dramatically reducing the kidneys' workload. This means eliminating most protein from the diet and supplanting it with carbohydrates, sugars, and fats. Sugar diabetes can be treated with diet changes or insulin, while diabetes insipidus can be treated with hormone drops on the eye that improve the ability to concentrate urine. Blood samples help diagnose Cushing's disease, which can be treated with tablets, or by removing the overactive adrenal gland.
Decreased urination Dehydration Kidney failure	When a dog is ill and dehydrated for any reason, it conserves as much fluid as it can. Any urine passed is dark in colour, often deep gold, and has an almost sticky consistency. There is no straining associated with urination. Quantities of urine voided also drop dramatically during the last stages of kidney failure, and this urine is much more watery. The dog's body has often lost all its fat deposits and most muscle. It is listless and lethargic.	Dehydration can be treated by giving lots of fluids. In the case of kidney failure, immediate veterinary attention is essential to get the kidneys working again. Large quantities of fluid can be administered intravenously. Because waste products build up, peritoneal dialysis is often used, in which litres of fluids are washed through the abdominal cavity. When possible, kidney dialysis is used to cleanse the blood. These treatments should be employed only if the quality of life of the dog can be returned to an acceptable level.

NERVOUS DISORDERS

A dog's muscles, ligaments, and tendons all depend on the brain and network of nerves to achieve maximum performance. Damage to the nervous system can lead to a lack of sensation, partial or complete paralysis, loss of balance, seizures, or changes in a dog's behaviour.

Viruses such as rabies and distemper cause inflammation of the brain and associated changes in temperament and coordination. Other bacterial and viral infections inflame the protective wrapping that envelops the brain, which can result in meningitis, seizures, and loss of balance. Physical injuries to the brain tissue can cause epilepsy, while damage to the spinal cord interferes with the transmission of nerve messages back to the brain. Depending upon the part of the spinal cord that is injured, this can result in loss of sensation in the skin, paralysis of a limb, or incontinence. Nerve damage needs immediate attention from a vet.

Light reflexes
By checking light reflexes in the eyes, a vet can determine whether there is damage to the brain.

THE NERVOUS SYSTEM

Nerve network symmetry
Travelling inside the well-protected spinal column, the spinal cord descends from the brain, sending nerves out between each vertebra of the spine to all muscles and organs in the body. Once outside the spinal column, nerves are more susceptible to damage. Unlike muscles, a severed nerve never repairs itself properly.

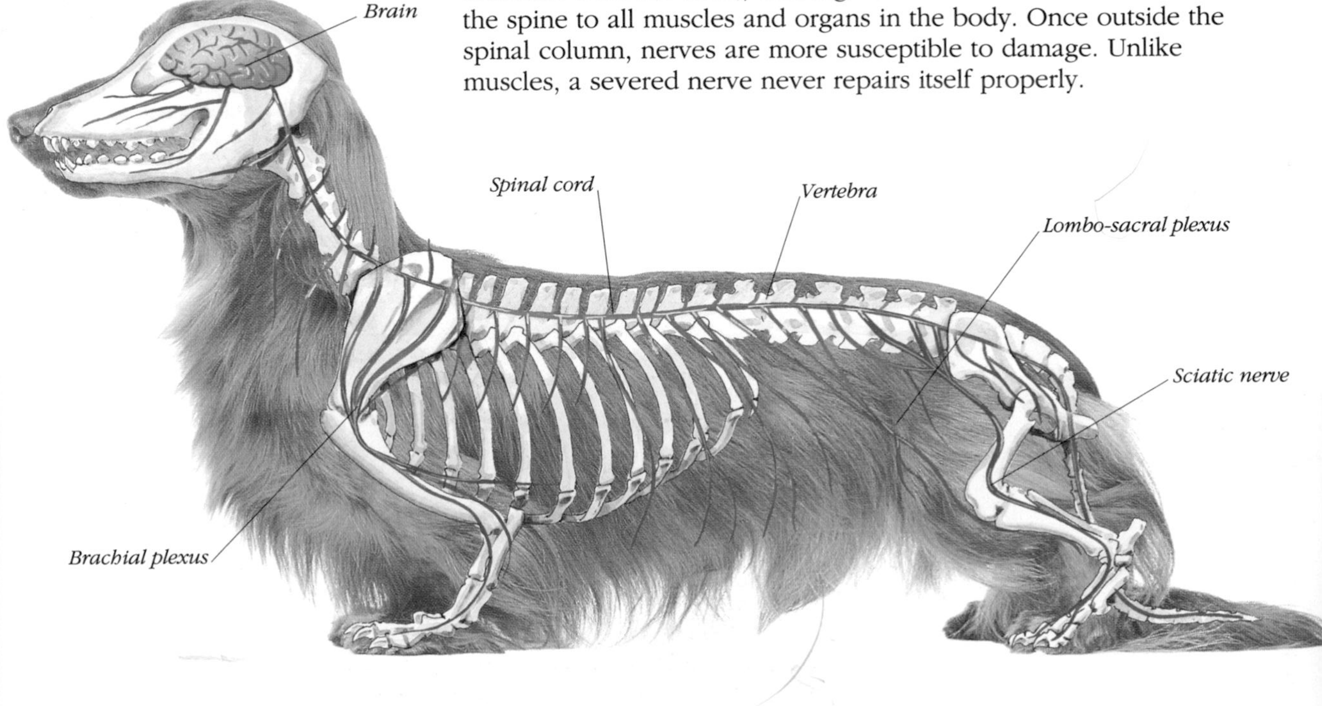

NERVOUS DISORDERS		
Signs and disorders	**Description**	**Action**
Seizures Epilepsy Encephalitis Distemper Trauma Poisoning (p. 165) Eclampsia Tumours	There are several different forms of epilepsy. Grand mal seizures cause loss of consciousness and twitching. Petit mal episodes can last only a few seconds, during which the dog seems to lose concentration. With narcolepsy the affected dog can temporarily fall asleep on its feet. Hydrocephalus causes seizures that can involve loss of consciousness, twitching, urinating, and defaecating. Encephalitis is an inflammation of the brain due to infections such as distemper. Physical damage to the brain, either because of trauma, tumours, or poisoning, can cause fits, as does the condition eclampsia, which is a drop in calcium levels *(see page 117)*.	Protect the dog from injuring itself while it is convulsing *(see page 173)*. Contact a vet immediately. Fits are controlled with anti-convulsants. Bacterial encephalitis can be treated with antibiotics, while infections can be avoided with preventative vaccination. Pressure on the brain can be relieved with medication or surgery. Seizures caused by falling calcium levels can be reversed by intravenous calcium. Low blood sugar levels and accompanying fits occur most frequently in small, lean, young puppies stressed by sudden journeys. They respond to intravenous glucose.
Loss of balance Stroke Inner ear infection Meningitis	After a stroke, a dog is unsure of itself, and often avoids food, or vomits if it eats. A stroke can affect any part of the body, causing paralysis or a head tilt. Inner ear infections cause a loss of balance and a head tilt on the affected side *(see page 107)*. If this is left untreated, the infection moves deeper, causing meningitis and a general loss of balance.	Contact a vet, who can examine the dog's reflexes and its response to light. It is difficult to tell whether a stroke has been caused by a blood clot or a haemorrhage, so it will usually be treated conservatively with appropriate drugs. Ear infection and meningitis can be treated with antibiotics.
Paralysis Compressed spinal cord Wobbler syndrome Nerve injuries Slipped disc Cancer of the spine Tetanus Scottie cramp Ascending neuropathy Tick poisoning (p. 103)	An instability of the vertebrae in large breeds, such as the Great Dane and Dobermann, often results in compression of the spinal cord. This can lead to incoordination of the hind legs, also known as Wobbler syndrome. Mild spinal nerve injuries produce an increased sensitivity to pain. If nerves in the neck are involved there is a lot of pain when the head is moved. If any nerves further down the spine are affected, perhaps due to a slipped disc *(see page 99)*, the affected dog is reluctant to jump or to climb stairs. More severe damage causes a weakness or paralysis of the limbs, and there can be loss of bladder and bowel control, as well. Cancer of the spine can produce similar paralysis through pressure on the spinal cord. Tetanus is uncommon in dogs, but those affected become rigid and almost convulsive. Scottie cramp afflicts some Scottish Terriers and West Highland White Terriers at around six months of age, affecting the nerves to the muscles and causing a rigidity to the legs and back. Ascending neuropathy is often seen in mature German Shepherd Dogs. The hind legs gradually lose their precision until there is a complete loss of their use.	Prevent the dog from moving, then get immediate veterinary advice. Wobbler syndrome responds best to early surgical correction. Nerve injuries are often initially treated with absolute rest, muscle relaxants, and anti-inflammatories. Intravenous drugs are sometimes given to reduce swelling around the spinal cord. If nerve injury is caused by a slipped disc, discuss preventative surgery with a vet. Some dogs, such as dachshunds, are especially vulnerable, and those that have suffered a slipped disc are likely to suffer another. Removing the diseased disc eliminates further problems. Drug therapy relieves Scottie cramp. Ascending neuropathy is irreversible, and its cause unknown. Affected dogs sometimes need bandages on their hind feet to protect them from scraping injuries due to their paralysis.
Behaviour changes Rabies Fly catching Avalanche of rage syndrome	Some behavioural changes are neurological and not within a dog's control. Rabies is the most serious *(see page 127)*. The affected animal usually becomes aggressive, although another manifestation, dumb rabies, causes unusual friendliness. Fly catching, or snapping at non-existent flies, is a form of psychomotor epilepsy most common in Cavalier King Charles Spaniels, while avalanche of rage is an uncontrollable syndrome suffered mainly by solid-coloured Cocker Spaniels. The dog's placid temperament suddenly changes to fierce and snarling, and then quickly reverts back to normal friendliness.	A medical examination can eliminate possible causes of behaviour change. If rabies is suspected, the dog should be confined away from humans and other animals, and a vet contacted immediately. Fly catching often responds to low doses of anti-convulsant medication. Avalanche of rage syndrome, however, is an inherited disorder. Although it sometimes responds to anti-convulsants, the best method of control is to avoid breeding from animals that perpetuate the disorder.

BLOOD AND HEART DISORDERS

There are very few inherent blood disorders in dogs. Although in some parts of the world, blood parasites are common, changes in the numbers of red or white blood cells are usually indicators of poisoning, liver disease, tumours, infections, bone marrow disease, poor nutrition, or allergies. Heart disease, on the other hand, is more common in dogs than in any other domestic species. However, congenital heart defects and heart attacks are rare, with sudden heart failure often occurring only in mature, large breeds, especially the Dobermann. Progressive valvular heart disease occurs most commonly in Cavalier King Charles Spaniels. In some countries, over half of of all members of this breed have signs of heart disease by the time they are five years old. Heart disease is frequently first detected during a routine veterinary examination.

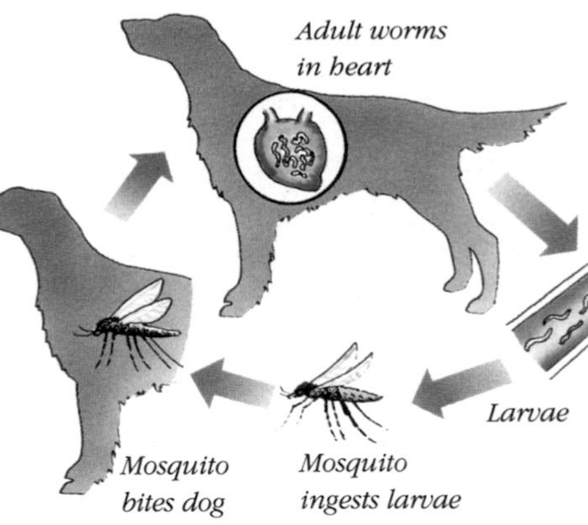

The heartworm life cycle
The microscopic larvae are transmitted via a mosquito bite and develop in the dog's heart.

THE CIRCULATORY SYSTEM

Circulation
The muscular bottom left chamber of the heart pumps fresh blood through arteries (shown in red) around the body. Veins (shown in blue) bring used blood back to the top right chamber, from where it flows to the bottom right, and then to the lungs, where carbon dioxide is removed and oxygen added.

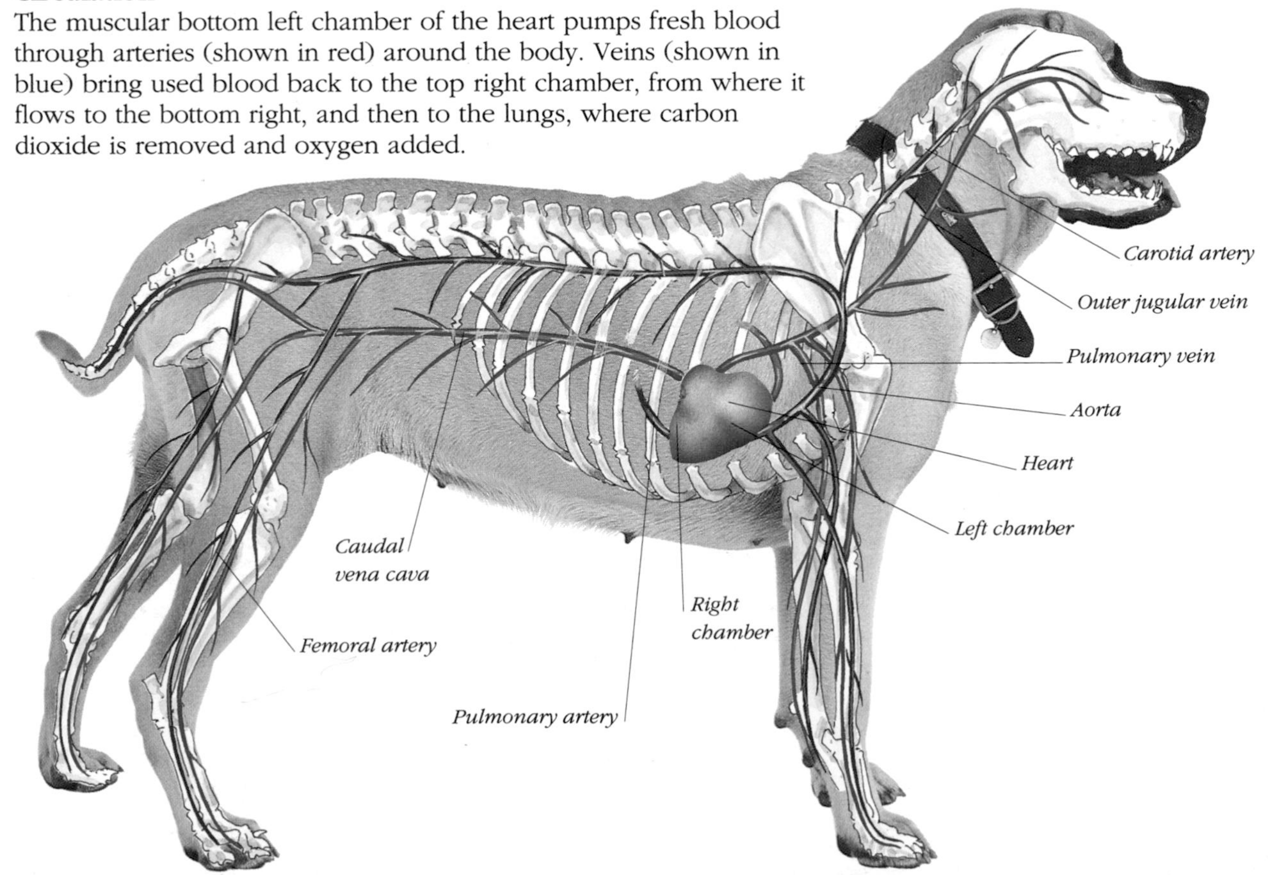

BLOOD AND HEART DISORDERS

Signs and disorders	Description	Action
Sudden blood loss Trauma Warfarin poisoning Liver failure Haemophilia Von Willebrand's disease Bone marrow damage Autoimmune haemolytic anaemia Tumours	Sudden internal or external blood loss causes lethargy, weakness, and sometimes collapse. The dog's breathing becomes laboured, and its heart rate increases. The gums are pale. External bleeding, for example due to trauma from a traffic accident, is obvious, but internal bleeding is not readily apparent. Warfarin poisoning *(see page 165)*, liver failure, haemophilia, and Von Willebrand's disease all produce coagulation (clotting) disorders. Other bleeding disorders are caused by infections damaging the bone marrow, and also occur when the body's natural defence system turns on itself (autoimmune haemolytic anaemia). Certain vascular tumours can rupture in the liver or spleen of older dogs, especially retrievers and German Shepherd Dogs, causing a sudden loss of blood.	Control any obvious external bleeding *(see page 168)* and get immediate veterinary assistance. Severe blood loss causes the body to go rapidly into a state of shock. This can be treated with massive amounts of cortisone and fluid replacement. When trauma is not the cause of blood loss, a vet can carry out blood tests to determine whether there is a coagulation or bleeding disorder. Vitamin K is a specific antidote for Warfarin poisoning. Internal bleeding, whether from trauma or from a tumour, usually requires immediate surgical correction. Blood transfusions are best for all forms of blood loss except autoimmune haemolytic anaemia. Because the body attacks red blood cells, transfusing more blood in this case makes the condition even worse.
Chronic blood loss or anaemia Heartworms Tumours Infections Inflammation Stomach ulcers	Chronic anaemias are slowly progressive. Affected dogs become lethargic, sleep more, and are reluctant to play. Their breathing is shallower than normal, and their heart rate faster. The gums are a dirty, pale pink. Heartworm infestation can cause a gradual weight loss, a persistent cough, and a pot-bellied appearance. Tumours, infections, inflammation, or stomach ulcers can all cause mild bleeding from the nose (epistaxis), or loss of blood in urine (haematuria), or in faeces, which leads to excessive demands on the bone marrow and spleen to produce new red blood cells.	Consult a vet. In a heartworm area, a vet can test a blood sample from the dog for heartworm larvae. If it is negative, preventative medication can be given during the mosquito season. If positive, the vet can hospitalize the dog for medical or surgical treatment. When there is chronic blood loss from any body opening, a vet can take a blood sample to check the number and condition of the red blood cells in order to determine the type and severity of anaemia. Treatment is directed at eliminating the cause of the anaemia.
Lethargy and coughing in older dogs Endocardiosis Cardiomyopathy	Endocardiosis (valvular heart disease) is a common progressive disease in many older dogs. When the left-side valve does not close properly, blood backs up into the lungs, causing a cough, breathing difficulties, a weak pulse, and a murmur that a vet can hear through a stethoscope. If the right-side valve is affected, blood backs up in the liver. As the liver swells, clear fluid builds up in the abdominal cavity, causing a pot-bellied appearance. Sudden heart failure (cardiomyopathy) often involves the heart muscle and occurs most often in large breeds, especially the Dobermann. The heartbeat becomes erratic and the pulse weak. An affected dog deteriorates within a few days, pants, and sometimes collapses or faints. The gums are pallid. When pressure is applied they blanch, and it takes a few seconds for blood to return.	Consult a vet if these signs appear. As valvular heart disease progresses, the lowest chambers of the heart enlarge to compensate for the inefficiency of the valves. Affected dogs should be fed salt-free diets, since salt retains unwanted fluid in the body. Drugs might be prescribed to eliminate excess fluid, dilate peripheral blood vessels, or to improve the efficiency of the heart. Acute heart failure is much more difficult to treat. Electrocardiographs and echocardiography can be used to determine the extent of the damage. Lessen the demand on the dog's heart by reducing exercise and excess weight with veterinary advice. Cardiac pacemakers are sometimes implanted in large dogs suffering from heart muscle failure.
Listlessness in young dogs Congenital heart valve defects Congenital septal defects Patent ductus arteriosis	Inherited heart defects are uncommon in dogs. Affected animals want to play but have little energy to do so. They are often weak and their growth is stunted. In severe circumstances the gums are blue (cyanosis), and puppies suddenly collapse from heart failure. Deformed valves, a septal defect (hole in the heart), and patent ductal arteriosis (failure of a foetal blood vessel to close) all cause blood to leak into other organs, producing a "murmur".	Consult a vet immediately if a puppy appears to be weaker or less active than normal. Audible heart murmurs in puppies almost always mean inherited defects, although severe anaemia can also produce a murmur. X-rays and electrocardiographs can diagnose the exact nature of the condition. Some forms of congenital heart defect can be surgically corrected.

INHERITED DISORDERS

In the wild, where only the fittest survive, inherited disorders are self-limiting. However, because the dog has been domesticated for longer than any other species, and because so many breeds have depended upon humans for their survival for hundreds of generations, the dog suffers from more inherited disorders than any other animal apart from man. Any body system is prone to hereditary defects. Popular breeds, such as the German Shepherd Dog, seem to suffer from more defects than other breeds, but that is only because there are more of them to study. Similarly, eye and skeleton disorders seem to be particularly common, but this is simply because it was in these systems that the inherited aspect of canine disease was first investigated. As the dog is studied more intensely, the causes of such diseases will eventually be controlled.

Breed problems
The genetics of disease have been investigated most in the German Shepherd Dog.

GENETICS AND INHERITED DISEASE

Recessive genes
Healthy dogs can pass on serious diseases to their offspring if they carry a recessive gene. In this diagram, two dogs are mated, but one carries a recessive gene for blindness (r). Two of their puppies

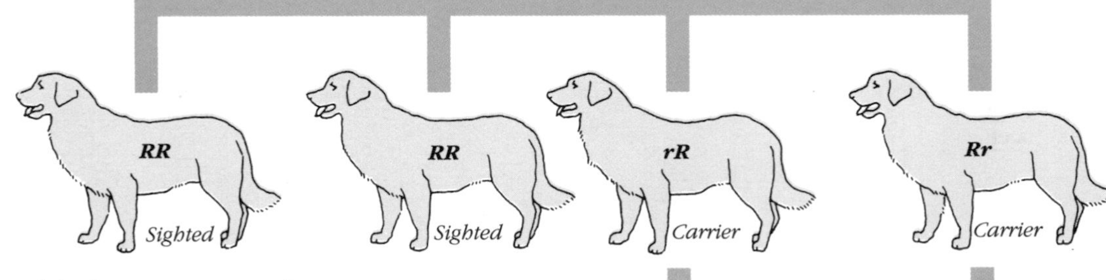

also carry this dangerous gene, but it is suppressed because they also carry the dominant normal gene (R). If these dogs are mated to each other and produce puppies, one puppy will have two normal genes (RR); two will have a dominant and a recessive gene (Rr and rR), and will be carriers; while the last one will have two recessive genes (rr), and will go blind.

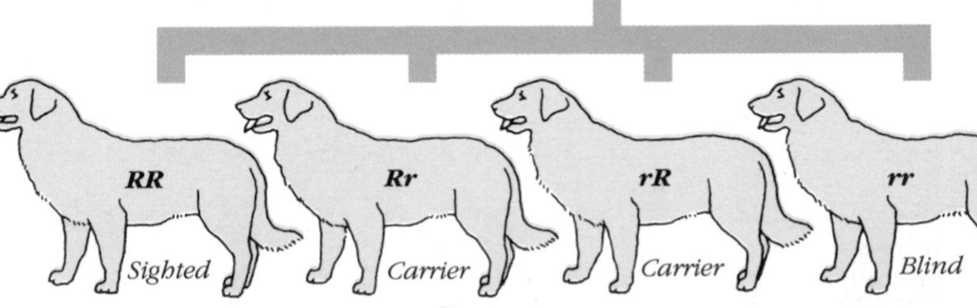

INHERITED DISORDERS

DISORDER	American Cocker Spaniel	Bloodhound	Border Collie	Boxer	Bull Terriers	Cavalier King Charles Spaniel	Chihuahua	Chow Chow	Dachshunds	Dalmatian	Dobermann	English Cocker Spaniel	German Shepherd Dog	Golden Retriever	Great Dane	Labrador Retriever	Mastiff	Miniature Poodle	Newfoundland	Old English Sheepdog	Pekingese	Rottweiler	Rough Collie	Shar Pei	St. Bernard	Toy Poodle	West Highland White Terrier	Yorkshire Terrier
BONE AND JOINT																												
Perthe's disease																		●			●					●	●	●
Osteochondrosis			●												●	●			●	●		●						
Hip dysplasia								●					●	●	●	●	●		●	●		●			●			
Luxating patella	●							●										●			●							●
Slipped disc									●		●				●						●							
Elbow dysplasia		●							●				●		●				●						●			
SKIN AND COAT																												
Recurring seborrhea												●												●			●	
Dermatitis																								●				
EYE																												
Progressive retinal atrophy			●						●			●		●		●		●					●			●		
Cataract	●					●							●	●		●				●								
Glaucoma	●						●					●																
Entropion	●	●						●				●		●		●								●	●			
Ectropion		●										●					●		●						●			
Dry eye																											●	
Retinal dysplasia	●															●												
Distichiasis	●											●						●			●		●			●		
EAR																												
Hereditary deafness			●		●					●	●				●							●	●					
RESPIRATORY																												
Collapsed windpipe																										●		●
Elongated soft palate						●															●							
DIGESTIVE																												
Pancreatic hypoplasia													●															
Colitis				●									●										●					
MOUTH AND TOOTH																												
Retained milk teeth																			●							●		●
Mouth tumours				●																								
Proliferating gum disease				●																								
REPRODUCTIVE																												
Difficult birth			●		●																							●
URINARY																												
Kidney failure					●				●	●	●	●							●									
Bladder stones										●																		
NERVOUS																												
Epilepsy			●				●		●				●	●		●		●					●					
Compressed spinal cord									●				●		●													
Fly catching						●																						
BLOOD AND HEART																												
Von Willebrand's disease	●			●					●			●	●	●	●	●		●				●						●
Endocardiosis						●																						
Cardiomyopathy				●							●				●					●								

Dangers from Dogs

Infectious diseases rarely spread from one species to another. For example, humans cannot catch distemper from dogs, and dogs cannot catch measles from humans. There are a few diseases, however, that can be shared between mammals. Certain parasites can also be passed from dogs to humans, and dogs can be carriers of micro-organisms that cause illness in humans and other animals. The most important dangers to humans from dogs are injuries from bites, or serious allergy. The risk of being bitten is lessened if you understand canine behaviour. Allergies can be helped by keeping your dog's coat and skin in pristine condition.

Rabies
Foxes are common carriers of rabies, which is transmitted to other animals in saliva via bite wounds.

RABIES WORLDWIDE

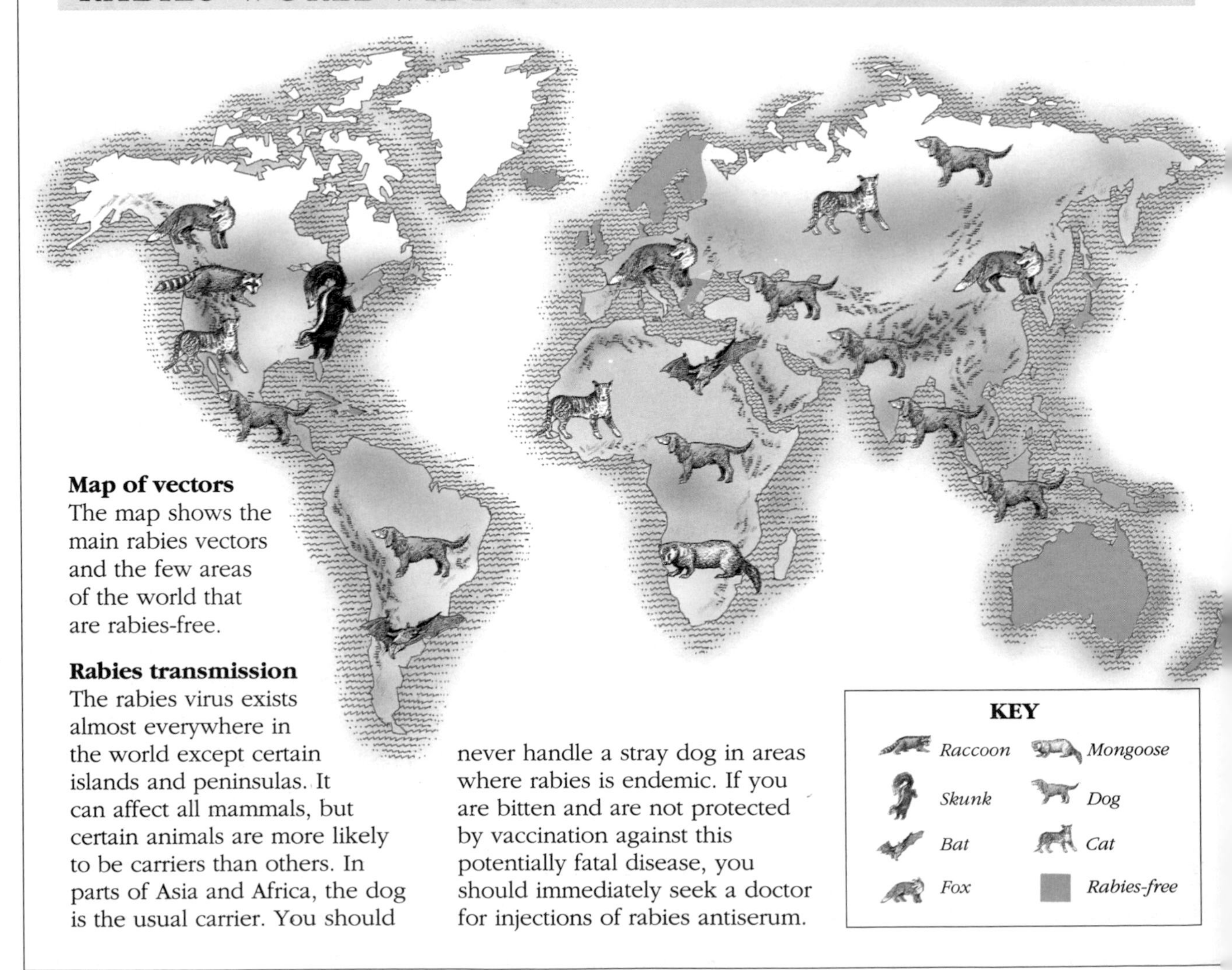

Map of vectors
The map shows the main rabies vectors and the few areas of the world that are rabies-free.

Rabies transmission
The rabies virus exists almost everywhere in the world except certain islands and peninsulas. It can affect all mammals, but certain animals are more likely to be carriers than others. In parts of Asia and Africa, the dog is the usual carrier. You should never handle a stray dog in areas where rabies is endemic. If you are bitten and are not protected by vaccination against this potentially fatal disease, you should immediately seek a doctor for injections of rabies antiserum.

DANGERS FROM DOGS

Disorders	Description	Action
Zoonoses Rabies Toxocariasis Ringworm Mange mites Echinococcosis Flea- and tick-borne diseases Tuberculosis	Zoonoses are diseases that can be transmitted between vertebrate species, including man. Of the zoonoses transmitted by dogs, rabies is the most dangerous. The virus is spread in saliva and is usually transmitted through bites. An infected dog undergoes a personality change, often accompanied by profuse salivation. If infectious *Toxocara* roundworm larvae are swallowed by humans they can induce the allergic reaction known as visceral larval migrans, and occasionally cause blindness. Ringworm infection causes circular skin lesions in humans, while *Sarcoptes* and *Cheyletiella* mange mites both produce itchy spots in human contacts (scabies and walking dandruff). Echinococcosis, or hydatid cyst disease, is contracted by humans eating uncooked meat from animals infected with the *Echinococcus* tapeworm. Fleas and ticks can transmit a number of diseases to humans, including Lyme disease. Tuberculosis can pass between dogs, humans, and farm animals. It produces chronic coughing, shortness of breath, and bloody spittle.	All dogs should be vaccinated against rabies where that disease occurs. In countries where this disease is present, humans at risk from dog bites should also be vaccinated against rabies. Routine worming every three months reduces the likelihood of ground being contaminated with *Toxocara* larvae. Owners should clean up their dogs' droppings in all populated areas. Ringworm should be treated medically immediately. Mange mites, fleas, ticks, and tapeworms can all be controlled with the use of parasiticides available from your vet. Consult a vet if you suspect any diseases such as tuberculosis. The dog may be successfully treated with antibiotics, or the vet may recommend euthanasia.
Communicable diseases Campylobacteriosis Salmonellosis Giardiasis Brucellosis Leptospirosis Chlamydial diseases	With these diseases, a dog can be a carrier, but may not show clinical signs of infection. *Campylobacter* and *Salmonella* bacteria cause abdominal cramps and diarrhoea in dogs and humans. Both often contract the infections from the same source, such as contaminated milk. Neither campylobacteriosis or salmonellosis is common in dogs but victims vomit and often pass blood in diarrhoea. *Giardia* can be picked up by dogs drinking contaminated water in streams and ponds, and causes the disease giardiasis, the principal sign of which is diarrhoea. Brucellosis causes periodic fever in humans. Leptospirosis is primarily a disease of rats but can be contracted by dogs from *Leptospira* bacteria and passed in urine. It causes diseases of the kidney and liver. In humans it is known as Weil's disease. *Chlamydia* seldom causes illness in dogs, but is reponsible for several diseases in humans and other animals.	*Campylobacter* and *Salmonella* are passed in dog faeces and spread through food. If human infection is suspected, a sample of dog faeces should be taken to a vet for bacterial culture. If positive, the vet will treat the dog with appropriate antibiotics. Dogs and humans should avoid drinking water possibly contaminated by *Giardia*. Dogs should be routinely blood tested for brucellosis, which is most likely to occur in breeding kennels. This is a difficult disease to eliminate even with appropriate antibiotics. Leptospirosis can be prevented with vaccination. Chlamydial infections respond to antibiotic medication.
Infections from bites *Pasturella* infections Tetanus	*Pasturella* is a normal bacterial inhabitant of most dogs' mouths. When dogs or humans are bitten this bacteria produces purulent infections and abscesses. Although tetanus is rare in dogs, the micro-organism that causes it can be passed on to humans through deep wounds.	Immediately clean any bite wound. People at risk from dog bites should have preventative vaccinations against tetanus. If these have not been given, seek medical advice for tetanus antiserum.
Allergies	Dogs can be allergic to people, cats, and other animals. They get itchy skin and watery eyes, and sneeze frequently. Humans are sometimes allergic to dogs, although not as frequently as we are to cats. We suffer the same complaints as dogs, although bronchospasm also affects severely allergic people. The allergy can be to dog hair, but is more likely to be to canine dandruff. In addition, dogs can carry pollens and mould spores in their fur that cause some humans to react in an allergic fashion.	Keep your dog's coat as healthy as possible. There is less likelihood of allergic reactions to clean, fresh hair and healthy skin. Routinely check for parasites, and do all grooming outdoors so that the home environment is contaminated with as little hair and dandruff as possible.

Chapter 7

HEALTH CARE AND NURSING

PET DOGS are living longer than ever before, thanks to greater knowledge leading to improved disease prevention, and an ever expanding array of diagnostic tests, drugs, and surgical procedures. To ensure that your pet maintains good health, it should have a yearly medical examination, although older dogs can often benefit from more frequent and detailed assessments, which can include urine and blood tests. In most cases, nothing unusual will be discovered, but if there are any problems, it is up to you to follow the vet's instructions. You may have to give your dog its medicine at home, and provide thoughtful, efficient nursing for its full recovery.

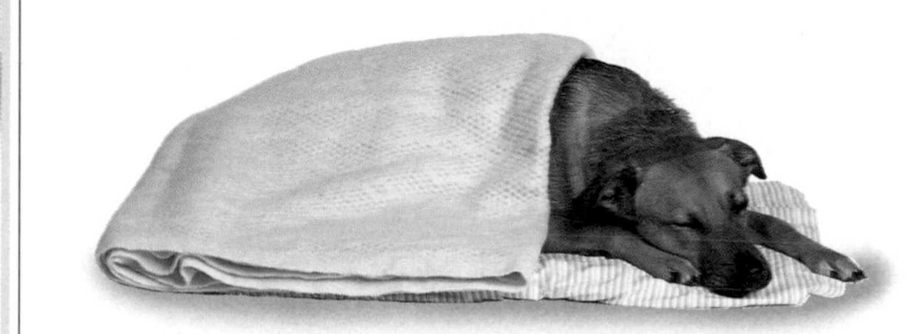

VISITING THE VET

Since your dog cannot tell you when it is ill, it is up to you to notice any changes in behaviour or demeanour that might indicate that it is unwell. The information you give the vet will help him decide where to concentrate his examination of the dog.

In most instances, the vet will first carry out a complete physical examination, while asking you questions about your dog. Whenever possible, you should keep a record of exactly when you first became concerned about your dog. Remember: your dog is totally dependent upon you for its medical care.

Prevention is not only better than cure – it is also less expensive. Consider obtaining health insurance, and take your dog to the vet for a medical check-up once a year.

EXAMINING A DOG

Eyes
Although there are many inherited and acquired eye diseases, changes in the eyes are often indicators of more complex diseases elsewhere in the body. The eye examination gives the vet clues about where else to concentrate his attention.

Nose
Dogs usually have wet, cold noses. The vet will look for discharges and physical changes, but will not be overly concerned if the dog has a hot, dry nose. This may indicate fever, but it may also be produced by age-related or even emotional changes.

Vet examines dog's nose for discharges or swellings

Ears
The ears are examined for any discharges or unusual odours. A heavily furred, lopped ear, like this Cocker Spaniel's, can act like a valve on the ear canal, raising the humidity within and creating an ideal environment for infection, but any ear is susceptible to infection. The vet will check for tufts of hair and foreign bodies, and also check the colour of the skin inside the ears.

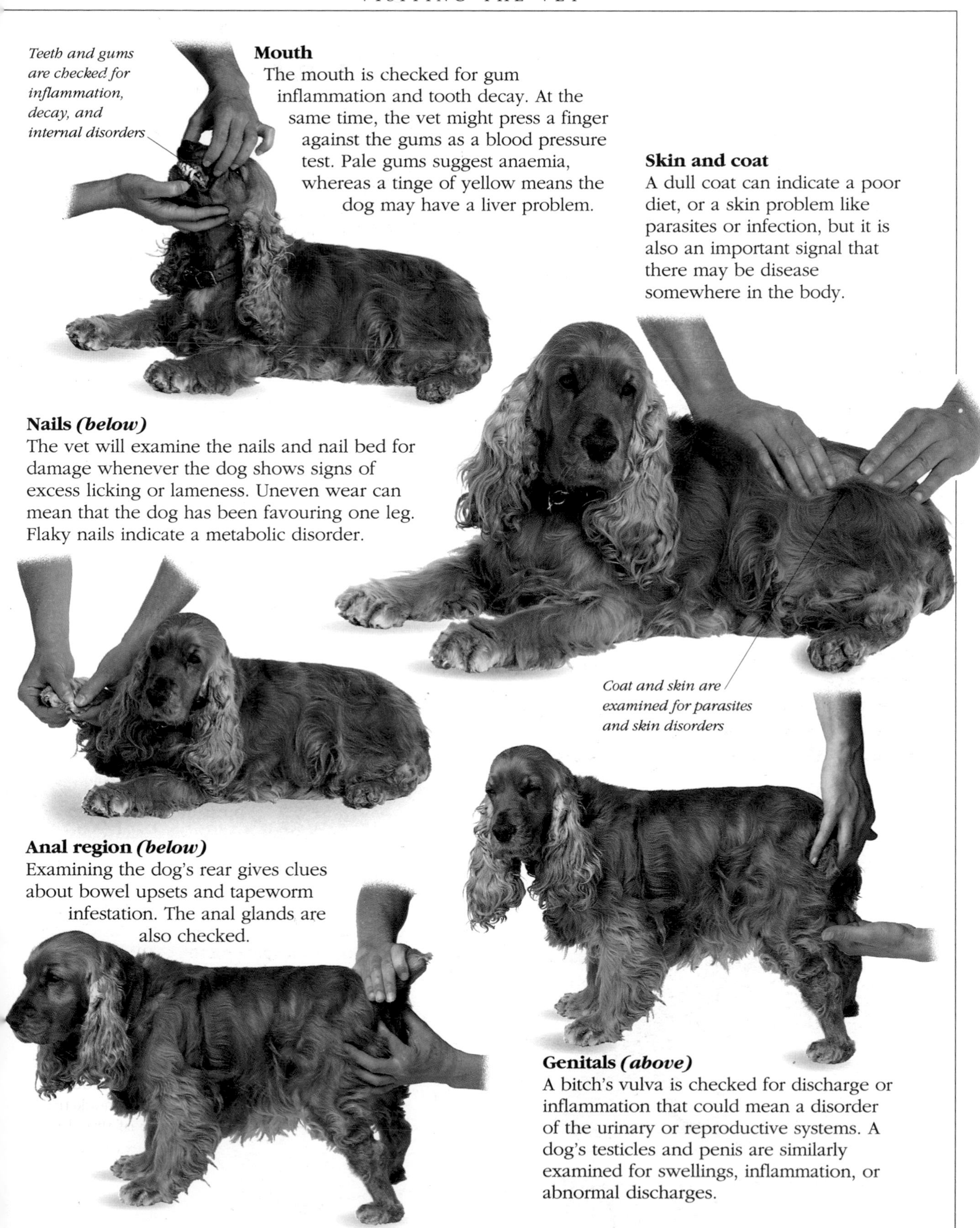

Mouth
The mouth is checked for gum inflammation and tooth decay. At the same time, the vet might press a finger against the gums as a blood pressure test. Pale gums suggest anaemia, whereas a tinge of yellow means the dog may have a liver problem.

Skin and coat
A dull coat can indicate a poor diet, or a skin problem like parasites or infection, but it is also an important signal that there may be disease somewhere in the body.

Nails *(below)*
The vet will examine the nails and nail bed for damage whenever the dog shows signs of excess licking or lameness. Uneven wear can mean that the dog has been favouring one leg. Flaky nails indicate a metabolic disorder.

Anal region *(below)*
Examining the dog's rear gives clues about bowel upsets and tapeworm infestation. The anal glands are also checked.

Genitals *(above)*
A bitch's vulva is checked for discharge or inflammation that could mean a disorder of the urinary or reproductive systems. A dog's testicles and penis are similarly examined for swellings, inflammation, or abnormal discharges.

THE VETERINARY EXAMINATION

Having completed the initial stages of a routine physical examination of your dog, the vet will investigate the state of the dog's health in more detail. He will check the dog's temperature and pulse, and listen to its heart and lungs. Lymph nodes in the neck and elsewhere are felt, and the abdomen is pressed to reveal any internal abnormalities. In addition, the joints are flexed for signs of discomfort or resistance.

Once this examination has been completed, the vet may want to carry out further tests. Most frequently, this simply involves taking a sample of the dog's blood, from which a tremendous amount of information can be obtained. It might also mean taking X-rays, scanning the body with ultrasound, or analyzing other body fluids.

CHECKING BODY FUNCTIONS

Taking the temperature

An elevated temperature is often a sign of infection, pain, or stress, or just excitement. A temperature below normal usually indicates a debilitating disease or disorder.

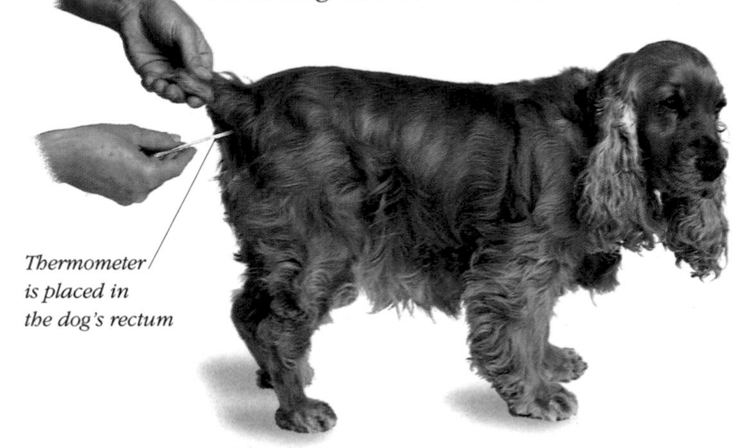

Thermometer is placed in the dog's rectum

Taking the pulse

The vet checks a dog's heart rate, rhythm, and blood pressure by feeling the pulsations in the hind-leg femoral artery. Blood pressure is calculated by feeling just how much pressure is needed to obliterate the pulsations. Blood pressure changes occur due to shock or heart disease.

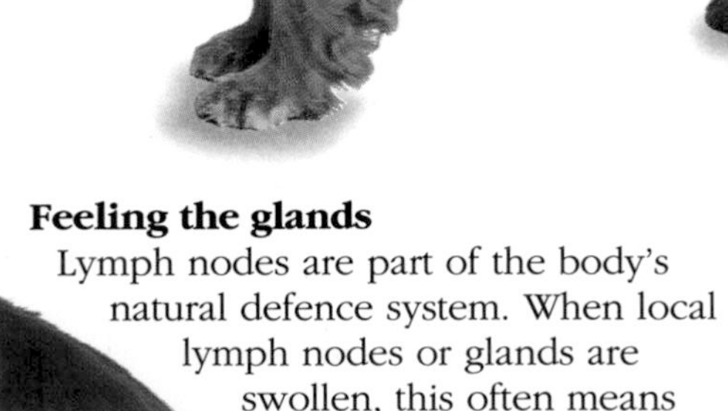

Feeling the glands

Lymph nodes are part of the body's natural defence system. When local lymph nodes or glands are swollen, this often means that there is infection in the part of the body that they serve. It can also indicate that the defence system itself has become infected.

RELAXING A DOG

A tense dog is difficult to examine. Train your dog at home to sit on command, and to allow itself to have its mouth opened, its ears, eyes, and feet checked, and to be gently prodded and squeezed. The vet will then be able to get the maximum amount of information from a physical examination of the dog.

Listening to chest sounds *(left)*
The vet listens to the dog's breathing and heart sounds, first with, and then without, a stethoscope. Well-developed heart murmurs can be felt through the chest wall, while difficulties in breathing are observed by simply watching the movements of the chest in breathing.

Palpating the abdomen *(right)*
After looking at the shape of the dog's abdomen, the vet will feel it for any abnormal fluids or lumps, then feel deeper to check the size and shape of the liver, kidneys, spleen, bladder, and intestines.

Flexing the joints *(above)*
Individual joints are flexed to check for discomfort. Dogs often tense up during a veterinary examination. This can make it difficult to diagnose mild joint problems.

RESTRAINING AND MUZZLING

1 Most dogs can be held by their owners or a nurse while being examined by a vet. However, if a dog is frightened or in pain, it is safest for the handler and the vet if the patient is muzzled.

2 To make an improvised muzzle, make a wide loop in a bandage or soft rope and slip it over the dog's nose with the knot on top. Take care the dog does not bite.

3 Make another loop in the muzzle and tie it securely, but not too tightly, under the dog's lower jaw. Wrap the ends around the dog's neck and tie them together securely.

ADMINISTERING MEDICINE

There is a wide range of medicines available to treat a variety of canine medical conditions. Drugs are available to cure infections like pneumonia, to correct metabolic disorders such as hormonal excesses or deficiencies, or to control certain types of cancer. Some medical conditions like sugar diabetes are controlled through daily injections.

Unfortunately, very few canine medicines are available as tasty, chewable tablets. Some pills even have an unpleasant taste. Dogs can be deviously clever at hiding pills in their mouths, only to spit them out when their owners are not looking. Never call your dog to you just to give it medicine, or it might become fearful each time it hears its name. It is much better for you to go to the dog.

GIVING A TABLET

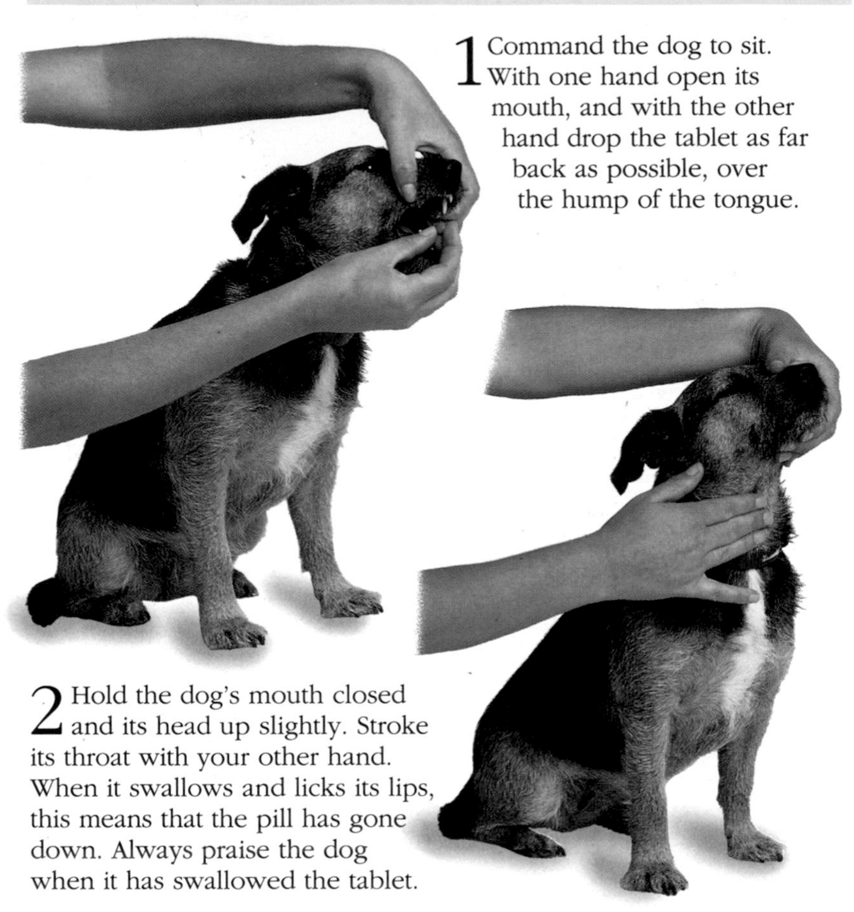

1 Command the dog to sit. With one hand open its mouth, and with the other hand drop the tablet as far back as possible, over the hump of the tongue.

2 Hold the dog's mouth closed and its head up slightly. Stroke its throat with your other hand. When it swallows and licks its lips, this means that the pill has gone down. Always praise the dog when it has swallowed the tablet.

GIVING AN INJECTION

1 Injections should only be given at home after discussing the procedure with a vet. Prepare the syringe and command the dog to sit. Lift the fold of skin at the scruff of its neck.

Slowly empty syringe into scruff

2 Insert the needle sideways through the skin of the dog scruff. This avoids underlying muscle. Be careful that the needle does not come out the other side of th scruff. Slowly empty th syringe into the skin.

GIVING A TABLET TO A DIFFICULT DOG

1 Hold the dog firmly between your legs, with your knees behind its shoulders, so that it cannot escape. Open its mouth by holding its snout with one hand and its lower jaw with the other. Be careful it does not bite.

2 Having dropped the tablet as far back on the tongue as possible, close the dog's jaws and massage its throat while still holding the chin up. Praise the dog after it has swallowed the tablet.

Hold dog firmly between your knees so you have both hands free

MEDICINE IN FOOD

Hiding a tablet
Simply dropping medicine into the dog's food bowl does not guarantee that it will be swallowed. It is better to hide a tablet in a small piece of a dog's favourite food. Most dogs willingly take their medicine hidden in chunks of meat. Others will accept tablets sandwiched in bread. You might even try mixing medicine in melted chocolate, or your dog's favourite treat. Always check with your vet first, however, since some foods should not be given with certain types of medicine.

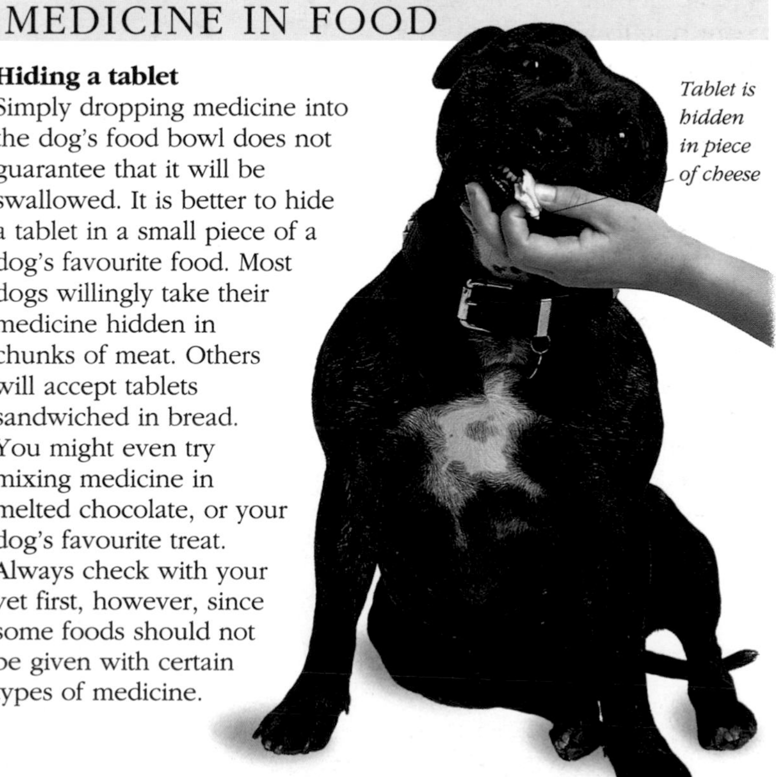

Tablet is hidden in piece of cheese

LIQUID MEDICINE

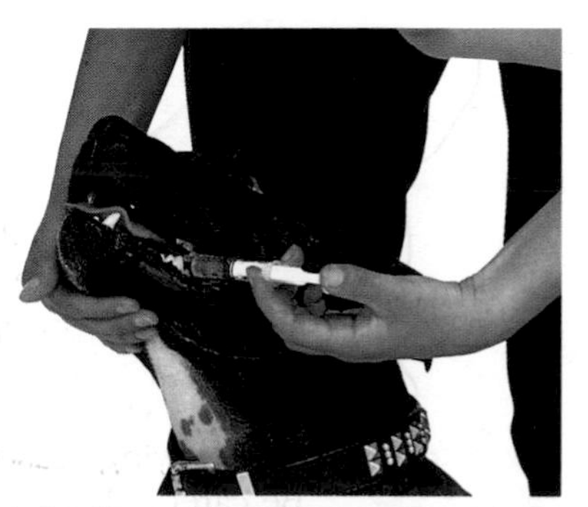

If a dog refuses to swallow tablets, they can be crushed, mixed in sugar water, and syringed sideways into the mouth. Cough syrup can also be given to a dog in a syringe.

TREATING EYES AND EARS

Infections, injuries, and allergic reactions involving a dog's eyes and ears are surprisingly common, and are usually treated with drops and ointments. It is always safest to consult a vet for advice before attempting to treat any condition yourself.

Never use old medicines to treat new disorders. Although the problem may look the same, the wrong treatment is likely to make it worse. For example, anti-inflammatory drops are perfectly safe when there is conjunctivitis, but if the condition is associated with invisible damage to the cornea, these drops will make that damage considerably worse. Even if the condition seems to completely disappear in a very short time, do not shorten a prescribed treatment without consulting a vet first for advice. Ear infections in particular have a nasty habit of recurring at a later date.

CLEANING THE EARS

When using cotton-wool buds, you should only clean the outer part of the ear that you can see. Do not use them in the ear canal itself, since they can act like plungers, forcing wax further down. A foreign body, such as a grass seed, can become lodged in the ear. This should only be removed if it is visible *(see page 163)*. Consult a vet if you suspect that anything is lodged inside the ear canal.

ADMINISTERING EAR DROPS

1 A dog's ears frequently need veterinary attention. Individuals that suffer from chronic ear problems should have their ears routinely cleaned with wax-dissolving drops. Preventative treatment reduces the likelihood of infection and the need for veterinary attention. First, lift the flap of the ear and clean away any visible wax with cotton wool dampened with warm water or wax-removal solution provided by a vet.

2 While holding the head still, and with the ear flap laid back, insert the nozzle of the bottle in the ear in a forwards direction towards the tip of the nose. Squeeze the appropriate number of drops into the ear.

3 Without letting the dog shake its head, withdraw the bottle, drop the ear flap back into position and, with the palm of your hand, gently but firmly massage the ear. This lubricates the entire ear canal with medication.

APPLYING EYE DROPS

1 Several common eye disorders can stimulate excess tear production, or a discharge from the eyes *(see page 104)*. If left overflowing, these discharges can stain the dog's facial hair. Before applying any medicine, gently soften, then wipe away any debris from the corners of the eyes with moistened cotton wool.

Gently clean away any eye discharge

2 Using either warm water or a special eye-wash solution provided by a vet, irrigate the eye. Do not use eye drops intended for humans. Be careful not to get any cotton-wool fibres on the eye itself.

Allow the eye to bathe in the drops for a few seconds

3 Gently restrain the dog and hold the eye open. Bringing your hand to the eye from above and behind so as not to frighten the dog, gently squeeze the required number of drops on to the eye. Allow the eye to bathe in the medication.

APPLYING EYE OINTMENT

1 You may have to administer eye ointment for certain conditions. This should be applied in a line along the inside of the lower eyelid. Do not let the nozzle touch the dog's eye.

2 Hold the dog's eye closed for a few seconds so that the ointment warms to the dog's body temperature and disperses over the eye. The eye will initially look greasy, but will soon clear.

EMPTYING ANAL GLANDS

If a dog licks or drags its rear along the ground, this may mean that its anal glands need emptying. Wearing a rubber glove and holding a tissue, place your thumb and forefinger on either side of the anus and squeeze gently. Ask a vet for guidance.

NURSING A SICK DOG

Only seriously ill dogs require hospitalization. In most circumstances, dogs get better faster when they are cared for by people they know in their own home.

You should provide your convalescent dog with a warm, dry, comfortable bed, and make sure it has free access to its toilet area. This might mean carrying the dog there several times each day.

Follow the vet's advice by giving medicine at appointed times, and offer fresh water and nutritious food. The vet will tell you which foods you can offer, and how much water the dog should drink each day. Herbal medicines may be beneficial, but should not replace life-saving drugs.

THE CONVALESCENT DOG

Intensive care
A dog must sometimes be hospitalized for a few days while its condition is stabilized. Visits from its human family should be discussed with the vet.

RECOVERY PEN

When a sick dog has to be kept quiet, with its movements curtailed, it can be kept at home in a recovery pen. For small dogs, a large cardboard box is usually sufficient. Larger dogs can be kept in a child's play pen, or a purpose-built dog crate. Provide warm bedding, food and water bowls, and newspapers in case of any accidents.

Keeping warm *(left)*
Body temperature can drop when a dog is unwell. With a vet's advice, provide your dog with comfortable bedding and a lukewarm, covered hot-water bottle for warmth.

Administering fluid *(right)*
A convalescing dog must consume enough fluid each day to equal the amount it loses in its urine and faeces and by panting. The vet will tell you how much liquid is required daily. If a dog is unwilling to drink, try spooning or syringing nourishing liquids into the side of its mouth.

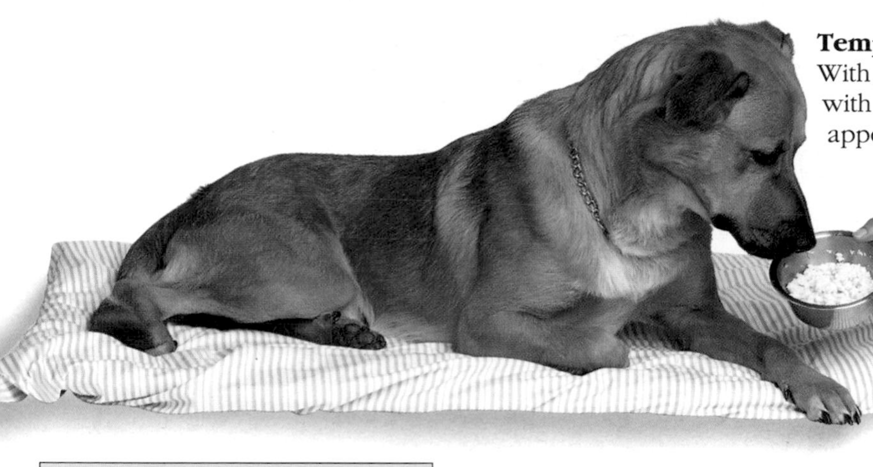

Tempting a sick dog to eat *(left)*
With veterinary guidance, be creative with the foods you offer your dog. Its appetite will be stimulated by smell. Warming food to between room and body temperature releases the odour and gets a dog's taste buds activated. Avoid foods that might cause diarrhoea, but pander to a dog's preferences.

HOME NURSING

A dog will not always understand why you are doing seemingly aggressive and unpleasant things to it, but you must follow the vet's instructions. Nursing a dog back to good health should be carried out as gently as possible, but invariably involves "being cruel to be kind". If you do not feel that you can carry out the vet's instructions and nurse your pet at home, it is in your dog's interests that it be hospitalized for the duration of its recovery.

Bed sores *(right)*
Pressure can produce bed sores in heavy dogs. Dress affected areas, such as the elbows, daily with softening skin cream.

Elizabethan collar
If your dog has been fitted with an Elizabethan collar to prevent self-mutilation and removal of its bandages or stitches, it must wear the collar in your absence. A collar can be made from cardboard or a plastic bucket.

ALTERNATIVE MEDICINE

Evening Primrose oil

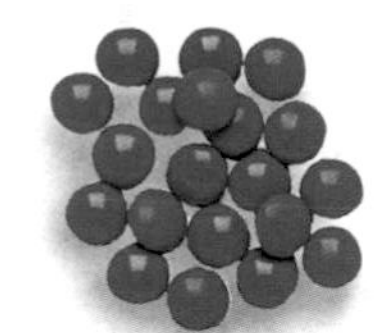

Garlic pills

Herbal nerve pills

Seaweed powder

Many herbal and natural forms of medicine are known to be therapeutic. Some are sources for refined prescription drugs, so always check with a vet before using these medicines with other medication.

CARING FOR AN ELDERLY DOG

Superficial ageing changes, such as greying hair or tooth loss, occur much earlier in some dogs than in others. As a dog gets older, messages travel more slowly through the nervous system, and hearing and vision deteriorate. Joint discomfort may develop, the skin loses its elasticity, and muscles shrink. The signs of old age vary according to each individual and may not be noticeable at first.

You can make an elderly dog's life more pleasant through special feeding, gentle grooming, and vigilant attention to its comfort and general well-being. Remember to be gentle with it and be patient with its behaviour.

SIGNS OF OLD AGE

The old dog
An elderly dog likes to take life easy, but still enjoys playing. You should not force an elderly dog to do things, but should respond sympathetically to its behaviour.

LIFESPANS OF COMMON BREEDS IN YEARS

Breed of dog	10	11	12	13	14	15	16	17
Cavalier King Charles Spaniel, Great Dane, Newfoundland								
Afghan Hound, Boxer, Chow Chow, St. Bernard								
Bloodhound, Bernese Mountain Dog, Labrador Retriever, Pointers, Rottweiler, Old English Sheepdog								
Airedale Terrier, Basset Hound, Dalmatian, German Shepherd Dog, Scottish Terrier, Staffordshire Bull Terrier								
Beagle, Chihuahua, Dobermann, Papillon, Pomeranian								
Collies, Jack Russell Terrier, Pekingese, West Highland White Terrier, Yorkshire Terrier								
Boston Terrier, Golden Retriever, Setters								
Cairn Terrier, Cocker Spaniel, Maltese Terrier, Poodle (Standard), Schnauzers, Shih Tzu								
Dachshunds, Poodle (Miniature and Toy)								

SPECIAL CARE FOR AN OLD DOG

Brushing teeth *(right)*
Gum infection allows bacteria to get into the bloodstream. Reduce this risk by routinely brushing your elderly dog's teeth *(see page 65)*.

Feeding *(above)*
Changes in the amount of exercise taken, the ability of the intestines to digest and absorb nutrients, and of the kidneys and liver to filter and detoxify waste products from the bloodstream all call for diet changes. Consult a vet for advice.

Eye care *(left)*
You should regularly clear away excess mucus with damp cotton wool and clean the skin around your elderly dog's eyes.

Ear care *(below)*
Wax can rapidly build up and cause infection. Regularly check inside the ears.

Grooming *(left)*
Elderly dogs groom themselves less than young dogs do because their bodies are not as supple. Gently groom your dog with a soft brush. Remember that its skin is thinner and more sensitive than when it was younger, so be gentle.

Massaging joints
Joint discomfort is very common, especially among large breeds. If your dog is not taking routine exercise, you can gently massage its muscles and joints by flexing its limbs when it is relaxing.

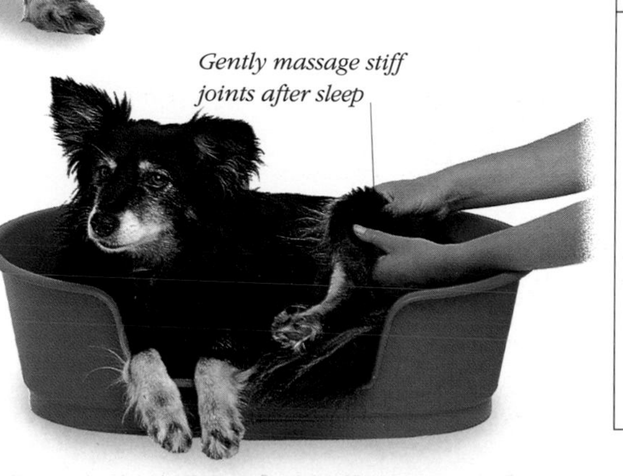

Gently massage stiff joints after sleep

EUTHANASIA

Improved medical attention means that many dogs live to reach their maximum age, but then their quality of life gradually drops below a comfortable level. Deciding when this occurs is difficult, but usually your vet will be able to offer advice. This is a family decision, perhaps the most difficult your family will ever make involving your dog. Euthanasia is painless. It is simply an injection of an overdose of anaesthetic.

Chapter 8

BREEDING

WITH A worldwide surplus of unwanted dogs, it is irresponsible to breed from a dog without first arranging for good homes for the litter. It is cruel to allow a bitch to go through the rigours of whelping only to have the puppies destroyed. You should also not allow your dog to breed if it has an hereditary disorder.

If you do decide to breed from your dog, it can be delightful to watch how magnificently most females cope with whelping, and with caring for their puppies. The experience can be made much easier for them if you provide the best possible diet and environment, as well as proper health care and nursing assistance.

Deciding to Breed

Thousands of unwanted dogs are humanely destroyed each year, so it is important that you consider having your dog castrated or spayed to avoid unwanted pregnancies. Only breed from a dog if you can provide good homes for the puppies and if neither the male nor the female are carriers of serious hereditary defects. Dogs usually reach sexual maturity by the age of about ten months, but do not reach emotional maturity for another year. Allow a bitch to have at least two oestrus cycles before mating.

Choosing a mate

If you decide to breed from your pedigree bitch, it is best to arrange for her to be mated with an experienced stud dog at its owner's premises.

THE BITCH'S REPRODUCTIVE CYCLE

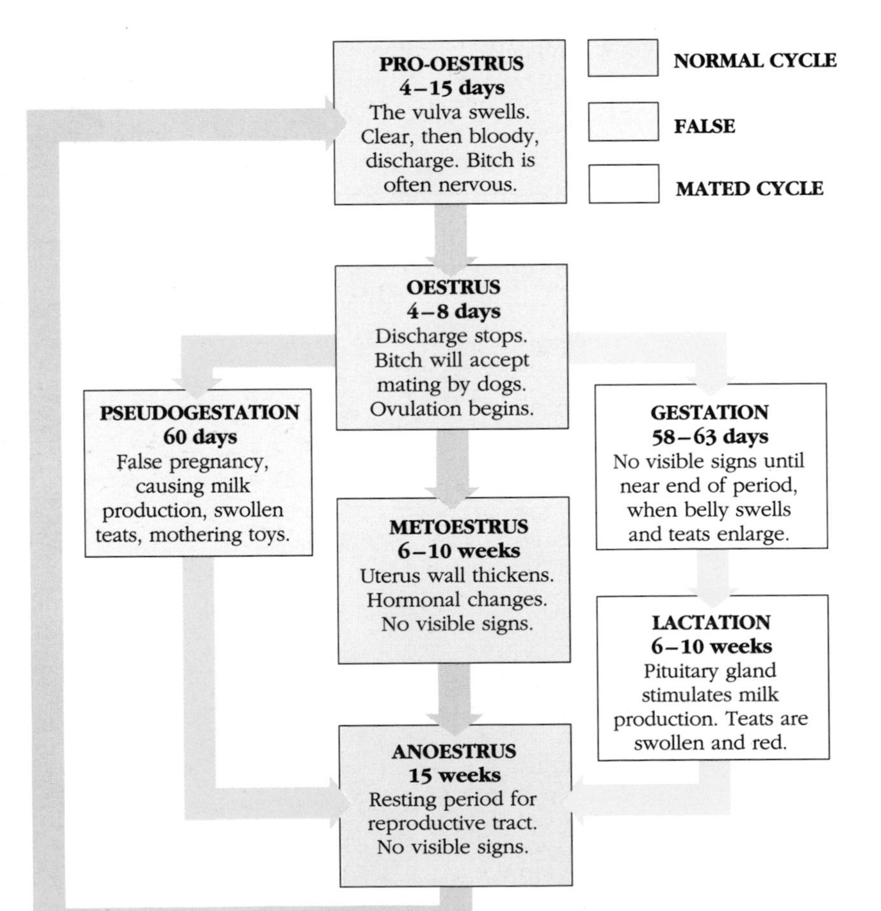

The normal cycle

Virtually all breeds have two oestrus cycles each year. Initially, the vulva appears swollen, and within a day there is a clear discharge, which becomes tinged with blood the next day. This discharge increases in intensity and then slowly diminishes, ending after about ten days.

During this time the bitch becomes more alert and urinates frequently, leaving signals of her impending willingness to mate. Ovulation takes place soon after the discharge has stopped. Only now will the bitch accept mating. Hormonal changes occur regardless of whether a bitch is pregnant, which is why there are no simple blood or urine tests to confirm impending motherhood.

CHECKLIST FOR MATING

Mating guidelines

1 Have the bitch examined by a vet and certified as healthy and not carrying inherited diseases.
2 Plan how you will find homes for the coming litter of puppies.
3 Check that a purebred dog is registered with the kennel club.
4 Arrange with a reputable breeder to use his stud dog.
5 If brucellosis is a problem in your area, make sure that the stud dog is routinely checked for sexually transmitted disease.
6 Exercise your bitch only on a lead while she is in season.
7 Take the bitch to the stud dog, rather than vice versa.
8 Make arrangements for two matings, two days apart.
9 If necessary, calm the bitch during mating and ensure a "tie" that lasts ten minutes.
10 Take the bitch to a vet three weeks after mating so that he can confirm the pregnancy.

The tie
Dogs may need to be held together while they are "tied" by the swelling of the male's penis to ensure that they do not hurt each other.

TAIL DOCKING AND EAR CROPPING

A dog's ears and tail are not only for hearing and balance, they are also vital for effective body language. In the past, ears were cropped to make the dog look more fierce. The tails of working dogs were often amputated to reduce injuries, while others were docked according to the breed standard. Such mutilations are now banned in many countries. Inhumane amputations like these are cosmetic fashions, surviving from an age when humans had less understanding of animal pain.

NEUTERING PROCEDURES

Castration
This is ideally carried out when a dog has reached physical maturity, but before puberty. Under a general anaesthetic, a small incision is made in the scrotum through which both the testicles are removed. The dog appears normal the next day, and the stitches come out ten days later. Castration may help to curb undesirable types of behaviour such as straying from home and hypersexuality.

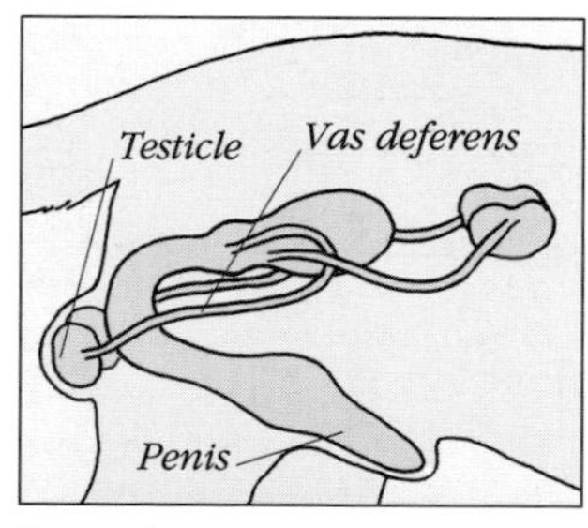

Entire dog

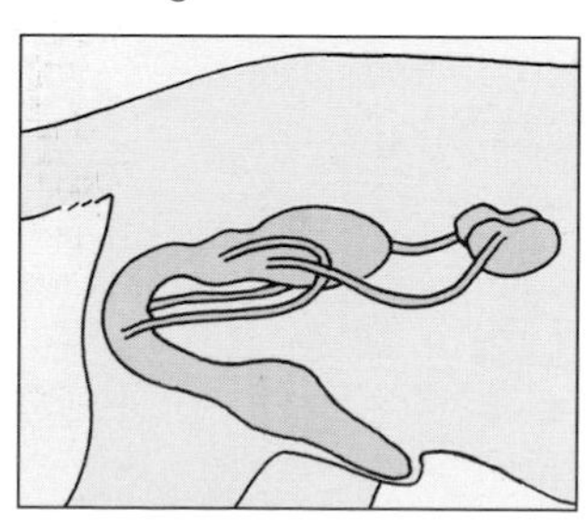
Castrated dog

Spaying
This operation is best carried out before puberty, but when the bitch is physically mature. Both the ovaries and uterus are removed under anaesthetic through an incision in the abdomen. Removal eliminates the likelihood of later development of mammary tumours, and ensures that the bitch's personality is unchanged. Surgery may, however, make dominant bitches even more dominant.

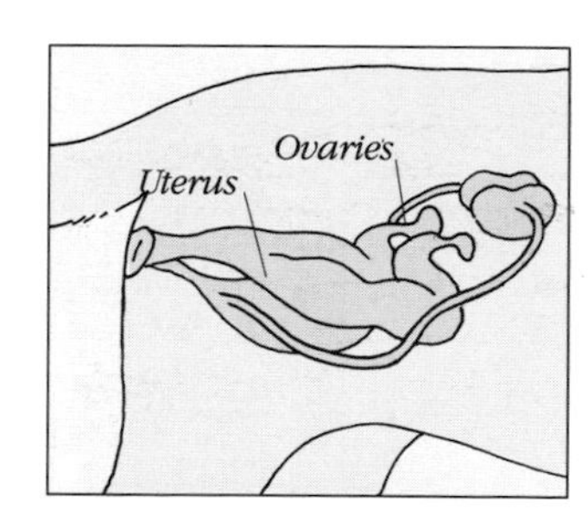

Entire bitch

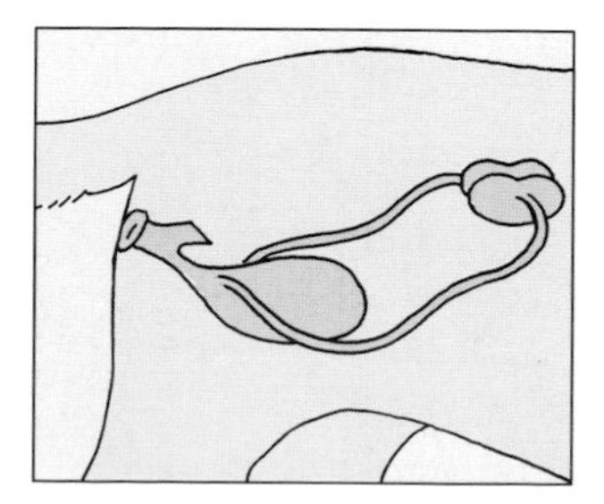
Spayed bitch

PREGNANCY AND PRE-NATAL CARE

There are always hormonal changes in a bitch after each bi-annual ovulation that cause identical signs to those that occur during pregnancy *(see page 144)*. This makes it difficult to determine whether a dog is really pregnant until she shows physical changes like an enlarged abdomen. When you see these changes, which usually occur about two-thirds of the way through her nine-week pregnancy, it is time to reduce her activities and increase her food.

SIGNS OF PREGNANCY

Conserving strength
For a few days before giving birth, the bitch spends a lot of time relaxing. You should not force her to take exercise now.

CARING FOR A PREGNANT BITCH

Feeding *(left)*
Mid-way through pregnancy, gradually increase the amount of the bitch's food by 10 per cent at first, increasing to 30 per cent extra by the time of the birth. Be sure to feed a nutritious diet with a proper balance of calcium and phosphorus for good bone development.

Grooming *(above)*
Groom the bitch regularly during pregnancy. This serves to reassure her of your involvement and makes it less likely that she will resent your help when the puppies are born. Take great care not to scratch her delicate abdominal area.

Cleaning up *(right)*
Just before the bitch is due to go into labour, gently clip any excess or matted hair from around her vulva and mammary glands. Clean her nipples with a safe disinfectant, making sure that you leave none on her skin.

DEVELOPMENT OF THE FOETUS

Length of pregnancy
Pregnancy usually lasts about 62 days. A vet can diagnose pregnancy by feeling the bitch's abdomen or using ultrasound.

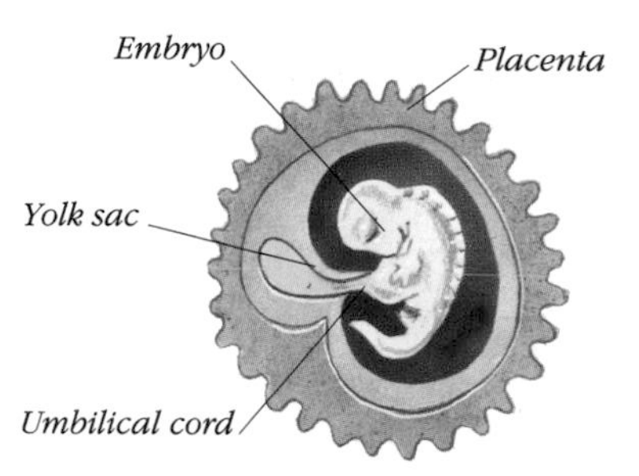

1 During the first few days, the embyro obtains its nourishment from the yolk sac.

2 By three weeks, nourishment comes from the placenta. The eyes, head, and limbs are now developing.

3 By the middle of pregnancy all internal organs have developed.

4 The skeleton has developed by six weeks.

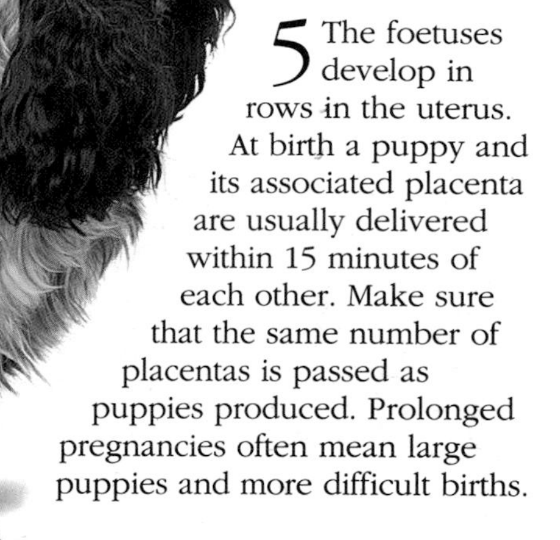

5 The foetuses develop in rows in the uterus. At birth a puppy and its associated placenta are usually delivered within 15 minutes of each other. Make sure that the same number of placentas is passed as puppies produced. Prolonged pregnancies often mean large puppies and more difficult births.

WHELPING PREPARATIONS

The whelping box
Familiarize the bitch with her whelping box at least a week before she is due to give birth. Position it in a quiet and secluded place where she feels secure. The box offers security for the newborn puppies by preventing them from wandering off. Poles prevent the mother from accidentally lying on the puppies. Keep equipment, such as disinfectant, towels, and scissors, within reach, and make sure a vet is on call.

WHELPING

The expectant mother goes off her food between one and two days before birth. She becomes restless and seeks out her whelping box. Shortly before labour her water bag breaks, leaving a puddle of fluid that can be mistaken for urine. Initially, contractions are simple but they soon become firm and productive. The first puppy should be delivered within two hours, then subsequent ones at intervals of between ten and eighty minutes.

GIVING BIRTH

1 The bitch starts to pant when the first contractions begin. Her temperature drops and she appears restless and a little tense. Watch her to make sure that she does not hide herself away.

2 The bitch stands and circles while she contracts. Other dogs prefer to lie down for the delivery. Let the dog find her own preferred position for giving birth.

3 Although this is her first litter, the mother instinctively examines her newborn puppy. She has already licked the enveloping membrane off its body. Now she chews off the umbilical cord separating the puppy from the placenta, which she later consumes.

Licking removes all delivery liquids

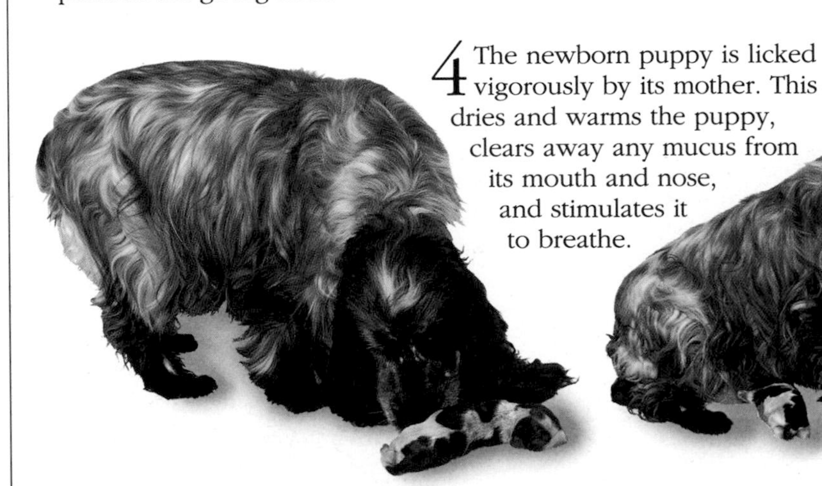

4 The newborn puppy is licked vigorously by its mother. This dries and warms the puppy, clears away any mucus from its mouth and nose, and stimulates it to breathe.

5 After the work and discomfort of delivery the mother rests. This gives time for her muscles to become resilient again, ready for further contractions.

Newborn puppy rests near the warmth of its mother

6 Now more relaxed, this mother lies down and prepares to deliver further puppies. Most mothers do not start feeding their litter until after the last delivery. Make sure that there is one placenta delivered for each puppy.

WHEN TO CALL A VET

You should let the vet know when a delivery is under way in case of any emergencies *(see page 174)*. Get medical advice if contractions have not begun within two hours of the water breaking, or if a puppy has not emerged after 15 minutes. Non-productive labour may mean a breech birth or large puppies. Caesarean delivery is common for breeds of dog with large heads and in small breeds with small litters of puppies.

Puppy is held firmly but gently in mouth

Newborn puppy has been completely cleaned and dried

7 Hearing a puppy cry, the mother retrieves it from where it has wandered and carries it back to the litter. Mothers will only respond to crying. If a youngster wanders off and does not cry, the mother may abandon it.

8 All the puppies have now been delivered. The mother settles down and allows the litter to suckle together for the first time. Contact a vet if the mother cannot produce sufficient milk.

9 As the bitch feeds her litter, she licks one of her puppies. She will lick each puppy's anogenital region to stimulate it to empty its bowels and bladder, and will consume all its body waste for the next three weeks. In the wild, eliminating all signs of the litter would protect the newborn puppies from predators.

Post-Natal Care

For the first three weeks of life the newborn puppies are totally dependent upon their mother for food and security. You can help by ensuring that they are kept warm and that their mother is well nourished, healthy, and producing sufficient milk. Sometimes, with extra-large litters, a mother's milk must be supplemented with special canine milk formula.

MATERNAL CARE

The new pack
In the absence of their mother the puppies huddle together for warmth. Pack behaviour has begun, even at this age.

Puppies huddle together for warmth and security

Bonding with mother
Because it is enjoyable for her, the mother sits contentedly while her litter suckles. The puppies bond to her, and at the same time her maternal feelings for them become firmly cemented. In the next few weeks she will feed, protect and, if necessary, defend them.

REARING PUPPIES BY HAND

Bottle feeding *(above)*
Feed milk formula initially every two hours if the mother has died, rejected her litter, or does not have enough milk. Ask a vet for guidance on the exact amounts to feed.

Stimulating body functions *(above)*
After feeding, wipe away any spilled milk, and clean each puppy's anogenital region with warm, damp cotton wool. This mimics maternal licking, stimulating it to urinate and defecate.

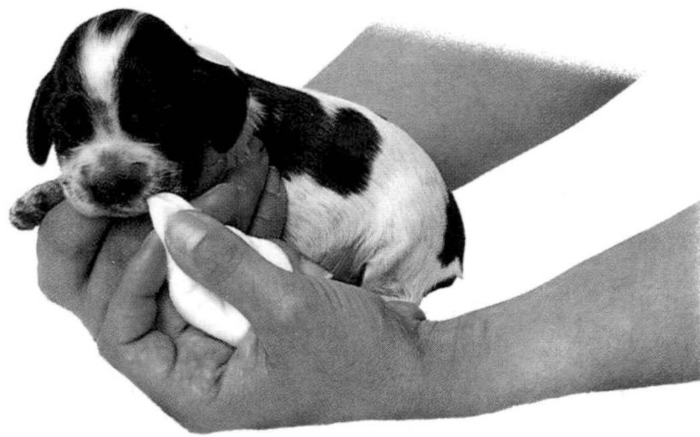

Cleaning up
Handle all the puppies frequently, but take care not to upset their mother. Each puppy's eyes, ears, and mouth should be cleaned daily with cotton wool moistened in warm water.

Puppy is yawning

Nail trimming
A puppy's nails may need to be trimmed to prevent it from scratching its mother *(see page 65)*.

Monitoring weight gain
Keep track of the puppies' weight gain by carefully weighing each member of the litter daily. Weak puppies and those that are not sufficiently pushy get relegated to less productive teats. Lack of weight gain means you might have to help them gain access to the most productive teats.

Early Puppy Care

Just as with humans, the environment in which a puppy is raised influences its behaviour in adult life. This early socialization period is very short, lasting for only a few months. During this time, puppies learn how to behave with other dogs and humans.

Lessons should start as soon as puppies are old enough to try to wander away from the mother dog. They should be routinely handled, groomed regularly, and exposed to the sights and sounds that will be part of their adult lives.

Puppies should eat and play with other puppies, so that they understand the nuances of pack hierarchy and body language. By ensuring that a puppy experiences this early socialization, you will make it an ideal companion for life.

Four Weeks of Age

Socialization ***(left)***
At four weeks of age the senses are developed. Puppies should receive mental stimulation and learn how to behave with other dogs through regular play activity. They may be kept in a pen so that they can become adjusted to their surroundings without being frightened.

Eating together ***(right)***
Feed puppies together rather than separately. This will ensure that they are not possessive over their food as adults.

Early grooming ***(left)***
A longhaired puppy, such as this Cocker Spaniel, needs daily grooming. This helps to keep the puppy's coat clean and satisfies its need for mothering.

Daily handling ***(left)***
By handling a puppy several times daily it will learn to accept being picked up and held by humans. Early obedience training from four weeks old will lead to good habits in later life. If you teach a puppy to stand or sit for its meal now, it will naturally do so as an adult.

EIGHT WEEKS OF AGE

Puppy's coat has darkened

Family mealtime *(below)*
Be sure to provide growing puppies with frequent, nutritious meals necessary for both growth and the maintenance of their bodies *(see below).*

Willing obedience *(above)*
At eight weeks old the puppy is used to being handled and stands quietly alert when held. The puppy's coat has now changed to its adult colour pattern.

Leaving home *(left)*
At eight weeks old the puppy is ready to leave its mother and move to its new home. It must be vaccinated against infectious diseases such as parvovirus and distemper. Early mental and physical stimulation ensures that it is now a confident young dog, able to cope with its exciting new world.

Brush and comb *(left)*
When acquiring a new puppy, start routine grooming immediately. Grooming and stroking are dominant gestures. The puppy will interpret this as a sign of dominance, and grow up to be an obedient dog.

WEANING PUPPIES

Age	Type of food	Number of feeds daily
Three weeks old	Milky porridge or cereal and mother's milk.	Two milky meals. Plus feeding by mother.
Four weeks old	Hard-boiled or scrambled egg yolk; milky cereal; finely minced, cooked meat or prepared puppy food; water and mother's milk.	One egg meal or one cereal meal, and one minced meat or puppy food meal. Plus normal feeding by mother.
Five weeks old	Hard-boiled or scrambled egg yolk; milky cereal; finely minced, cooked meat or prepared puppy food; water and mother's milk.	One egg meal or one cereal meal, and four minced meat or puppy food meals. Plus feeding by mother if she will allow it.
Six weeks old	Minced, cooked meat or prepared puppy food and puppy biscuits. Give milk if tolerated. Mother's milk should have nearly dried up.	Four meat and biscuit meals. Plus one egg or cereal meal if the puppies will eat it. Drinks of cow's or goat's milk and water.
Seven weeks old	Increase amounts of meat and biscuits. Water should always be available. Give milk if tolerated. Mother's milk should have completely dried up.	Four meat and biscuit meals. Plus one egg or cereal meal if the puppies will eat it. Drinks of cow's or goat's milk and water.
Eight weeks old	Increase amounts of meat and biscuits. Water should be always be available.	Four meat and biscuit meals. Plus drinks of cow's or goat's milk and water.

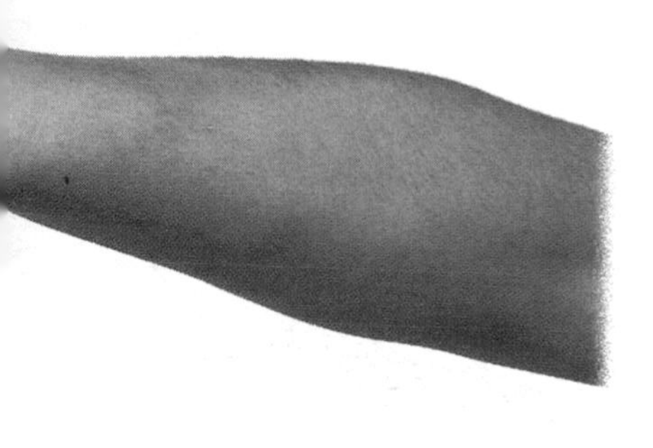

Chapter 9

FIRST AID

EVEN THOUGH serious accidents and emergencies do occasionally happen, you can reduce a dog's immediate pain and distress – or even save its life – with prompt action. Trauma from accidents, falls, or dog fights, chemical injuries from poisons, bites or stings, lacerations, choking, heatstroke, hypothermia, and whelping disorders all require urgent veterinary attention. But by rendering immediate first aid you can prevent further body damage, restore vital functions, reduce discomfort, and stabilize a dog's condition until professional veterinary assistance is available. Even if you never have to use these skills, it is best to be prepared in case of an emergency.

PRINCIPLES OF FIRST AID

Serious injuries always call for urgent, professional veterinary attention, but before an injured dog can be moved, the degree of injury should be assessed and life-supporting first aid administered. First aid involves removing a dog from the source of harm, preventing its condition from worsening, restoring vital bodily functions, alleviating pain and distress, and helping recovery to begin.

Over-enthusiastic first aid can do more harm than good. First determine the seriousness of the dog's condition, then provide essential treatment, and get urgent veterinary help.

FIRST-AID EQUIPMENT

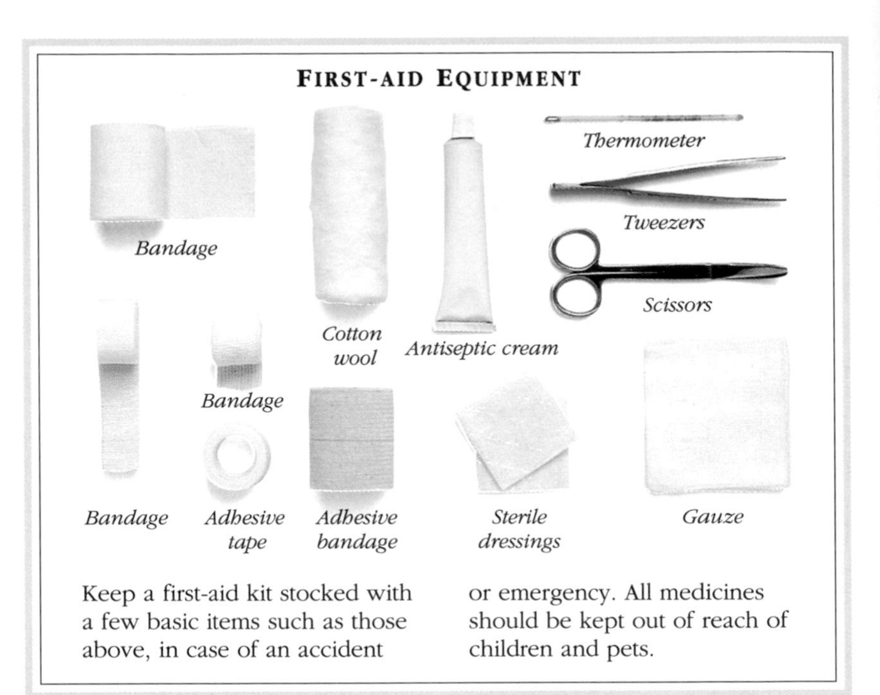

Keep a first-aid kit stocked with a few basic items such as those above, in case of an accident or emergency. All medicines should be kept out of reach of children and pets.

ASSESSING AN INJURED DOG

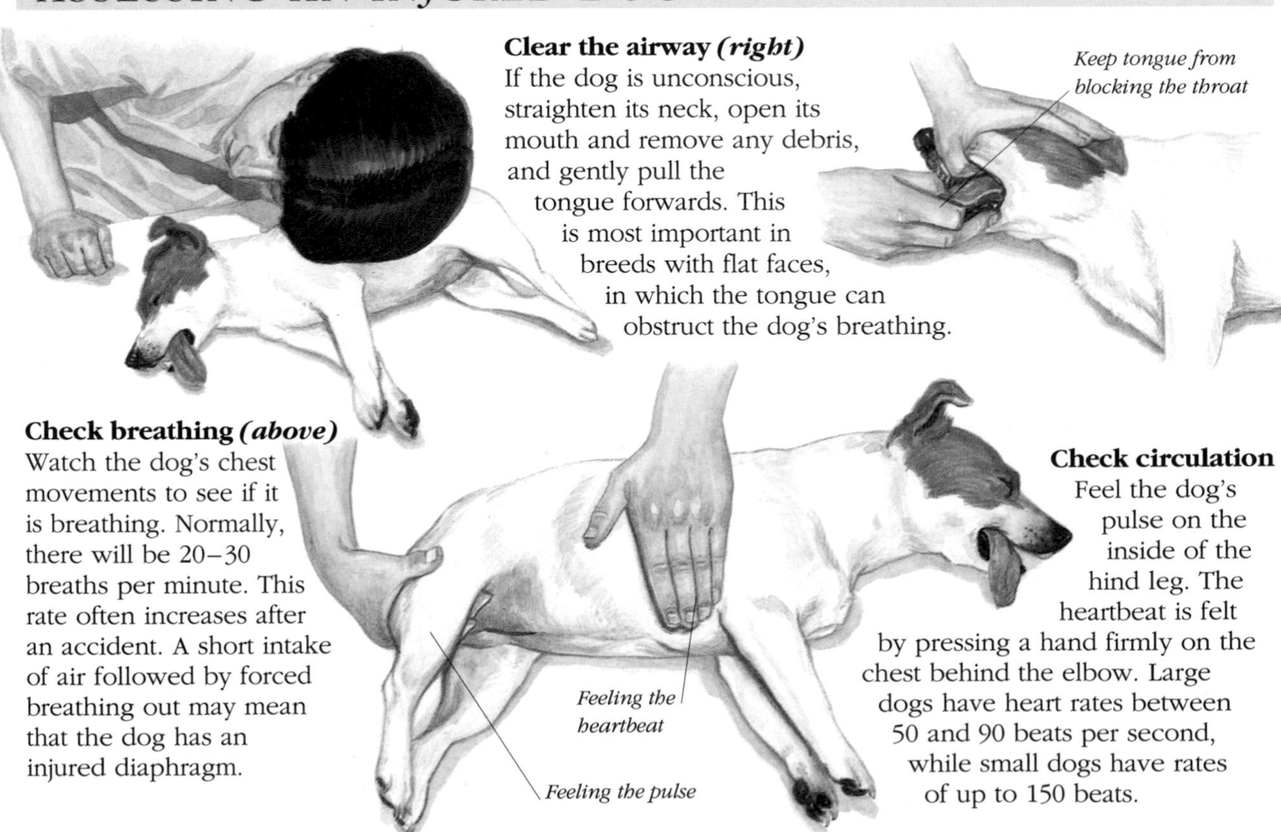

Clear the airway *(right)*
If the dog is unconscious, straighten its neck, open its mouth and remove any debris, and gently pull the tongue forwards. This is most important in breeds with flat faces, in which the tongue can obstruct the dog's breathing.

Check breathing *(above)*
Watch the dog's chest movements to see if it is breathing. Normally, there will be 20–30 breaths per minute. This rate often increases after an accident. A short intake of air followed by forced breathing out may mean that the dog has an injured diaphragm.

Check circulation
Feel the dog's pulse on the inside of the hind leg. The heartbeat is felt by pressing a hand firmly on the chest behind the elbow. Large dogs have heart rates between 50 and 90 beats per second, while small dogs have rates of up to 150 beats.

CHECKING REFLEXES

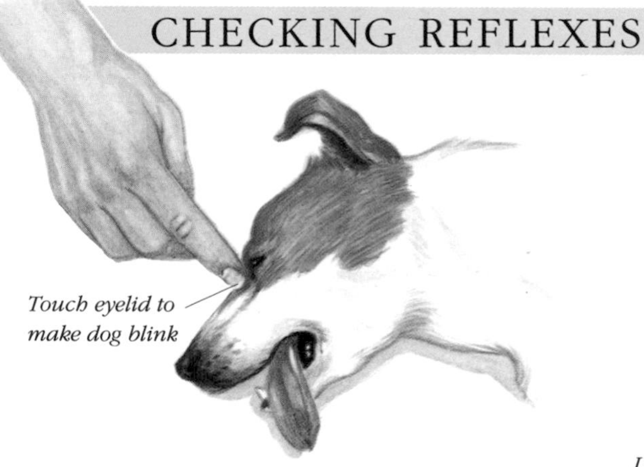

Corneal reflex *(above)*
To test the corneal reflex, gently touch the junction of the eyelids by the nose. If the dog is conscious it will automatically blink.

Light reflex *(below)*
Shine a light into the dog's eye. The pupil will constrict. If it does not, this may mean the heart has failed. If the pupil is already constricted, this may indicate brain damage.

Light makes pupil constrict

FIRST-AID WARNING
An injured dog may suddenly regain consciousness and become hysterical through pain or shock. Take care that it does not injure itself further by trying to get up, and also be very careful that it does not bite you. If the dog is in shock, keep it quiet and warm.

Pedal reflex *(left)*
Pinch a toe or the web of skin between the toes. If there is no response, this means the dog is deeply unconscious, or that its heart has stopped. If it is only lightly unconscious, it will retract its foot.

COLLAPSE AND SHOCK

Recognizing shock *(below)*
Shock occurs when the body's circulation fails. This can happen even hours after an accident. The dog becomes weak, its breathing and pulse are rapid, and it is cold to the touch.

Treating shock *(right)*
Unless shock is the result of heatstroke, wrap the dog loosely in a blanket to keep it warm. Make sure it can breathe easily, and get urgent medical advice.

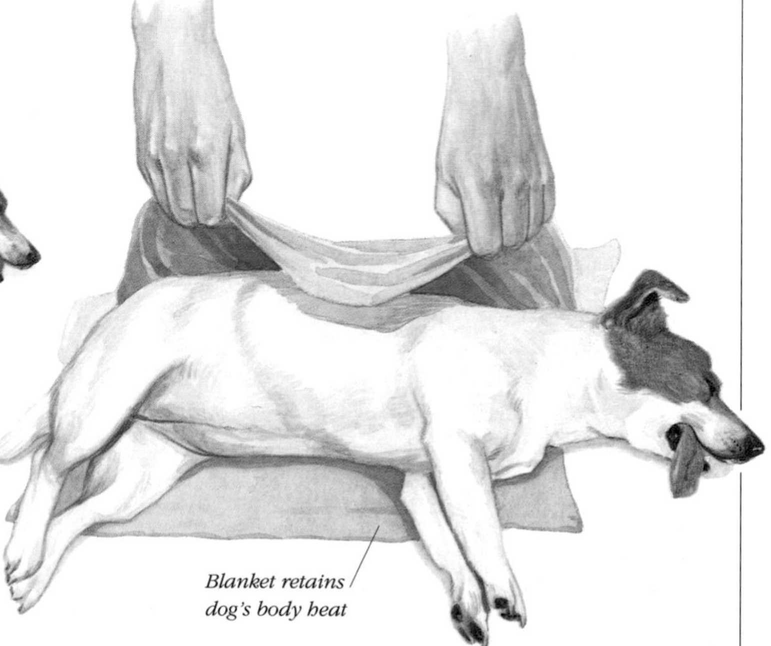

ROAD ACCIDENTS

Prevention is always better than cure. Many traffic accidents could be prevented by proper obedience training. Make sure that your dog is well trained and always under the control of a responsible person when walking outside, especially near a busy road.

If an accident occurs, do not panic, but use common sense. If a dog has been injured in a traffic accident, or has fallen, and is still at risk from further injury, carefully remove it from the source of danger.

A badly injured dog might bite if it is shocked or in pain, so before assessing the dog's injuries, muzzle it with a scarf, rope, or tie. Examine the dog for signs of injury and get immediate medical attention.

PREVENTING ACCIDENTS

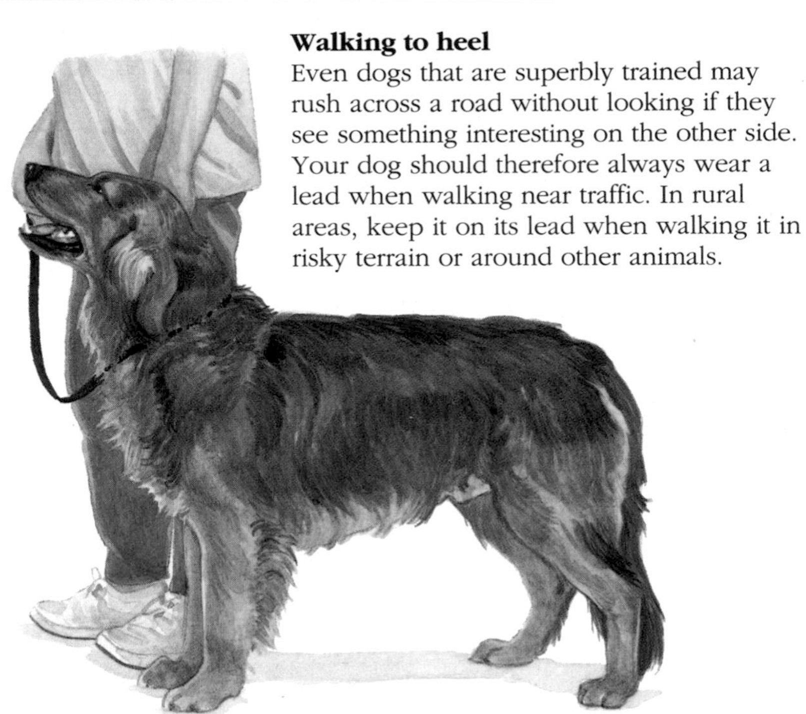

Walking to heel
Even dogs that are superbly trained may rush across a road without looking if they see something interesting on the other side. Your dog should therefore always wear a lead when walking near traffic. In rural areas, keep it on its lead when walking it in risky terrain or around other animals.

MOVING AN INJURED DOG

1 Whether a dog is conscious or unconscious, it must be moved if it is at risk. First check for obvious injuries such as bleeding or distorted limbs. Have someone warn oncoming traffic while you administer immediate first aid to stabilize the dog's condition.

Start cardiac massage if the heart has stopped (see page 161)

Perform artificial respiration if the dog is not breathing (see page 160)

Do not handle a fractured limb

Control severe bleeding by bandaging wounds (see page 168)

EMERGENCY ACTION

If an injured dog is unconscious but breathing normally, press a finger on the gums to see if blood instantly returns when you remove your finger. If it does not, this may be due to severe haemorrhaging. Stop the flow of blood from external lacerations by holding an absorbent pad or bandage to the wound with firm pressure.

2 If another person is available to help, support the dog's body and lift it on to a blanket or coat. If you are by yourself, place the blanket along the dog's back, firmly grasp the skin over the neck and hips, and drag the dog on to the blanket. Then pull the blanket and dog out of harm's way. Avoid touching any obvious injuries.

Lift injured dog in a blanket and get it to a vet as quickly as possible

3 A dog involved in a road accident may have internal injuries that require urgent veterinary attention. Do not move the dog more than is necessary. Using the blanket as a stretcher, carry the dog to a vehicle and get it to a vet as quickly as possible. Make sure that its neck is extended so that breathing is not obstructed.

4 If the dog is obviously in pain, fit it with an improvised muzzle before attempting to move it. Wrap a rope or scarf around the dog's nose, knot it once under the jaws and then again behind the neck.

FIRST-AID WARNING

Some dogs have stoic personalities and may conceal their injuries. However, they are just as much at risk from complications such as post-accident concussion as more complaining dogs. Internal bleeding may produce no visible sign until the dog goes into shock. All dogs should be examined by a vet after an accident, and be kept under observation for 24 hours.

Examine the eyes for signs of shock

5 Even if a dog appears to be normal, it may have damage to internal organs. With the dog removed from further risk, examine it thoroughly. Any dog that has been involved in a road accident should also be taken for a veterinary examination as soon as possible.

6 Gently feel each limb for broken or dislocated bones. If the dog has a suspected fracture, the limb should be moved as little as possible. A dog with spinal injuries should be lifted on a flat board.

RESUSCITATION

Prompt cardiac massage and artificial respiration may occasionally be necessary to save a dog's life. A dog's breathing and heartbeat can fail following a road accident, electric shock, poisoning, drowning, or shock. If a dog's heart has failed, or if it has stopped breathing, get someone to telephone a vet for advice while you attempt to resuscitate the dog. It is crucial to get oxygen-rich blood to the brain as soon as possible to prevent brain damage. If the dog is to survive, its heart must be restarted within minutes.

ARTIFICIAL RESPIRATION

1 If you cannot see the dog breathing, press your ear firmly on the chest to listen for a heartbeat. If the dog's heart is still beating, start to give mouth-to-nose resuscitation *(see below)*. If you cannot hear the heart, start cardiac massage at once *(see opposite)*.

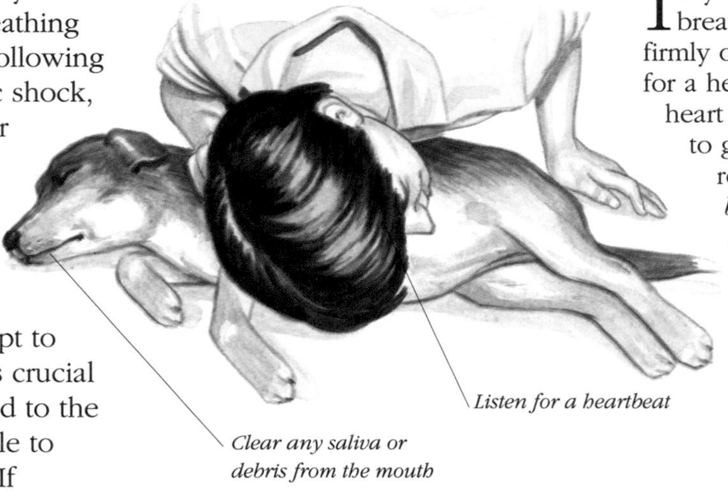

Listen for a heartbeat

Clear any saliva or debris from the mouth

2 With the dog lying on its side, make sure the neck is stretched forwards. Remove any obstructions from the mouth and pull the tongue forwards. If there is damage to the nose, an unconscious dog will breathe through the mouth, and the tongue may obstruct its breathing.

3 Keeping the dog's neck as straight as possible, cup the nose with your hands and breathe into the nostrils for about three seconds to inflate the lungs. The chest should expand. Pause for two seconds, then repeat.

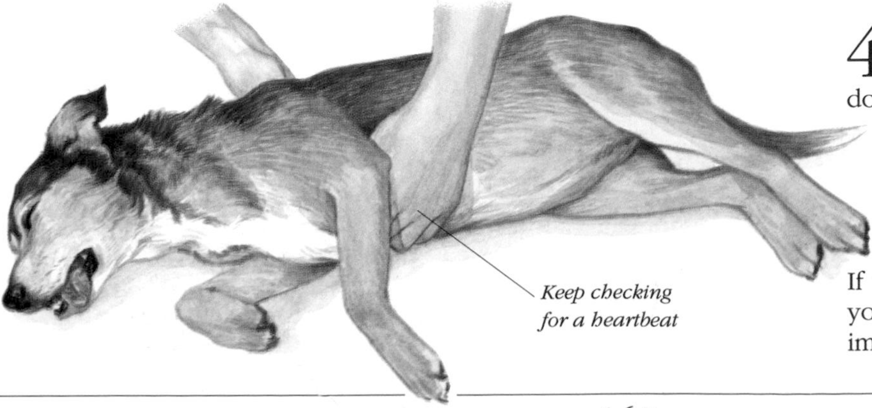

4 Make sure that the heart is still beating by feeling behind the dog's elbow with your hand or by placing your ear on the dog's chest. As long as the heart is beating, continue mouth-to-nose resuscitation until the dog breathes on its own.
If the dog's heart should stop, you must start cardiac massage immediately *(see opposite)*.

Keep checking for a heartbeat

5 The procedure for cardiac massage is as follows. Place the heel of your hand just behind the elbow on the left side of the chest. Place your other hand on top, then firmly press both hands down and forwards towards the brain. This squeezes blood out of the heart to the brain. Repeat six times at one-second intervals.

6 After six cardiac massages, give one breath of mouth-to-nose resuscitation. Continue alternating until the heart beats, then start resuscitation.

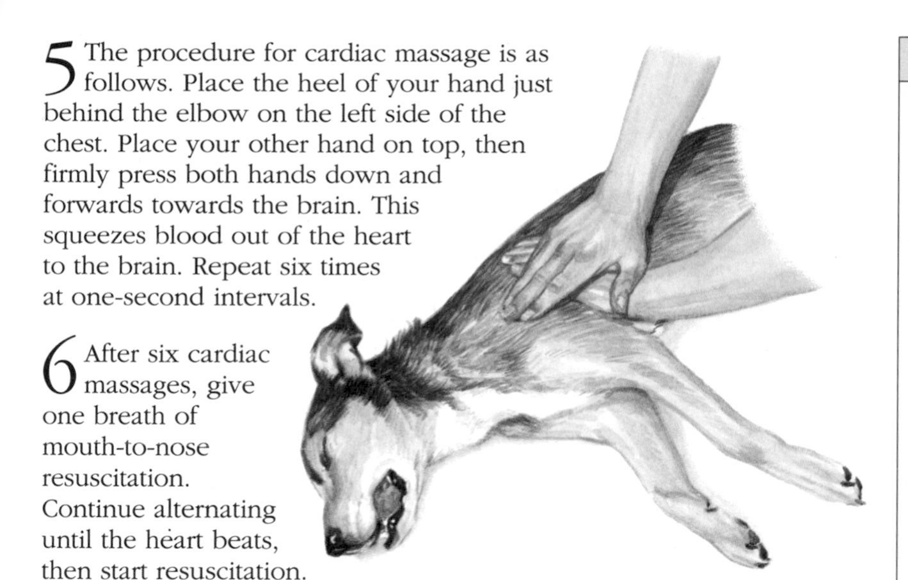

EMERGENCY ACTION

You must get the heart started before attempting mouth-to-nose resuscitation. Do not worry about bruising a rib or applying too much pressure when giving cardiac massage. This is a life-or-death situation. Large dogs in particular need very forceful external pressure to squeeze blood out of the heart. Cardiac massage should be kept up for at least ten minutes. Do not give up trying to resuscitate a dog while there is still a faint heartbeat. Artificial respiration can keep an injured dog alive long enough for veterinary help to be obtained.

DROWNING

1 Because dogs enjoy swimming, they may sometimes enter pools of water from which they cannot get out. When weakened, they swallow water and sometimes debris, too. Drain water from the mouth and clear the airway before starting artificial respiration.

2 Hold a small dog just above the hocks on the hind legs to allow as much water as possible to drain from the lungs. The unconscious dog can be shaken moderately, but not vigorously. If it is still not breathing, lay it on its side and give artificial respiration *(see opposite).*

3 Lay a large dog on its side with its head at the lowest possible position. Lift the hind legs as high as possible to help drain water from the lungs. Allow 30 seconds for drainage, then start mouth-to-nose resuscitation until the dog starts to gasp.

SAFETY ADVICE

Garden ponds and swimming pools should be covered or fenced off to prevent accidents. Take special care when walking your dog near water. You should prevent your dog from entering the sea when it is turbulent, swiftly flowing rivers, or water with strong undercurrents.

CHOKING AND FOREIGN BODIES

With its inquisitive nature, scavenging habits, and enjoyment in chewing, every dog, at one time or another, is likely to get something stuck in its mouth, or to have a foreign object embedded in its skin. Choking often occurs on bone splinters or twigs. A dog should be trained not to chew dangerous objects.

Small balls and toys can also be swallowed and become stuck in a dog's throat. These must be dislodged with the handle of a spoon or cooking tongs as soon as possible to allow the dog to breathe. You should not allow a dog to play with balls that are small enough to be swallowed.

Thorns, glass, needles, and plant seeds can all become embedded in a dog's skin. You should examine your dog's coat and skin for foreign bodies after each walk.

CHOKING

1 Twigs and bone splinters often become lodged between the large upper teeth, or in the back of the throat. To remove them, get a helper to restrain the dog firmly, and open its mouth wide.

2 Holding the mouth open, carefully remove the object with round-ended tweezers or a pair of pliers. Do not risk putting your fingers in the dog's mouth. You are likely to get bitten.

FISH HOOK IN THE MOUTH

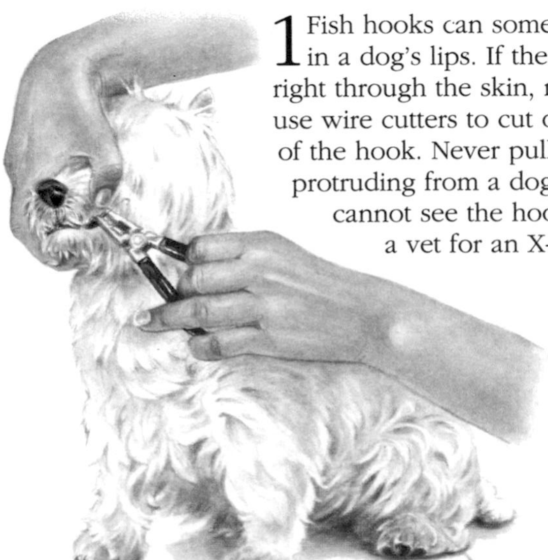

1 Fish hooks can sometimes get caught in a dog's lips. If the hook has gone right through the skin, restrain the dog and use wire cutters to cut off the barbed end of the hook. Never pull on a fishing line protruding from a dog's mouth if you cannot see the hook. Take the dog to a vet for an X-ray.

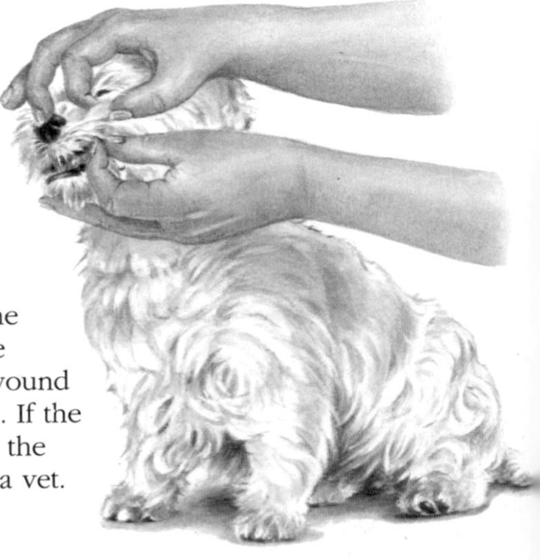

2 Gently ease out the straight part of the hook and clean the wound with a mild antiseptic. If the hook is embedded in the skin, take the dog to a vet.

FOREIGN BODY IN THE EAR

1 During dry weather, check a dog's body and ears for plant seeds after each walk. Visible seeds can be removed with tweezers. If the dog shakes its head, this may mean the seed is lodged deeper in the ear canal.

2 Deep seeds should always be removed by a vet. To soothe the dog temporarily, fill the affected ear with olive or mineral oil. Sometimes this will float the seed up so that it can be easily removed.

FOREIGN BODY IN THE EYE

Floating out objects
If a dog is pawing at its eye or rubbing its head on the ground, hold open the eyelid and look for grit or grass seeds. Try floating out loose debris with eye drops or olive oil. Do not attempt to remove foreign objects that have penetrated the eyeball, but seek veterinary assistance without delay.

EMERGENCY ACTION

Foreign bodies such as grass seeds often enter the ears, nose, eyes, vulva, or skin, and especially the area between the toes. The dog then shakes its head, sneezes, paws at the wound, or licks it vigorously. The body tries to eliminate the object by creating a local bursting abscess, but objects such as grass seeds can migrate throughout the body.

FOREIGN BODY IN THE PAW

Removing an object
Thorns, needles, and shards of glass can penetrate a dog's paw pads, while grass seeds can enter the webs of skin between the toes. If the dog is limping, examine the paw and remove any visible object with tweezers.

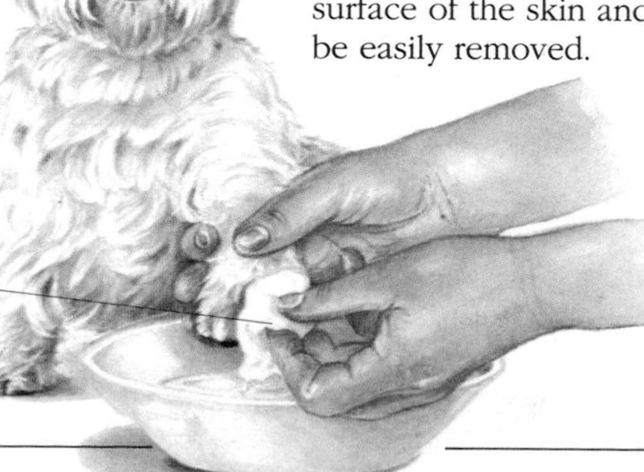

Bathe minor wounds with salt water

Bathing the paw
If the object is not visible, bathe the foot several times daily in tepid salt water (a teaspoon to a cup) until the object comes to the surface of the skin and can be easily removed.

POISONING

Poisons can enter the body through the skin, by being inhaled, or by being eaten. Because of their inquisitive natures, ingestion is the most common way that dogs are poisoned. Do not leave toxic substances in places where a dog can find them. Avoid keeping poisonous plants in your garden *(see page 45)*, especially if you have a young puppy. Do not allow a dog to touch the carcasses of animals such as rodents and birds that may have been poisoned.

COAT CONTAMINATION

Removing paint
Never use solvent, paint stripper, concentrated detergent, or fabric softener on a dog's coat. These substances are all highly toxic if ingested. To remove paint or tar, soften it with petroleum jelly, or products safe for human skin. Cut off any heavily contaminated, matted fur. Then wash the area with canine or baby shampoo, and rinse it thoroughly.

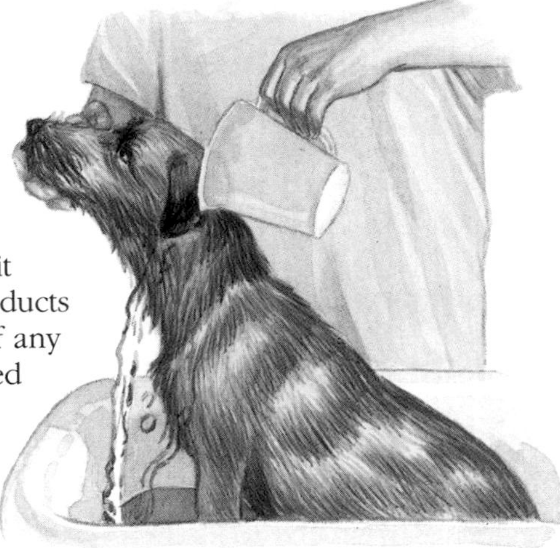

FIRST-AID WARNING

Only induce vomiting if the poison has been swallowed within the last hour, and if the dog is conscious and alert and you are certain that it has not consumed a caustic or irritating substance. Administer a large crystal of washing soda (sodium carbonate) or a concentrated solution of tepid salt water (one teaspoon to a cup). Get immediate veterinary attention, and take a sample of the vomit with you for analysis.

ACCIDENTAL POISONING

1 Puppies, playful adults, and bored dogs are most at risk from accidental poisoning. Common household substances such as aspirin tablets might taste unpleasant but are still eaten by some dogs. Keep all potentially toxic substances out of reach of your dog. Signs of poisoning include severe vomiting, diarrhoea, collapse, fits, and coma.

Dog may chew at plastic container holding tablets

2 If the poison has taken effect and the dog has collapsed, take it immediately to a vet, along with a sample of the substance it has eaten and the packaging listing the ingredients. Treatment will be most effective if the vet can quickly identify the type of poison ingested.

3 If you catch the dog eating something potentially toxic, restrain it and examine the package to find out the ingredients. Contact a vet or your local poison control centre for advice.

Restrain the dog and stop it from eating toxic substance

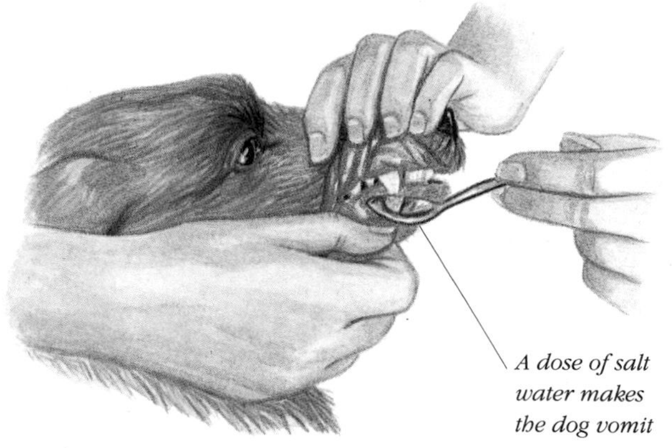

A dose of salt water makes the dog vomit

4 While a helper restrains the dog, open its mouth and administer an emetic, if this is appropriate *(see below)*. Small amounts of salt water are usually effective.

COMMON HOUSEHOLD POISONS

Poison	Source	Signs	Action
Alkaline household cleaners (solvent, paint stripper)	Dog walks in spilled fluid, or owner uses it to clean paint from fur.	Inflamed skin, vomiting, diarrhoea, possible convulsions, ulcers on the tongue.	Do not induce vomiting. Thoroughly wash the coat and skin with soap and water. Contact a vet immediately.
Chlorinated hydrocarbon insecticide	Concentrated insecticide rinses, and flea collars.	Agitation, restlessness, twitching, salivation, convulsions, coma. Potentially fatal.	If poisoning is through skin contact, wash the coat thoroughly with soap and water. Take the dog to a vet immediately.
Organophosphate insecticide	Insecticidal sprays, shampoos, and flea collars.	Muscle tremors, drooling, breathing difficulties, frequent urinating and defecating.	Thoroughly wash the coat with soap and water. Take the dog to a vet immediately.
Warfarin rodenticide	Dog eats poison itself or poisoned rodent.	Bleeding gums and bruising to the skin. Can be fatal, especially in smaller dogs.	If recently ingested, induce vomiting with soda or salt crystals. If signs of poisoning develop, get urgent veterinary treatment.
Strychnine rodenticide	Rodent bait, sometimes used in malicious poisoning.	Initial stiffness, progressing to convulsions. Can be fatal within an hour.	Induce vomiting and get the dog to a vet as quickly as possible.
Slug and snail bait (metaldehyde)	Dogs like the taste of it and sometimes deliberately eat it.	Tremors, salivation, convulsions, coma. Can be fatal.	If recently ingested, induce vomiting with washing soda or salt crystals. Contact a vet immediately if signs develop.
Antifreeze	Sometimes leaks from car radiators. Dogs like the taste of it.	Wobbling, convulsions, vomiting, collapse, coma. Can be fatal.	If recently ingested, induce vomiting with washing soda or salt crystals. Get veterinary attention immediately.
Aspirin	Wrongly given by owners to alleviate pain.	Appetite loss, depression, vomiting with or without blood.	Induce vomiting with washing soda or salt crystals. This counteracts the poison.
Lead	Chewing old paint, lead fishing weights, old pipes, or batteries.	Vomiting, diarrhoea, and abdominal pain, followed by staggering and paralysis.	Induce vomiting if lead has just been eaten. Contact a vet, who will take blood tests and commence immediate treatment.
Illegal drugs	Either discovered by or given to the dog.	Incoordination, agitation, fear biting, dilated pupils.	Get veterinary treatment immediately. Veterinary sedatives relax the dog.
Sedatives and antidepressants	Either discovered by or given to the dog.	Depression, staggering, coma.	Induce vomiting with washing soda or salt crystals. Contact a vet immediately.

Bites and Stings

Dog bites most frequently occur around the neck, face, ears, and chest. Skin punctures from canine teeth look simple and clean, but there is often considerable soft-tissue damage under the skin. Bites, stings, and injuries from insects and venomous animals are often difficult to find and require symptomatic treatment. Contact a vet if a dog shows any agitation.

DOG BITES

1 Be careful not to get injured when trying to separate two dogs or stop a dog fight. Cold water from a hosepipe or bucket may be effective in separating them. Allow the dog time to calm down before examining it. Check to see whether the skin is lacerated or punctured. If the skin is punctured, clip hair away from the wound.

Cut away fur surrounding the wound

2 Remove all clipped hair, then carefully bathe the region with warm water and a gentle skin disinfectant. Apply petroleum jelly around the site of the wound to prevent hair from getting inside and causing irritation.

3 If the skin is punctured, take the dog to a vet for antibiotic treatment. If it is lacerated, apply antiseptic cream to the area. Expect bruising to occur. A deep, penetrating wound may need stitching.

INSECT STINGS

Wasp stings

Wasp and hornet stings cause pain and swelling. Some dogs are allergic to stings and can react badly. Urgent veterinary care is essential if there is acute swelling to the mouth or throat.

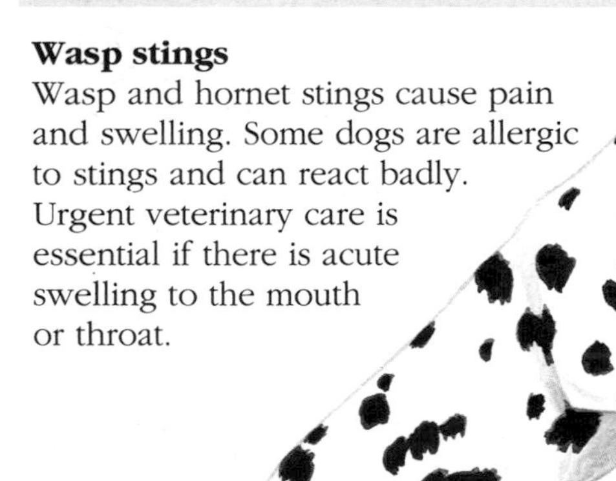

The mouth and face are usual sites of wasp stin

Bee stings

Bees leave an embedded sting in the skin. With a magnifying glass, remove the sting with tweezers. An icepack may help to reduce the swelling.

Try to draw out the sting with tweezers

SNAKE BITES

Treating a snake bite
If you know where a dog has been bitten, try to keep it calm and apply an icepack to the wound to slow down the flow of blood. If the dog's limb is affected, do not apply a tourniquet. Instead, apply ice, and wrap the leg tightly in a bandage. Contact a vet at once. He may be able to give it anti-venom medication.

EMERGENCY ACTION

Snake bites are rarely observed as they occur. Suspect a poisonous snake bite if the dog is trembling, excited, drooling, vomiting, has dilated pupils, or has collapsed. There will also be considerable swelling. Venomous snakes may leave two puncture marks at the site of the bite, usually on the head or legs. Do not cut into the wound and attempt to suck out the venom. This only increases the blood flow to the region and speeds the spread of poison. Carry the dog to a vet.

TOAD AND CATERPILLAR POISONING

Poisonous toads and caterpillars
Some species of toad secrete a toxic substance on their skin. This passes into the mouth of any dog that picks up the toad to play with it. Certain types of longhaired caterpillar can also produce similar irritants.

Treating poisoning
Itchiness, redness, and swelling can be reduced by bathing the mouth with cold water. A water spray is ideal for flushing out the mouth, but do not let the dog swallow any water. Contact a vet if the dog is in discomfort – it may need antihistamines to reduce swelling.

BITES AND STINGS

Poisonous spiders rarely bite dogs because their mouthparts cannot penetrate the coat. However, dogs can be bitten or stung by other animals. Puppies are very susceptible to bites and stings, especially between the toes. Apply a cold compress and take the dog to a vet. If a dog is in pain after swimming in the sea, it may have been stung by a jellyfish or anemone. Apply ammonia diluted one to ten with water and consult a vet.

PORCUPINES AND SKUNKS

Meeting other animals
Curiosity often gets the better of dogs. Porcupine quills are quite painful when caught in a dog's flesh, but can be removed with pliers. However, they are best removed under veterinary sedation, or even anaesthesia. Skunk odour can be eliminated using special products, or by dousing the dog with tomato juice or mouthwash, and then bathing thoroughly with canine shampoo.

Bandaging Wounds

Traffic accidents, dog fights, and unexpected traumatic injuries are the most common causes of bleeding wounds. If a dog is bleeding, remove it from risk of further injury, and clean and bandage the wound to prevent any additional damage until you can get the dog to a vet. Bandaging will prevent further blood loss and shock. Spurting blood denotes a severed artery. Apply firm, constant pressure until you reach a vet. Slower bleeding means that veins and smaller vessels are damaged. Firm pressure with an absorbent gauze pad and bandaging will stop minor bleeding.

STOPPING BLEEDING

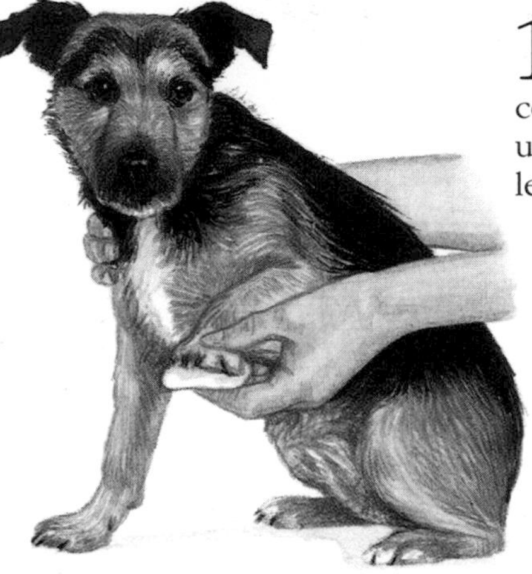

1 While someone contacts a vet, apply a gauze pad soaked in cold water to the wound. Do not use cotton wool as it will adhere, leaving fibres in the wound.

2 If bleeding does not stop, or to prevent it from starting again, cover the area with a non-sticking absorbent pad and secure it with a bandage.

BANDAGING AN EAR WOUND

1 Ears are most frequently torn in dog fights, and bleed profusely. First calm the dog, then clean the wound. Apply an absorbent pad to the wound.

2 Wrap the ear in a bandage, winding it around the head to keep it secure and prevent the ear from bleeding when the dog shakes its head.

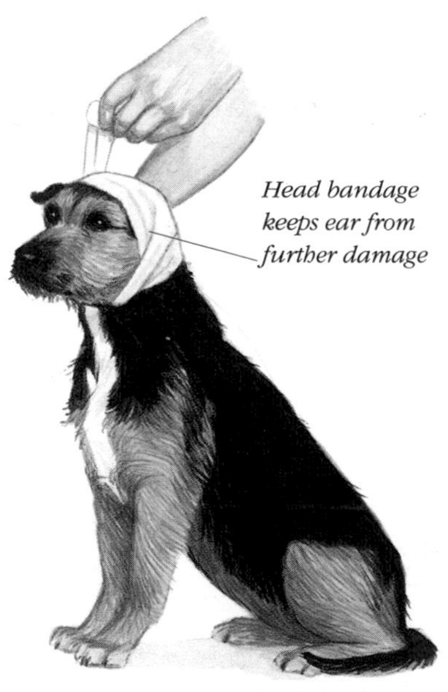

3 Continue bandaging the ear to the head until it is held securely. Avoid putting pressure on the windpipe. If necessary, use an Elizabethan collar.

BANDAGING A TAIL WOUND

1 Dogs' tails are most frequently damaged by being caught in closing doors. They bleed profusely, especially if the tail is wagged a lot. Disinfect the wound and apply a non-sticking absorbent pad to it.

2 Starting at the tip, bandage up the tail towards the body. Cover the absorbent pad, making sure that you catch all hair in the bandage.

3 Vigorous tail wagging may remove lightly applied bandaging. It also prolongs bleeding. If the dog's tail is long enough, bandage the tail to the body, but not too tightly.

BANDAGING A TORSO WOUND

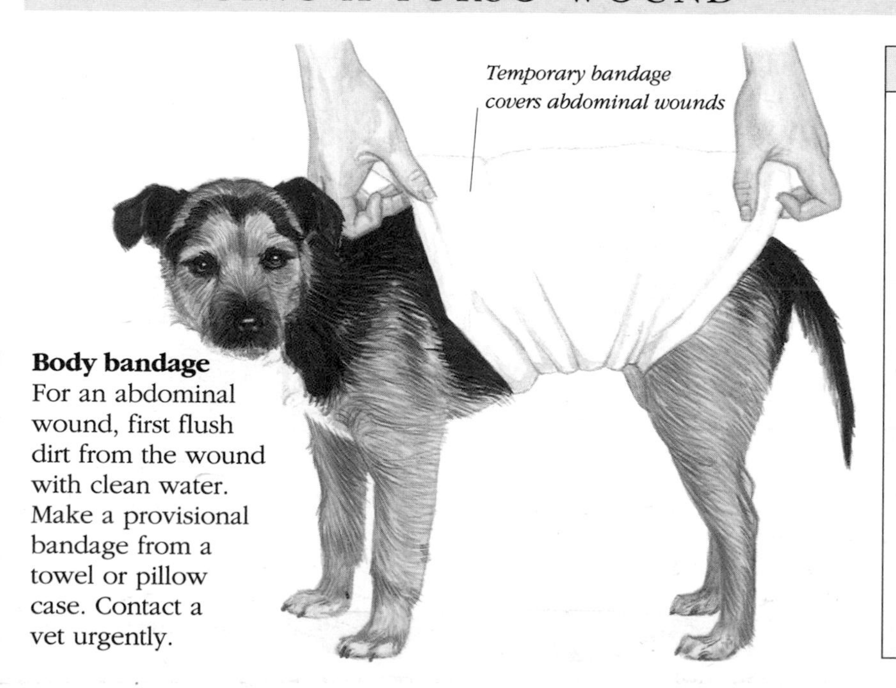

Body bandage
For an abdominal wound, first flush dirt from the wound with clean water. Make a provisional bandage from a towel or pillow case. Contact a vet urgently.

FIRST-AID WARNING

External bleeding is obvious, but internal bleeding is more dangerous because it cannot be seen. If a dog has had a serious fall, has been in a traffic accident, has had other traumatic injuries, or suddenly becomes pale and lethargic, suspect internal bleeding, even if there are no outward signs of damage. The spleen and liver in particular are prone to crush injuries. Keep the dog quiet if there is internal bleeding and get immediate veterinary attention. Internal bleeding often requires urgent surgery. Blood can be replaced by transfusion from a donor, or by blood-replacement fluids.

TEMPERATURE-RELATED INJURIES

Dog breeds that evolved in the north of Eurasia and North America, and those with double coats of downy underhair and long outer hair, are well-equipped for the freezing weather of extreme northern or southern regions. However, they do not cope very well with heat.

Dogs cannot lose heat by sweating, since they have no sweat glands. All they can do is pant. Heatstroke is one of the commonest causes of avoidable death in dogs. Remember, in the presence of heat and without ventilation, a dog's temperature rapidly rises to 43.3°C (110°F). If left in that condition, it literally cooks to death. A hot car is a deathtrap for dogs. Single-coated breeds are more prone to frostbite and hypothermia than breeds with thicker coats.

HEATSTROKE

Heatstroke prevention

Do not leave a dog in a car in warm, sunny weather. Even parking in the shade and leaving a window partly open is not safe. Never leave a dog alone in a car with the heater on in cold weather. In both circumstances, a dog overheats and is unable to cool itself down.

1 The first sign of heatstroke is rapid, heavy panting, often with salivation. After a few minutes the dog becomes weak and collapses, still panting.

2 Remove the dog from the hot environment as quickly as possible. Clear the mouth of saliva to ease breathing, and sponge face with cool water. Get someone to contact a vet.

3 If possible, immerse the dog's body in cool water. Do not use ice-cold water. Alternatively, wrap it in towels soaked in cold water. Pour cold water over the towels to prevent them from getting warm. Let the dog drink if it wishes.

HYPOTHERMIA

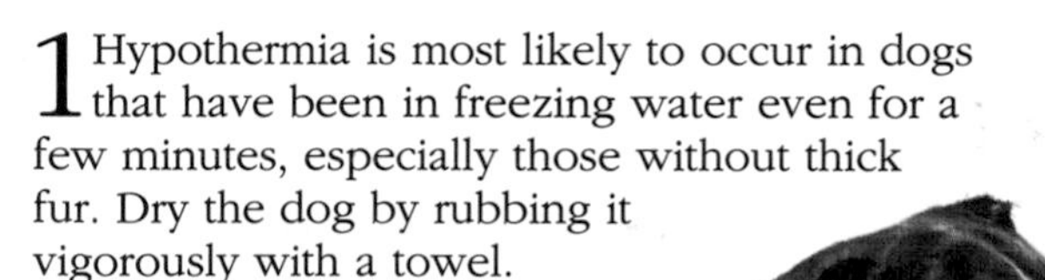

1 Hypothermia is most likely to occur in dogs that have been in freezing water even for a few minutes, especially those without thick fur. Dry the dog by rubbing it vigorously with a towel.

Dry the dog if it has been swimming in cold water

EMERGENCY ACTION
Hypothermia can occur as a result of shock, after anaesthesia, and in newborn puppies. It is seen most often in toy breeds and those with very short coats. Orphan puppies are particularly at risk from the cold. It is essential that they are kept in a warm, draught-free environment for the first weeks of life.

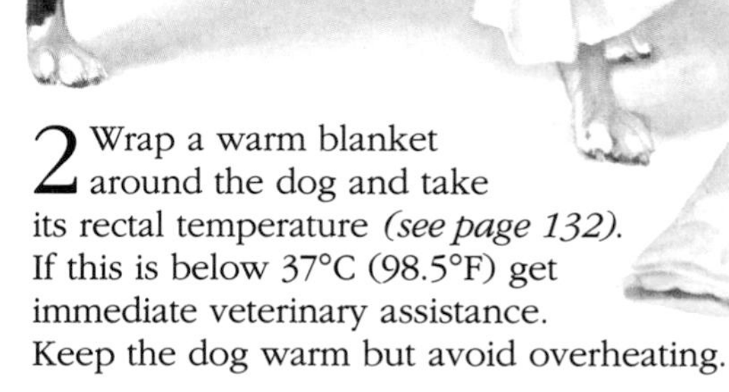

2 Wrap a warm blanket around the dog and take its rectal temperature *(see page 132)*. If this is below 37°C (98.5°F) get immediate veterinary assistance. Keep the dog warm but avoid overheating.

FROSTBITE

1 Frostbite is most likely to occur to the extremities after exposure to below-freezing temperatures, especially when it is windy. Examine the feet, ears, and tail, which may appear pale, or be cold and insensitive. Massage them gently with a towel.

Rub feet with a dry towel to warm them

Immerse paws in a bowl of tepid water

2 Warm the frozen parts with tepid water heated to 32.2°C (90°F). Thawing should occur within ten minutes, and the skin may appear reddened. Keep the dog warm until veterinary assistance is available.

OTHER EMERGENCIES

You should always be prepared for potential canine emergencies, such as burns, seizures, and gastric torsion. A dog's coat insulates and protects the skin, but hot water or oil, and irritating chemicals can seep through the hair, causing skin damage. Chewing on an electric flex can burn a dog's mouth, or cause unconsciousness and cardiac arrest. When suffering a fit, a dog convulses and may pass out *(see page 121)*.

Another emergency occurs when a dog's stomach twists on itself (gastric torsion), causing bloat. This condition is fatal without immediate veterinary attention.

CHEMICAL BURNS

Washing off caustic chemicals
Wash off any caustic chemicals from the coat with warm, soapy water. Contact a vet for advice. Never apply anything to a dog's coat that you would not use on your own skin.

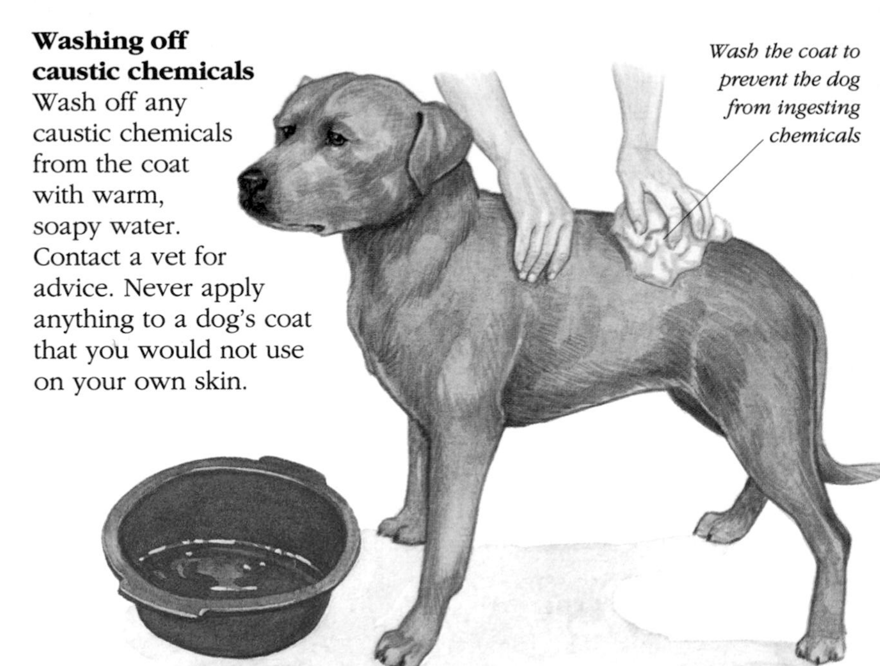

Wash the coat to prevent the dog from ingesting chemicals

ELECTRICAL BURNS

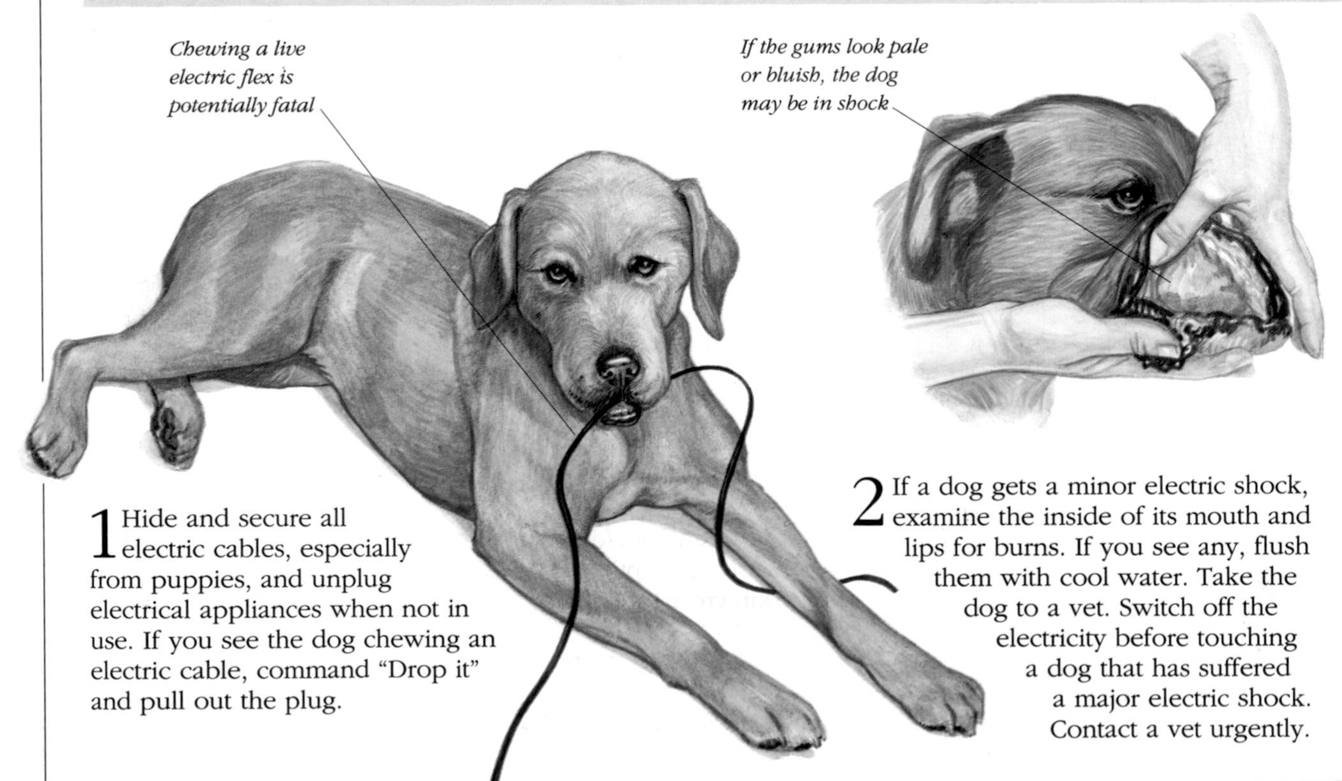

Chewing a live electric flex is potentially fatal

If the gums look pale or bluish, the dog may be in shock

1 Hide and secure all electric cables, especially from puppies, and unplug electrical appliances when not in use. If you see the dog chewing an electric cable, command "Drop it" and pull out the plug.

2 If a dog gets a minor electric shock, examine the inside of its mouth and lips for burns. If you see any, flush them with cool water. Take the dog to a vet. Switch off the electricity before touching a dog that has suffered a major electric shock. Contact a vet urgently.

GASTRIC TORSION

Gas builds up in stomach and cannot escape

Recognizing bloat
Deep-chested dogs risk twisting their stomachs if they play immediately after eating a large meal. The dog is lethargic and pants heavily. Bloat leads to collapse and fatal shock.

EMERGENCY ACTION

Gastric torsion is a critical condition that requires immediate veterinary treatment. This is a situation where a few minutes can make the difference between life and death. If action is not taken immediately the dog will die. There is little that can be done in the way of first aid. Telephone a vet immediately or even set off while someone telephones the surgery to alert the staff that you are on your way. A vet may be able to correct the gastric torsion by immediate surgery.

FITS AND SEIZURES

Treating a seizure
Seizures vary from mild behaviour quirks such as a dog snapping at non-existent flies, to dramatic convulsions accompanied by back arching and salivation. Make the dog comfortable. Eliminate noise and reduce lighting. Clear the dog's airway and make sure the tongue is not blocking the throat, but take care that you are not bitten. Get urgent veterinary help.

SCALDS AND BURNS

1 Most burns are caused by boiling water or oil. Treat minor burns by applying cold water immediately to the affected area. Follow it with an icepack.

2 Once the affected area has been cooled, apply antiseptic skin cream and contact a vet. Try to keep the wound clean. Do not apply ointment to serious burns.

WHELPING PROBLEMS

Big breeds like Labrador Retrievers that produce large litters of relatively small puppies have fewer whelping problems than small breeds such as terriers, which have small litters or quite large puppies. Large-headed breeds such as bulldogs often have more difficulty giving birth than do other breeds.

When your dog goes into labour, contact a vet so that he is prepared for possible problems. Keep a supply of towels at hand, together with thread for tying off umbilical cords, and a safe disinfectant for your hands. Try not to interfere with whelping unless it is absolutely necessary. In some circumstances, however, you may have to assist with the birth, or even hand-rear a puppy *(see page 151)*.

LABOUR PROBLEMS

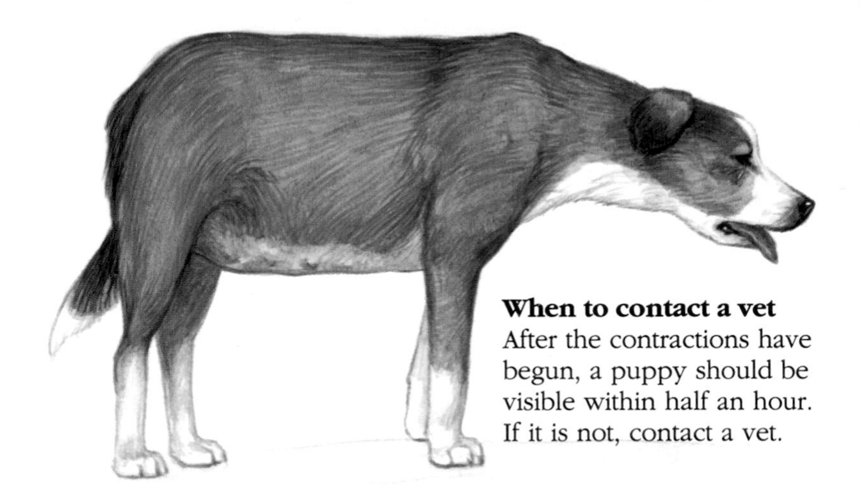

When to contact a vet
After the contractions have begun, a puppy should be visible within half an hour. If it is not, contact a vet.

EMERGENCY ACTION
A bitch should produce a puppy within two hours of the water bag breaking. Further puppies may arrive at intervals of several minutes to two hours in length. Contact a vet if the bitch has been straining unproductively for more than half an hour, since the puppies may be too large for the mother to deliver. The vet may recommend a Caesarean section, in which an incision is made in the abdomen and the puppies removed by hand.

ASSISTING WITH THE BIRTH

1 Puppies are usually born headfirst in a diving position, or tail and hind legs first. If the mother is having difficulty, you can gently pull out the exposed puppy as the mother strains. If only the legs appear, call the vet.

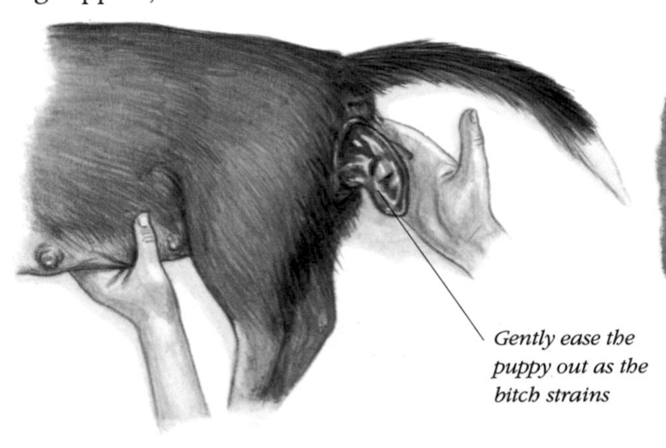

Gently ease the puppy out as the bitch strains

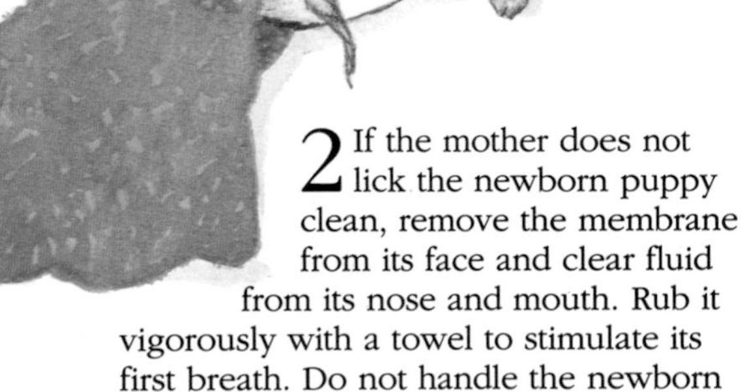

2 If the mother does not lick the newborn puppy clean, remove the membrane from its face and clear fluid from its nose and mouth. Rub it vigorously with a towel to stimulate its first breath. Do not handle the newborn puppy more than is necessary.

HELPING A WEAK PUPPY

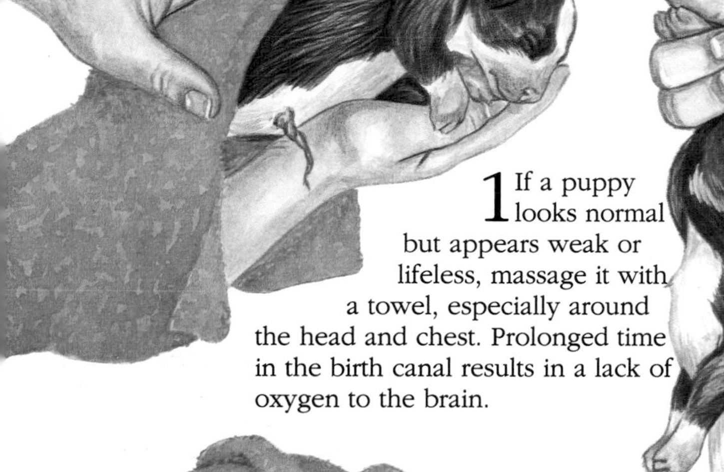

1 If a puppy looks normal but appears weak or lifeless, massage it with a towel, especially around the head and chest. Prolonged time in the birth canal results in a lack of oxygen to the brain.

2 If, after rubbing the puppy with a towel, it is still not breathing, suspend it by its hind legs for a few seconds to allow fluids to drain from the air passages. Keeping a secure grip on the puppy's hind legs, shake it gently. This should stimulate it to start breathing.

Suspend puppy by hind legs

3 Once the puppy is breathing, keep it warm by wrapping it in a towel until the mother has finished giving birth.

4 When whelping has finished, show the weak puppy to its mother and make sure it finds a productive teat. Watch it for a few days to ensure it is not bullied by stronger puppies.

3 The mother should chew through the umbilical cord. If she does not, tie off the cord with thread about 5 cm (2 in) from the puppy's belly, then cut it on the opposite side of the knot, away from the puppy. Do not pull on the umbilical cord.

4 The mother may reject the puppy if it is taken away, so allow her to lick the puppy. Place it where it can suckle.

Chapter 10

SHOWING

DOG SHOWS are not simply for professional breeders. Anyone who enjoys the company of canines can find a suitable show. At official shows, purebred dogs are compared to a breed standard, which is a list of ideal characteristics for a perfect specimen of each breed. Only registered pedigree dogs may be entered at this type of show. In other competitions, both mongrels and purebreds compete in agility, retrieval work, obedience, or simply for the waggiest tail. There are even ball-catching and frisbee championships. The competition is always intense and it requires a lot of training and preparation to produce a prize-winning dog. Although the material rewards are few, the dogs seem to have as much fun as their human owners.

Dog Shows and Competitions

Dog shows developed in the 1830s and 1840s when dog-fighting and bull-baiting became illegal, yet owners still wanted to display their dogs. The first shows were small, local events held in public houses. Dog shows soon caught on, and the first organized show was held in 1859 at Newcastle-upon-Tyne in England.

At first, there were no breed standards, which resulted in a lot of controversy, since dogs were judged according to different rules at each show. Gradually, local breed clubs and societies were set up to oversee shows, and breeders began collaborating to produce dogs that conformed to specific standards of size, shape, and bone structure.

EARLY DOG SHOWS

19th-century show
Early shows had few rules, and the dogs did not even have to be properly trained in obedience and ringcraft. The result was often a melée of excited and uncontrollable dogs, as seen in this sketch by Louis Wain. This print shows one of the earliest competitions to be organized by the British Kennel Club, held in London in 1890.

KENNEL CLUBS

The Kennel Club of Great Britain was set up in 1873 to register the standards of each breed and to oversee dog shows. Organizations in other countries later followed suit. As well as registering breed standards, national kennel clubs promote breeding, classify breeds, register pedigree dogs, and establish the rules governing dog shows and competitions.

International show *(left)*
Before pedigree breed standards and classes were established by a recognized organization, dogs of all kinds could compete against each other. In this print, dogs from all over the world compete in a show held at the Agricultural Hall, Islington, London in 1865.

MODERN COMPETITIONS

Sheepdog trials *(left)*
In these popular competitions, working sheepdogs compete against each other to herd and pen a flock of sheep in the shortest possible time. The dogs are controlled by a handler with a whistle, or by using hand signals and voice commands. The sheepdogs are penalized for disobeying any command or not performing a manoeuvre cleanly.

Field trials *(right)*
Field trials give gundogs a chance to show off their skills. They compete in the field under normal shooting conditions to scent, locate, or retrieve dummies on land and in water, according to the type of work for which they were bred.

Agilty competitions *(left)*
In agility competitions, dogs negotiate an obstacle course to show their fitness, speed, and training. All kinds of dog can compete in these events, many of which rely on the inate abilities of the breed, such as running for Greyhounds, and tunnelling for terriers.

Obedience contests *(right)*
Different breeds and mongrels can all compete in obedience competitions. The dogs are commanded to perform basic obedience tests, such as sitting, lying down, and coming when called. Other types of advanced obedience contests involve tracking and retrieving, and the dogs are sometimes commanded by hand signals alone.

JUDGING SHOW DOGS

Show dogs are judged against a breed standard, which is a list of features maintained by the kennel club of each country, specifying the attributes of a perfect dog of each breed. No dog can match all these characteristics, but judges look for the dogs that come as close as possible to the breed standard.

A dog is judged on its body shape, general appearance, coat colour, temperament, and the way it stands and moves in the show ring. A dog is penalized for any departure from the breed standard.

HOW DOGS ARE JUDGED

Smooth-haired Dachshund
Originally bred for hunting small mammals, this dog has a long body and very short legs.

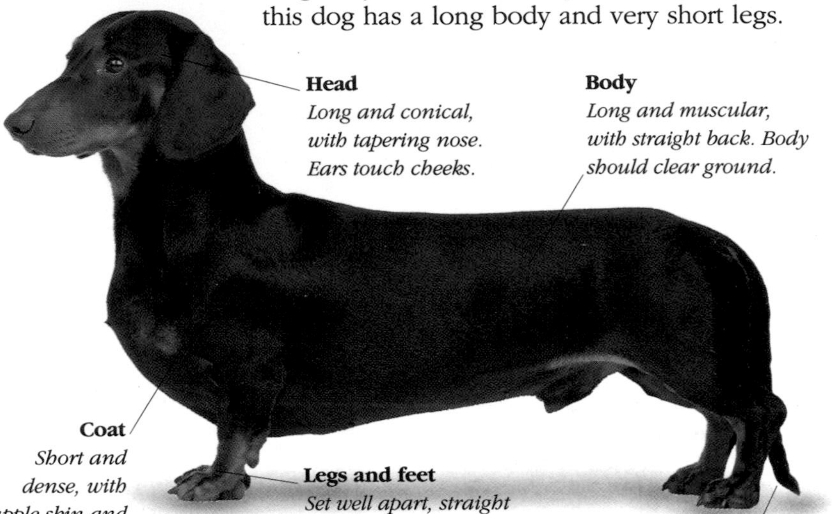

Head
Long and conical, with tapering nose. Ears touch cheeks.

Body
Long and muscular, with straight back. Body should clear ground.

Coat
Short and dense, with supple skin and no wrinkles. Colours vary.

Legs and feet
Set well apart, straight and parallel, with hard muscles on forelegs.

Tail
Curved, with no kinks. Should not touch the ground when at rest.

German Shepherd Dog
This intelligent and lively breed has a powerful body, and the ability to scent and chase for long distances.

Body
Deep chest, straight back, and sloping hindquarters. Body length should be greater than shoulder height.

Head
Wedge-shaped, straight muzzle should be about half total length of skull.

Tail
Long and bushy. Hangs when the dog is at rest, but should be carried slightly raised when moving.

Coat
Thick undercoat covered with dense, straight hair. Longer hair on backs of legs. Colour can be black, black and tan, grey, or sable.

Legs and feet
Forelegs should be longer than chest depth. Well-muscled hind legs and compact feet.

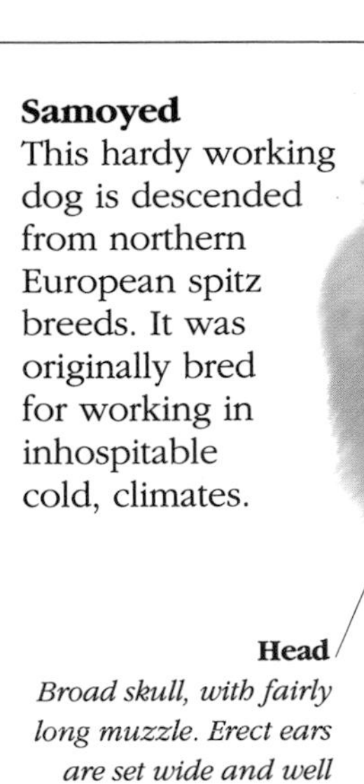

Samoyed

This hardy working dog is descended from northern European spitz breeds. It was originally bred for working in inhospitable cold, climates.

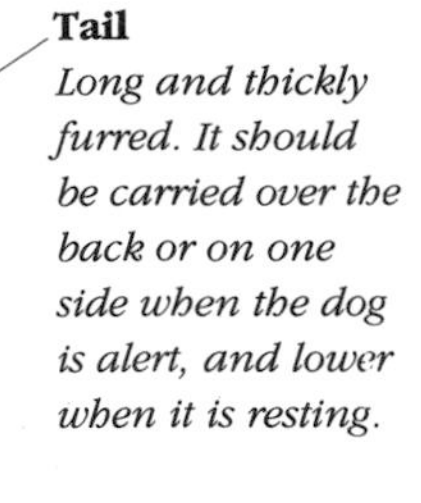

Tail

Long and thickly furred. It should be carried over the back or on one side when the dog is alert, and lower when it is resting.

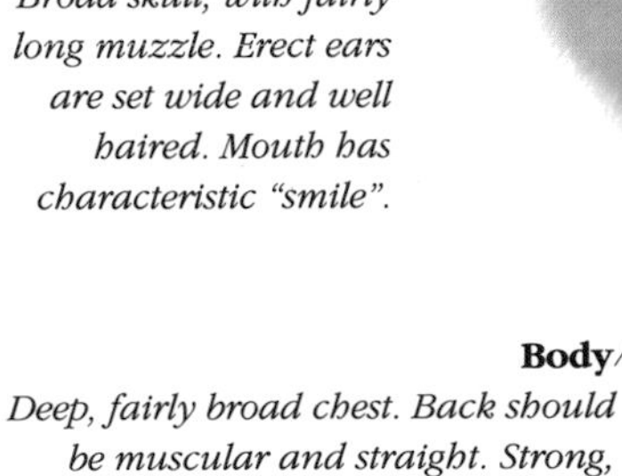

Head

Broad skull, with fairly long muzzle. Erect ears are set wide and well haired. Mouth has characteristic "smile".

Coat

Thick, short undercoat. Weather-resistant outer coat should be straight and harsh, but not wiry. Colour can be white, biscuit, or cream.

Body

Deep, fairly broad chest. Back should be muscular and straight. Strong, powerful loins.

Legs and feet

Straight, muscular legs. Well-feathered feet.

Miniature Schnauzer

The schnauzer was bred in southern Germany as a cattle dog. Alert and energetic, the miniature variety makes a good companion.

Coat

Dense undercoat and harsh, wiry outer coat. Short hair on shoulders and neck, and longer hair on legs. Colour can be "pepper and salt" or black.

Head

Muzzle should taper to blunt, black nose with wide nostrils. Prominent moustache and eyebrows. Dark eyes set forward. High, V-shaped ears.

Tail

High tail historically docked. In many countries, tail docking is now banned.

Body

Deep, broad chest with strong breastbone. Strong back should be straight, rising slightly higher at shoulders than at hindquarters. Length of body should be same as height at top of withers.

Legs and feet

Strong and straight, with muscular, slanting thighs. Compact feet, arched toes, and dark nails.

Taking Part in a Show

There are many types of dog show, each with its own rules, but the basic procedure for entering a show is the same whether it is a championship, open, exemption, or local event.

There are several important things to remember before entering any show. Your dog must be in excellent health, with all its vaccinations up to date, since it may be exposed to contagious diseases at a show, or pass on ailments to the other dogs with which it comes into contact. It must also have an immaculate general appearance, resulting from grooming all year long. No artificial cosmetic aids, such as coat dye, are allowed.

Your dog must also be well trained in ringcraft so that it does not disrupt the other entrants, and so that you can concentrate on showing it to its full advantage without worrying about controlling bad behaviour.

Arriving at the Show

Settling in *(above)*
When you arrive at the show, settle your dog with its bed on the numbered bench that you have been allotted. Secure it with a benching chain and give it a drink of water. To prevent it from becoming sleepy, do not feed it until after its class. Check your entry in the show catalogue and note the times of the various classes. All classes are numbered and follow in order.

Grooming *(above)*
Just before you enter the ring, groom your dog so that it looks its absolute best. This may also help to calm it. There are usually small exercise areas where your dog can relieve itself before going into the show ring.

Show Equipment

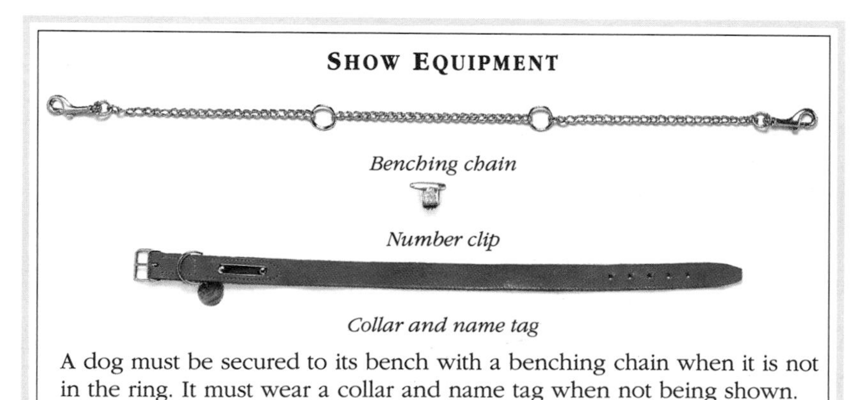

A dog must be secured to its bench with a benching chain when it is not in the ring. It must wear a collar and name tag when not being shown. The dog handler must wear a number attached to his clothing.

THE JUDGING PROCEDURE

Standing *(right)*
Be ready to enter the ring when your class is called. Once in the ring, set your dog in its stance on a level piece of ground for the judge to make an assessment. Adjust the dog's legs and tail with as little interference as possible.

Judging *(left)*
A dog should stand still and remain calm when the judge examines it. Keep the dog still with its head held up to present it correctly. The judge is looking for a healthy, good-tempered dog that matches the official breed standard.

Gaiting *(below)*
The judge will want to see the dog's "gait" or movement. You may be asked to trot the dog in a triangle so that the judge can watch how it moves from the side, in front, and behind. An experienced show dog should move smoothly and in a straight line. Depending on the size of the dog, you may need to move at a fast walk or run.

Final line-up *(above)*
After the dogs have been seen individually, the judge will select the winners. Rosettes are given for first, second, and third place, reserve, and highly commended.

Best of breed *(right)*
Finally all the winners of each class compete for the best-of-breed title. At championship shows, the best dog and the best bitch compete for the title.

GLOSSARY

Abscess Collection of pus forming painful swelling.
Acquired disorder Condition or illness that develops after birth.
Action Way in which a dog moves.
Acute Condition occurring suddenly and rapidly. *See also* Chronic.
Albino Lack of pigment melanin, causing white fur and pink eyes.
Alopecia Baldness.
Anoestrus Not in oestrus.
Anorexia Loss of appetite.
Anuria Passing no urine.
Anus Outlet of the rectum.
Ascariasis Infestation of worms.
Aural Pertaining to the ear.
Autoimmune disease Condition in which body destroys its own tissues.

Balanitis Infection of the penis.
Bay Characteristic bark of a hound.
Benched show Championship show at which dogs are confined to benches when not in ring.
Best in show Top award at show.
Best of breed Award given to best specimen of each breed at show.
Bitch Female dog.
Blue eye Clouding of the eye, caused by inflammation of the cornea.
Boarding kennel Establishment that boards dogs while owners are away.
Brace Two dogs of the same breed.
Brachycephalic Dogs with short noses and pushed-in faces, such as the Pekingese and Pug.
Breed Type of pedigree dog whose characteristics are transmitted from generation to generation.
Breed standard Description of ideal characteristics against which dogs are judged at shows. Determined by national dog society of each country.
Breeding kennel Place where purebred dogs are mated to preserve the breed.

Carcinoma Malignant cancer in the skin or internal organs of the body.
Cardiac Pertaining to the heart.
Castrate To surgically remove male dog's testicles to prevent reproduction.
Chromosomes Tiny strands of DNA that store genetic information.
Chronic Condition that continues or recurs over a period of time, rather than developing suddenly. *See also* Acute.
Cleft palate Deformity of puppies, in which two sides of the skull do not join together properly.
Clinical signs Symptoms or signs that are visible to the naked eye.
Coat Hair that covers a dog's body.
Collie eye anomaly Inherited disease of retina, found in collie breeds.
Conformation Structure and form of the framework of a dog.
Congenital disorder Condition that is present at birth, not necessarily inherited.
Conjunctivitis Inflammation of the thin outer layer of the eye, causing watering and soreness.
Cropping Trimming ears for medical or cosmetic reasons. Cropping for cosmetic reasons is illegal in many countries.
Cross breed A first-generation cross between two different pedigree breeds.
Cryptorchid Male dog with neither testicle descended.
Cyst Liquid-filled sac that arises through disease or infection.
Cystitis Bladder infection.

Dam Mother of a litter of puppies.
Dermatitis An inflammation of the skin.
Dermatology Study of diseases of the skin and their treatment.
Dew claw Extra toe on inside of the legs above paw. Often removed by surgery when a puppy is a few days old.
Dewlap Flap of skin that hangs beneath the throat of some breeds.
Diabetes insipidus Disease of the pituitary gland, in which the body cannot concentrate urine properly.
Diabetes, sugar Excess sugar in the blood, due to malfunctioning pancreas.
Distemper Contagious viral disease, fatal if left untreated.
Distichiasis Ingrown eyelashes.
DNA Deoxyribonucleic acid, the substance that makes up chromosomes, from which all life is made.
Docking Cutting the tail for medical or cosmetic reasons when a puppy is a few days old. Docking for cosmetic reasons is illegal in many countries.
Dog show Exhibition of dogs in which animals are judged against a recognized breed standard.
Dominant gene The gene that overrides a recessive gene so that its characteristics are evident in the offspring.
Double coat Undercoat plus longer outer coat.
Dry eye Lack of lubrication in the eye, leading to infection and inflammation.

Ear mites Tiny parasites that live in the ear canal, causing irritation.
Eclampsia Calcium deficiency, often suffered by lactating bitches.
Ectropion Condition resulting from outward-turning eyelids.
Elizabethan collar Cardboard or plastic funnel fitted over the head to keep a dog from interfering with stitches or wounds.
Entropion Condition resulting in inward-turning eyelids. The eyelashes irritate the eyeball.
Epiphora Watery eyes.
Even bite When upper and lower teeth meet without any overlap.
Expression General appearance of all features of the head as viewed from the front, typical of the breed.

Feathering Long, fine fringe of hair on ears, legs, tail, and body.
Feral Domestic animals that have reverted to a wild state.
Field trial Outdoor competition in which dogs are judged for their tracking, pointing, or retrieving abilities.
Flank Side of a dog's body between last rib and hip.
Flea collar Special collar impregnated with chemicals to kill fleas.
Fleas The most common external parasite living on a dog's skin and feeding on its blood. Dogs are sometimes sensitive to flea bites or droppings.
Flukes Parasites found in intestines and liver, causing diarrhoea and anaemia.
Fringe *See* Feathering.

Gait Style of a dog's movement.
Gastritis Inflammation of stomach walls, causing vomiting and reluctance to eat.
Gastroenteritis Infection causing vomiting and diarrhoea.
Gene Bead of DNA on chromosomes that carries information on a dog's physical characteristics, such as coat colour and eye colour.
Gingivitis Inflammation of gums at edge of teeth, caused by tartar build-up.
Glaucoma Enlargement of eyeball caused by increased pressure.
Groom To brush and comb a dog's coat.
Guard dog Dog kept as a watchdog.
Guard hairs Long hairs that extend beyond the undercoat.
Gundog Breeds of dog traditionally used to retrieve shot game.

Haematoma Blood blister, often in ear flap, where it is caused by head shaking.
Halitosis Bad breath.
Harvest mites Parasites that appear in the autumn and cause skin irritation.
Heartworms Parasites living in the heart. Larvae are transmitted by mosquitoes.
Heat *See* Oestrus.
Hereditary disorder Condition passed down through generations, contained in genetic information on chromosomes.
Hip dysplasia Hereditary condition of certain breeds causing lameness.
Hock Central, back joint on hind leg.
Hookworms Blood-sucking worms that live in the small intestine.

Inbreeding Breeding of pedigree dogs that are closely related.
Incisors Upper and lower front teeth.
Interbreeding Cross breeding of different varieties of dog.

Jaundice Yellow colour to gums, caused by liver disease.
Jowls Fleshy parts of mouth.

Kennel cough Infectious disorder of respiratory system.
Keratitis Clouding of the eye, caused by inflammation of the cornea.

Lens luxation Condition in which lens drops out of normal position in eye.
Lesion Injury to tissue.
Lice Parasites that suck blood, causing anaemia in a severe infestation.
Line breeding Mating of dogs related by a common ancestor.
Litter Puppies born in a single whelping. Size of litter varies according to breed.

Malocclusion Misaligned bite.
Mange mites Minute parasites that burrow into a dog's skin, causing chronic hair loss, irritation, and inflammation.
Mastitis Inflammation of milk glands.
Melanoma Dark, pigmented tumour.
Milk fever *See* Eclampsia.
Milk teeth Puppy's first teeth. Usually lost between four and six months old.
Mongrel Dog of unknown parentage.
Monorchid Male dog with only one testicle descended.
Muzzle Front part of the head.
Myiasis Infestation of open wounds by fly maggots, causing infection.

Neuter To castrate males or spay females to prevent reproduction and unwanted sexual behaviour.
Nictitating membrane *See* Third eyelid.

Oestrus Periods during which female dog is sexually responsive to males, commonly known as heat or season.
Otitis externa Inflammation of the outer ear, caused by mites, bacteria, or foreign bodies. Also known as canker.
Otitis interna Infection of the inner ear.
Otitis media Infection of the middle ear.
Outcross Use of a totally unrelated pedigree dog for breeding purposes.
Overshot Jaw where the upper incisors extend past the lower ones.
Ovariohysterectomy *See* Spay.

Paraphimosis Condition in which the penis cannot be withdrawn into sheath.
Pedigree A record of ancestry, showing a family tree over several generations.
Poodle eye Condition of breeds like poodles, in which tears stain the face.
Progressive retinal atrophy Inherited disorder causing loss of sight.
Prolapse Condition in which an internal organ is pushed through to the outside.
Prostatitis Condition in which a male's prostate gland is enlarged, causing constipation or urinary problems.
Pruritus Itchiness.
Purebred Dog whose parents are of the same breed and of unmixed descent.
Pyometra Pus in the womb.

Quarantine Period of time for which animals entering certain countries, such as Great Britain, Australia, and New Zealand, must be isolated to prevent the spread of rabies.

Rabies Fatal viral disease affecting nervous system. Usually transmitted through a bite from an infected animal.
Recessive gene One whose characteristics are overridden by a dominant gene in each pairing of chromosomes, so that it is not evident in the features of the resulting offspring.
Register List of pedigree dogs. In order to enter shows, purebred dogs must be registered upon birth with the national dog authority.
Ringworm Form of fungal infection that causes scaly skin and mild irritation.
Roundworms Parasites that live in a dog's digestive tract, feeding on digesting food. Can cause diarrhoea.

Scent marking A dog marks its territory with urine, or with scent from special glands in the face and paws, sending a clear message to other dogs.
Season *See* Oestrus.
Selective breeding Breeding of pedigree dogs by planned matings to enhance certain physical characteristics, such as coat colour and body shape.
Spay To surgically remove bitch's ovaries and uterus to prevent oestrus and unwanted pregnancy.
Stifle Hind leg above the hock.
Strip To remove hair on a wire-coated dog with a stripping knife.
Stud Pedigree male dog used for breeding purposes. Owner usually charges fee.
Stud book Register of breeding particulars of pedigree stud dogs.

Tapeworms Intestinal parasites that feed on a dog's partly digested food.
Terrier Small dog traditionally bred to go to ground after small game.
Territory Area considered by a dog to be its own, usually garden or house. A dog may defend its territory against intruders.
Third eyelid Filmy lid that is sometimes visible at the corner of a dog's eye.
Ticks Parasites that bury their heads in a dog's skin to feed on its blood. Some types of tick can transmit diseases.
Topline Top of the back.
Trauma Shock, injury, or wound.
Tumour Abnormal growth of tissue. Can be benign (local) or malignant (having the ability to spread elsewhere).

Undercoat Dense second coat that is hidden by the topcoat.
Undershot Jaw where the lower incisors overlap the upper incisors.

Weaning Gradual change in a puppy's diet from its mother's milk to solid food.
Whelping Act of giving birth.
Whiskers Long hair on muzzle and jaw.
Wire-haired Rough-coated dog.
Withers Highest point of the shoulders, from where a dog's height is measured.
Wobbler syndrome Nervous disorder caused by a neck vertebra rotating. Results in partial paralysis.

X-chromosome Chromosome responsible for development of female characteristics.

Y-chromosome Chromosome responsible for development of male characteristics.

Zoonoses Diseases that can be passed between vertebrate species, including humans. Rabies is by far the most dangerous. *See also* Rabies.

Dog Care Record

Dog's name: ....

Pedigree name: ....

Registration number: ....

Breed: ....

Colour of coat: .... Sex: ....

Date of birth: ....

Veterinary Record

Name and address of vet: ....

....

Surgery telephone number: ....

Emergency telephone number: ....

Medical history (any illnesses with dates of visits to the vet): ....

....

....

....

Vaccinations due: ....

Adult weight: ....

Name and address of medical insurance company:

....

....

Telephone number: ....

Policy number: ....

Premium due: ....

General Information

Sire's name: ....

Sire's breed: ....

Dam's name: ....

Dam's breed: ....

Breeder's name and address: ....

....

Telephone number: ....

Name and address of boarding kennels: ....

....

Telephone number: ....

Name and address of dog sitter: ....

....

Telephone number: ....

Name and address of training club: ....

....

Telephone number: ....

Trainer's name: ....

ADDITIONAL INFORMATION

USEFUL ADDRESSES

Veterinary organizations

British Small Animal Veterinary Association
Kingsley House,
Church Lane,
Shurdingham, Cheltenham,
Gloucestershire GL51 5TQ

British Veterinary Association
7 Mansfield Street,
London W1M 0AT

Royal College of Veterinary Surgeons
32 Belgrave Square,
London SW1X 8QP

Welfare Associations

Blue Cross
1 Hugh Street,
London SW1V 1QQ

Guide Dogs for the Blind
Alexander House,
9 Park Street,
Windsor,
Berkshire SL4 1JR

Hearing Dogs for the Deaf
The Training Centre,
London Road,
Lewknor,
Oxfordshire OX9 5RY

Irish Society for the Prevention of Cruelty to Animals
1 Grand Canal Quay,
Dublin 2,
Republic of Ireland

National Canine Defence League
1 and 2 Pratt Mews,
London NW1 0AD

P. A. T. Dogs
Rocky Bank,
4 New Road,
Ditton,
Kent ME20 7AD

People's Dispensary for Sick Animals
PDSA House,
Whitechapel Way,
Priorslee, Telford,
Shropshire TF2 9PQ

Royal Society for the Prevention of Cruelty to Animals
RSPCA Headquarters,
Causeway,
Horsham,
West Sussex RH12 1HG

Scottish Society for the Prevention of Cruelty to Animals
19 Melville Street,
Edinburgh,
Scotland EH3 7PL

Ulster Society for the Prevention of Cruelty to Animals
11 Drumview Road,
Ballymagarrick,
Lisburn,
Northern Ireland BT27 6YF

Wood Green Animal Shelters
Highway Cottage,
Chiswell Road,
Heydon,
Royston,
Hertfordshire SG8 8BR

Registration organization

The Kennel Club of Great Britain
1 Clarges Street,
Piccadilly,
London W1Y 8AB

FURTHER READING

Periodicals

Dogs Today
10 Sheet Street,
Windsor,
Berkshire SL4 1BG

Dog Training Weekly
7 Greenwich South St,
London SE10 8BR

Dog World
9 Tufton Street,
Ashford,
Kent TN23
1QN

Our Dogs
5 Oxford Road,
Station Approach,
Manchester
M60 1SX

Books

Blogg, Rowan, and Allen, Eric, *Everydog*, William Morrow, 1983
Carlson, Delbert, and Giffin, James, *Dog Owner's Home Veterinary Handbook*, Howell Book Inc., 1980
Clutton-Brock, Juliet, *Eyewitness Dog*, Dorling Kindersley Ltd., 1991
Cruft, Charles, *Charles Cruft's Dog Book*, W. Foulsham and Co., 1983
Edney, Andrew (ed.), *Dog and Cat Nutrition*, Pergamon Press, 1981
Edney, Andrew, and Mugford, Roger, *The Practical Guide to Dog and Puppy Care*, Salamander, 1987
Evans, J.M., and White, Kay, *The Doglopaedia*, Henston, 1985
Fogle, Bruce, *Know Your Dog*, Dorling Kindersley Ltd., 1992
Fogle, Bruce, *The Dog's Mind*, Pelham Books, 1990
Hawcroft, Tim, *The Complete Book of Dog Care*, Ringpress Ltd., 1992
Kay, William, *The Complete Book of Dog Health*, Howell Book Inc., 1980
Palmer, Joan, *A Dog Owner's Guide to Training*, Salamander, 1987
Palmer, Joan, *An Illustrated Guide to Dogs*, Salamander, 1981
Ruiz, Suzanne, *A Dog Owner's Guide to Grooming*, Salamander, 1987
The Reader's Digest Illustrated Book of Dogs, Reader's Digest, 1988
Taylor, David, *The Ultimate Dog*, Dorling Kindersley Ltd., 1990
Taylor, David, *You & Your Dog*, Dorling Kindersley Ltd., 1986
Turner, Trevor (ed.), *Veterinary Notes for Dog Owners*, Random Century, 1990

INDEX

ACKNOWLEDGMENTS

Author's acknowledgments
This might look like a book to you, but it is really a jigsaw puzzle in which a team of people work together, neatly and efficiently, to finish the puzzle. Thanks to Alison Melvin, Nigel Hazle, Lynn Parr, and Hazel Taylor for their day-to-day planning, and to the photographers, Tim Ridley, Andy Crawford, and Steve Gorton for their superb work. Like parents not wanting to interfere with the developing child, but all the while keeping a close eye on what we were doing, were Krystyna Mayer, the Managing Editor, and Derek Coombes, the Managing Art Editor. Like a grandparent, David Lamb, the Editorial Director, organized lunches and made sure everyone was happy. And like Banquo's ghost, Peter Kindersley, the Chairman, kept a hawk's eye on everyone. Thanks to them all. The system works.

My gratitude also to my clients who offered their model dogs; to my nurses Jenny Berry, Amanda Topp, and Ashley McManus for finding some of the models (including their own – Winnie the Boxer puppy living permanently under my receptionist's desk); and to Dr. Ivan Burger at the Waltham Centre for Pet Nutrition, who cheerfully faxed me answers to any questions I asked of him. And, finally, special thanks to Andrew Edney, who, by writing the *RSPCA Complete Cat Care Manual*, saved us all from walking down many dead ends.

Publisher's Acknowledgments
Dorling Kindersley would like to thank the following people and dogs who helped with the photography:

Atalanta De Bendern (Semi Soul Dancing); Rosemary Baker (Ben); Jenny Berry (Mr. Badger and Hattie); Rowan Clifford (William); Sandra Dunne (Tanya); Kate Forey (Daisy); Bruce Fogle (Lexington); Maggi Fox (Archie and Angus); Mrs. Guy (Buster); Fil Manning (Scampy); Danuta Mayer (Gip and Bilbo); Anita McCarthy (Gunner); Mrs. Murkett (Luke, Sam, and Nike); Loretta Nobes (Dawn and puppies); Christina Oates (Cloud the Burmese cat); Peter's Posh Pets (Dizzy, Fifi, Beryl, Dilly, and Chippie); Paolo Pimental (Islay); Angela Ratner (Lizzie); June Raymond (Rocky); Colin Tennant (Spike, Huxley, Nelson, Holly, Claude, and Rufus); Amanda Topp (Edwin and Winnie); Hazel Taylor (Maisey and Zak); Samantha Ware (Jaffa, Flynn, Jace, Percy, Ginnie, and Jessie); Mrs Williams (Genghis); Andrew Woodhead (Rex).

Kate Forey, Barnabas Kindersley, Nina Fortnam, Rachel Simm, and Colin Tennant for modelling and dog handling. Animal Fair, Kensington; Jennifer Corker; and The Company of Animals for supplying equipment and materials. Diana Morris for picture research. Colette Cheng for design assistance.

Dorling Kindersley also wish to thank Terence C. Bate BVSc, LLB, MRCVS of the RSPCA for his valuable advice on the text.

KEY: t *top*, b *bottom*, c *centre*, l *left*, r *right*

Illustrations
Rowan Clifford: pp 65cr, 112t, 124, 145b, 155t, 156–157, 158–159, 160–161, 164–165, 166–167, 168–169, 172–173, 174–175
Angelica Elsebach: pp 155cr, 155b, 162–163, 170–171
Chris Forsey: pp 14–15, 44bl, 98, 100, 102, 104, 106, 108, 110, 112b, 114, 116, 118, 120, 122, 126, 147
Jane Pickering: pp 44–45

Photography
All photography by Tim Ridley, Andy Crawford, and Steve Gorton except for:
Animal Photography: Sally Ann Thompson 47cl, 179cl, 183bl; R. Wilibie 182br
Animals Unlimited: 177br, 183t
Sarah Ashun: 182t, 183cl, 183br
Jane Burton: 116t, 126t
Bruce Coleman Ltd.: Peter F.R. Jackson 15cr; Johnny Johnson 14bc; Hans Reinhard 15tl
Hazel Edington: 44t
E.T. Archive: 13tl, 13tr, 13b
Mary Evans Picture Library: 178t, 178bl
Guide Dogs for the Blind Assoc.: 23tr
Marc Henrie: 179t, 179b, 183cr
Michael Holford: 12bl, 12br
Images Colour Library: 12t
Dave King: 2–3, 5cr, 11t, 11b, 14, 15, 16t, 16br, 17bl, 18t, 19b, 21b, 23tl, 23br, 24br, 25, 27b, 28t, 29tl, 29cr, 62, 63t, 63bl, 91t, 91cr, 94–95, 98b, 116b, 176–177, 177cr, 180, 181
Natural History Photographic Agency: David Tomlinson 179cr
David Ward: 10–11, 16bl; 17t; 18b, 20t, 20cl, 21t, 21c, 22t, 23bl, 24t, 24cl, 27t, 28bl, 29tr, 40t, 42t, 42c, 42bl, 43t, 43c, 47br, 48b, 49tl, 49bl, 50–51, 51b, 54, 55b, 58b, 96tl, 100t, 108b, 110, 112b, 118, 120b, 122b, 138t, 184–185, 187b, 191b
Wood Green Animal Shelters: 29bl
Jerry Young: 1, 14bl, 17c, 17br, 20b, 23cl, 29br, 51c

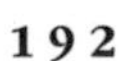